European Religious Cultures

Essays offered to Christopher Brooke
on the occasion of his eightieth birthday

T0346382

Professor Christopher Brooke

(*Photograph:* Yao Liang)

European Religious Cultures

Essays offered to Christopher Brooke
on the occasion of his eightieth birthday

Edited by

Miri Rubin

LONDON
INSTITUTE OF HISTORICAL RESEARCH

Published by

UNIVERSITY OF LONDON PRESS
SCHOOL OF ADVANCED STUDY
INSTITUTE OF HISTORICAL RESEARCH
Senate House, Malet Street, London WC1E 7HU

Available to download free or to purchase at
https://www.sas.ac.uk/publications

ISBNs
978-1-912702-71-8 (paperback)
978-1-912702-70-1 (PDF)
978-1-912702-72-5 (.mobi)
978-1-912702-73-2 (.epub)

INSTITUTE OF HISTORICAL RESEARCH | SCHOOL OF ADVANCED STUDY UNIVERSITY OF LONDON

Contents

Notes on contributors

John H. Arnold is professor of medieval history at the University of Cambridge and author of numerous books, including *Belief and Unbelief in Medieval Europe* (London, 2005) and *What is Medieval History?* (Oxford, 2008). Recent edited collections include *Heresy and Inquisition in France, c.1200-c.1300* (with Peter Biller, Manchester, 2015) and *History after Hobsbawm: Writing the Past for the Twenty-First Century* (with Matthew Hilton and Jan Rüger, Oxford, 2018).

Caroline M. Barron is professorial research fellow at the Department of History, Royal Holloway, University of London. She is the author of many articles and the editor of several collections of essays. Her book *London in the Later Middle Ages: Government and People, 1200–1500* was published by Oxford University Press in 2005. In 2019 she was the recipient of a volume entitled *Medieval Londoners*, offered on the occasion of her eightieth birthday, and published by University of London Press.

Paul Binski is professor of the history of medieval art at the University of Cambridge. He specializes in the art and architecture of Western Europe in the Gothic period in England especially. His fields of interest include manuscript, panel and wall painting, sculpture and architecture, patronage and the relationship of art and ideas. His most recent books include *Gothic Wonder* (New Haven, Conn., 2014) and *Gothic Sculpture* (New Haven, Conn., 2019).

Susan Boynton is professor of historical musicology at Columbia University. She works on medieval liturgy and chant in regions of what are now Italy, France and Spain. Susan is the author of *Shaping a Monastic Identity: Liturgy and History at the Imperial Abbey of Farfa, 1000–1125* (Oxford, 2006), which won the Lewis Lockwood Award of the American Musicological Society. Recent publications include *Silent Music: Medieval Song and the Construction of History in Eighteenth-Century Spain* (Oxford, 2011) and *Resounding Images. Medieval Intersections of Art, Music, and Sound* (Turnhout, 2015), co-edited with Diane J. Reilly which received the Ruth A. Solie Award of the American Musicological Society.

Giles Constable is professor emeritus at the School of Historical Studies of the Institute for Advanced Study, Princeton, New Jersey. His many works explore the culture of monasticism in eleventh- and twelfth-century Europe and its lasting effect on the later middle ages.

Virginia Davis is professor of medieval history and dean for research in the Faculty of Humanities and Social Science at Queen Mary, University of London. Her research addresses themes in late medieval ecclesiastical and educational history, brought together in the biography *William Wykeham* (London, 2007). Other published works deal with the motivations of medieval priests in seeking ordination, and with the priesthood of medieval London. Her collection *The Individual in Late Medieval England*, co-edited with Julia Boffey, was published in 2009.

Janet L. Nelson is professor emerita of medieval history at King's College London. Her research interests lie chiefly in Carolingian culture and politics. Her debts, intellectual and personal, to Christopher Brooke go back to his years in London when she attended his seminars at the Institute of Historical Research. Her latest book, *King and Emperor: a New Life of Charlemagne*, was published by Allen Lane in 2019.

William J. Purkis received his PhD from the University of Cambridge, and after a period of teaching at Queen Mary, University of London he is now reader in medieval history at the University of Birmingham. His publications include a monograph on *Crusading Spirituality in the Holy Land and Iberia, c.1095–c.1187* (Woodbridge, 2008), *The Charlemagne Legend in Medieval Latin Texts*, co-edited with Matthew Gabriele (Woodbridge, 2016) and a number of articles on eleventh- and twelfth-century Iberian Christian perceptions of the past.

Miri Rubin is professor of medieval and early modern history at Queen Mary, University of London. Her research explores the religious cultures of Europe, *c.*1100–1600 and her many publications include *Mother of God: a History of the Virgin Mary* (New Haven, Conn., 2009) and *City of Strangers: Making Lives in Medieval Europe* (Cambridge, 2020) based on her 2017 Wiles Lectures given at Queen's University Belfast.

Acknowledgements

to the 2008 edition

On 18 June 2007 a colloquium took place in honour of Christopher Brooke on the occasion of his eightieth birthday, in the Social Science Suite of Queen Mary, University of London. Queen Mary is the proud bearer of the heritage of Westfield College, which merged with Queen Mary in 1989. At Queen Mary the study of medieval religious cultures flourishes, just as it had done at Westfield College, where Christopher served as Professor of Medieval History between 1967 and 1977. It seemed most fitting to celebrate Christopher's achievements – past and still very much present – at Queen Mary. Thanks to the support of the Department of History and the Humanities and Social Science Sector at Queen Mary we were able to offer a venue and generous hospitality to speakers and other participants. The papers collected in this issue were delivered and discussed on that day, an event which drew medieval scholars from London and far beyond.

This enterprise of sharing new approaches to the study of medieval religious cultures received an excellent launch from the inaugurating lecture delivered by Professor Giles Constable on the evening of the colloquium. The Institute of Historical Research graciously hosted the event. Its Director, Professor David Bates, also suggested that the papers be published by the Institute. It is pleasing to know that the events we enjoyed so much that summer will thus be shared in part with a much wider audience. I am very grateful to Dr Jane Winters and Ms Emily Morrell for their guidance and support, and to the contributors who toiled to turn their animated talks into articles for publication.

Miri Rubin

Foreword

to the 2020 edition

One of the few consolations during the Covid-19 lockdown and its aftermath has been the intensification of contacts between historians, and the large number of publications that have become available online. After the few first weeks of shock and anxiety, and for some illness and the desperate care for sick relatives and loved ones, academics have organised themselves into seminar groupings around shared interest and expertise, yet global and all-embracing in their digital reach. Publishers followed with generous offers of access to books and articles to underpin whatever research was still going on during the closure of libraries and archives.

The Institute of Historical Research – the historians' home and a publisher too – has played its part, with online seminars and enabling activities. Since 2017 new books produced by the IHR and its partner, the University of London Press, have been freely available as open access from their first publication. Now, in response to the lockdown, the Institute is preparing a selection of its earlier print titles for reissue as open access. I was delighted to hear that *European Religious Cultures* was chosen to be such an offering, as part of the recently created 'IHR Shorts' series.

This generous act is in the spirit of the academic gathering in 2007, which took place at the Institute and Queen Mary, University of London, to mark the 80th birthday of Christopher Brooke (1927–2015). Christopher's scholarship had always dealt with aspects of the religious life, from the monastic to the popular, an enterprise which he maintained even as he served as the most prolific and exacting editor of medieval texts in his generation. So it seemed right to gather scholars whose lives had crossed with his, and who had developed interesting approaches to what we now call the 'religious cultures' of the middle ages. In the comments he offered at the end of that day, Christopher noted the exciting novelty, but also the thread of continuity: making the sources speak. Sources meant not only texts, but images, for Christopher always blended his work with archaeology, art history, liturgy and architecture.

When soon after we were approached by the (then) IHR director, Professor David Bates, to consider publishing the papers in a volume, I was delighted that the day we had lived together might be shared. The resulting volume opens with a lecture delivered by Giles Constable, Christopher's life-long friend. The historiographical story of their lives, the move from the hegemony of ecclesiastical history in the study of religion, to the study of religious culture could not have been more authoritatively delineated. And it is followed by Paul Binski's reflections on what it takes to understand the buildings and images that medieval people crafted: how are they to be read? Binski's 2019 *Gothic Sculpture* is a magisterial fruition of some of the thoughts developed here.

The six shorter articles that follow bring together scholars of different generations and training. A section on the life-cycle of religious men, with papers by Jinty Nelson and Virginia Davis, marked a turn towards taking age seriously and was followed a few years later by the founding of the IHR's own Life-Cycles seminar. The contribution by Susan Boynton, a historian of music was a sign of the emerging turn towards a new history of liturgy, while William Purkis's article on monastic spirituality and crusade exemplified the trend towards the study of the crusades as expressions of European culture. John Arnold introduces with helpful clarity the theory and practice of studying medieval emotions, an interest which animates the Centre for the History of the Emotions, founded at QMUL in 2008 – the year this book was published. In her essay Caroline Barron explored St Zita, a saint much loved in London, with a material approach to devotion. Each contribution marked possibility, and so still reads with a certain freshness.

Had the event been planned for 2020, it would have probably contained more discussion of the materiality of religion, perhaps the sounds of medieval religious life. It may have dwelt on questions of religious difference more, and may even have had a global turn to it. I trust – I know – that the pieces collected here, gifts to Christopher and offerings to other scholars of medieval Europe, will delight in 2020 and beyond just as they did when they were first delivered.

Miri Rubin, Cambridge, June 2020

I

The study of religious cultures

From church history to religious culture: the study of medieval religious life and spirituality

Giles Constable

One of the most striking changes in medieval studies over the past fifty years – and one to which Professor Brooke has made notable contributions – is the rise in interest in religion. There has been a concomitant decline – to which incidentally Professor Brooke has not contributed, rather the contrary – in interest in the traditional fields of constitutional, institutional and economic history, which dominated the study of medieval history during the first half of the twentieth century. This is not to say that religious life and spirituality (as distinct from the church and ecclesiastical institutions) were entirely neglected at that time, but with a few exceptions, to some of whom I shall return, they were treated by most scholars from a secular point of view. Even the Reformation was seen primarily as a matter of politics, and the crusades as a chapter in the social and economic history of Europe.

The history of religion and religious life and attitudes was traditionally the domain of clerical and monastic scholars, who in many respects laid the foundations of the modern study of medieval history. The works of the Bollandists and Maurists are of great scholarly value. G. G. Coulton (who was not always an admirer of monastic historians) said that 'There is no monastic historian who, for learning and impartiality, comes even into the same class as Mabillon'.[1] Scholars still make use of his works and those of Martène and other historians who were monks or secular clerics, and also of the *Gallia Christiana*, the first edition of which appeared in 1626, and of the *Italia Sacra*. Among lay scholars at that time pride of place belongs to William Dugdale, whose *Monasticon Anglicanum*, first published in 1655–73, is indispensable for the study of monasticism in England.

---

[1] G. G. Coulton, *Five Centuries of Religion* (4 vols., Cambridge Studies in Medieval Life and Thought, Cambridge, 1926–50), i. 3, cf. p. xxvi, where he said that Mabillon's *Annales* and *Acta* formed 'the most valuable contribution, beyond all comparison, ever made to monastic history'.

G. Constable, 'From church history to religious culture: the study of medieval religious life and spirituality', in *European Religious Cultures: Essays offered to Christopher Brooke on the occasion of his eightieth birthday*, ed. M. Rubin (London, 2020), pp. 3–16. License: CC-BY-NC-ND 4.0.

Few areas of historical research can boast such a distinguished genealogy, which holds out the hope that some modern works, including perhaps our own, may be consulted long after most books on more recent history are forgotten. Certainly some of Professor Brooke's will be. Academic historians in the nineteenth and early twentieth century, however, inherited much of the secularism and anti-clericalism of the eighteenth century, often without the learning, and tended to neglect the study of religion, which they equated with irrationality, if not superstition. Again according to Coulton, 'The vast wealth of documents between St. Bernard and the Reformation is practically non-existent for modern historians'.[2] Among other reasons for this neglect were the predominantly national focus of medieval studies, the reaction against the clerical domination of education, the view that the study of religious thought and institutions was the business of clerics rather than lay scholars, and more generally the perceived decline in the importance of religion in the modern world. When I first went to the University of Iowa (then called the State University of Iowa) in 1955 religion was taught by professors who were each supported by their own denominations, since the university was forbidden to teach religion; and in some universities church history is still taught in a separate department and even a separate faculty. The serious study of religious life and spirituality was almost completely ignored in most secular universities until well into the twentieth century.

Laymen who addressed themselves to religious history were frequently motivated by partisan sympathies, such as (in the nineteenth century) the Catholic Charles René de Montalembert, whose study of early medieval monasticism relied heavily on Mabillon, and the Protestant Charles Henry Lea, perhaps the greatest American medievalist, who had little good to say about medieval religion. In the twentieth century G. G. Coulton was a polemicist as well as a scholar, and his works, in spite of their learning, are less widely read today than they deserve.

Serious and important research was still done by clerics and monks, but after the revival of monasticism in the mid nineteenth century, monks were almost more cut off from secular society than before, and scholarly work was not always encouraged in religious communities. Even great scholars like Ursmer Berlière and André Wilmart were not widely known among lay scholars. The great exception was David Knowles, the first Benedictine monk to hold a professorship at an English university since the Reformation. His history of the monastic and religious orders in England, which appeared between 1940 and 1959, took the scholarly world to some

---

[2] Coulton, i. xliii.

extent by surprise and helped to create a more receptive attitude towards the history of monasticism.

In England the way had already been prepared by, among others, Maurice Powicke, who in addition to his works on constitutional and institutional history wrote studies of Aelred of Rievaulx and Stephen Langton and a book on *Christian Life in the Middle Ages*. Some of his students, notably Richard Southern, followed this path. The economic historian Eileen Power meanwhile published a book on *Medieval English Nunneries*, in which she said a good deal more about the material culture of nunneries and the misdemeanours of the nuns than about their religious life or spirituality. On the continent the most important works were Carl Erdmann's *Die Entstehung des Kreuzzugsgedankens*, which is a study in the changes in Christian thought and spirituality in the tenth and eleventh centuries, and Herbert Grundmann's *Religiöse Bewegungen im Mittelalter*, both of which came out in 1935 but were not translated into English until many years later. Grundmann especially studied the religious and social basis of the religious movements of the twelfth and thirteenth centuries, including the role of women, and showed their common features rather than the differences which scholars who were themselves members of religious orders tended to emphasize.

In America, medieval religious history, after a promising start with Lea, was even less studied than in Europe.[3] Coulton, in an appendix on 'American medievalists' to the first volume of his *Five Centuries of Religion*, published in 1927, said that Lea 'seems to have found no worthy successor' in social or religious history, and C. W. David, in an article on 'American historiography of the middle ages', published in 1935, recognized the achievements of American medievalists primarily in the areas of art history and of institutional and intellectual history, to which he added palaeography, owing to the influence on his American students of the German palaeographer Ludwig Traube. Ernst Robert Curtius took a more positive attitude in a lecture delivered in 1949, in which he said nothing about religious history but commented on the interest of what he called the 'phenomenon' of American medievalism. 'The American conquest of the Middle Ages', he wrote, somewhat oddly, 'has something of that romantic glamor and of that deep sentimental urge which we might expect in a man who should set out to find his lost mother'. The Belgian scholar Fernand Van Steenbergen was surprised by the growth of American medieval centres,

---

[3] See H. R. Guggisberg, *Das europäische Mittelalter im amerikanischen Geschichtsdenken des 19. und des frühen 20. Jahrhunderts* (Basler Beiträge zur Geschichtswissenschaft, xcii, Basel and Stuttgart, 1964).

institutes and journals and questioned whether 'there were sufficient vocations of medievalists in the New World to assure the vitality of all these centers of research'.[4] He was writing in 1953, before Kalamazoo!

In preparing this paper I looked at several articles published in the nineteen-sixties by prominent (and for the most part senior) scholars on medieval studies.[5] Very few of them say anything about religion or even about the crusades, which was a flourishing field at that time. The emphasis is on constitutional, institutional and legal history, with occasional references to the history of art and to economic and intellectual history. Most striking is the virtual omission of religious history in David Knowles's lecture entitled 'Some trends in scholarship, 1868–1968, in the field of medieval history', where he said that until the middle of the twentieth century English constitutional history held 'pride of place', as he put it, in British universities, though he also discussed developments in legal, administrative and economic history and, since the Second World War, in intellectual and art history. While he mentioned the contributions to the study of monastic history made by the members of several religious orders, he called them one of many foreign groups 'which is perhaps unfamiliar in this country', that is, in England. Probably out of modesty, he cited no English-speaking scholars in the field and suggested, without explicitly stating it, that this was an area best left to members of religious orders.[6]

This then was the situation when I completed my Ph.D., in 1958, and began to look for an academic position. I hope at this point you will allow me a short autobiographical excursus, which also applies *mutatis mutandis* to Professor Brooke, who began his academic career, though in England rather than America, shortly before I did. I wrote my thesis at Harvard under Herbert Bloch, a classicist who also worked in medieval history, and

[4] Coulton, i. 521; C. W. David, 'American historiography of the middle ages, 1884–1934', *Speculum*, x (1935), 125–37; E. R. Curtius, *European Literature and the Latin Middle Ages*, trans. W. R. Trask (Princeton, N.J., 1990), p. 587; F. Van Steenberghen, 'Les études médiévales en Amérique', *Revue philosophique de Louvain*, xlix (1951), 405–14, at p. 414.

[5] N. B. Lewis, *The Study of Medieval History* (Inaugural Lecture: University of Sheffield, 1960); S. Packard, *The Process of Historical Revision: New Viewpoints on Medieval European History* (The Katherine Asher Engel Lecture, 1960, Northampton, Mass., 1962); S. Harrison Thomson, 'The growth of a discipline: medieval studies in America', in *Perspectives in Medieval History*, ed. K. Fischer Drew and F. Seyward Lear (Chicago and London, 1963), pp. 1–18. See also E. Demm, 'Neue Wege in der amerikanischen Geschichtswissenschaft', *Saeculum*, xxii (1971), 342–76, who stressed the replacement of political-institutional by social-economic emphasis and the influence on historical research of psychology, anthropology and quantification.

[6] M. D. Knowles, 'Some trends in scholarship, 1868–1968, in the field of medieval history', *Transactions of the Royal Historical Society*, 5th ser., xix (1969), 139–57, at p. 154.

I spent a year at Cambridge under David Knowles. My subject was the letters of Peter the Venerable, who was abbot of Cluny in the first half of the twelfth century. It was unusual at that time (and still is, I believe) to present a textual edition, even with a substantial introduction and notes, as a doctoral dissertation, and my professors in the department of history at Harvard, Charles Taylor and Helen Cam, both of whom worked in traditional fields, thought that I would find a position only in a seminary, and a Roman Catholic seminary at that, and since I am not a Roman Catholic, probably no job at all! In fact the winds of historiographical fashion were changing, and my fields of research – monastic history, the crusades, letter-writing, medieval forgery, all growing out of my work on Peter the Venerable – have been a modest growth industry over the past half century. More work is being done today on saints' lives and miracles than on the history of parliament. The study of religious life and spirituality took off, as it were, in the nineteen-fifties and sixties, just at the time the articles I mentioned above were written. I shall not bore you, however, with lists of individual scholars and their works, which saves me, incidentally, from the invidious task of mentioning some but not others. I shall rather look at the subject matter of the field, and at some of the developments in recent years.

Before doing so, however, something more should be said about the nature of medieval religion and spirituality. The term *religio* in the middle ages preserved its ancient meaning, which later prevailed again, of a system of faith and worship, but it primarily referred to the lives and beliefs of monks, canons, hermits and recluses, both male and female, and others who devoted themselves, fully or in part, to a life of religion, as it was called in the middle ages, when *religiosi* covered a wide range of vocations,[7] as *religieux* still does in French. There is no good equivalent in English. 'Spirituality' also presents problems and is an overworked term today.[8] It was used in the fifth century for a life according to the spirit and 'the effort to practice detachment from sin and attachment to God'. Later it took

[7] See P. Biller, 'Words and the medieval notion of "religion"', *Journal of Ecclesiastical History*, xxxvi (1985), 351–69.

[8] For references in this paragraph, see J. Leclercq, 'Spiritualitas', *Studi medievali*, iii (1962), 279–96, at p. 281; R. R. Post, *The Modern Devotion: Confrontation with Reformation and Humanism* (Studies in Medieval and Reformation Thought, iii, Leiden, 1968); W. Principe, 'Toward defining spirituality', *Studies in Religion*, xii (1983), 127–41; *La spiritualità medievale. Metodi, bilanci, prospettive* (offprint from *Studi medievali*, xxvii, Spoleto, 1987); an unpublished lecture by John Coakley entitled 'What is spirituality?' (1988); and P. M. Alberzoni, 'Le idee guida della spiritualità', to appear in the proceedings of the conference on 'Orden und Klöster im Vergleich' (Eichstätt, 2006), where there is a good bibliography of works in Italian.

on the meaning of *incorporalitas* in contrast to *corporalitas, materialitas, carnalitas* and *mortalitas* and implied the presence in an individual of the Holy Spirit. More recently it has been variously described as 'the attitude of the faithful to God and Christ', 'the experience of the sacred', the point where faith and action interact, or simply as piety and what people do about what they believe. Spirituality, said Walter Principe, 'points to those aspects of a person's living a faith or commitment that concern his or her striving to attain the highest ideal or goal'.

Spirituality is not the same as popular religion, to the study of which Professor Brooke and his wife Rosalind have made notable contributions, and which concerns the practices and beliefs of the average Christian. John Van Engen described popular religion as 'perhaps the most successful as an interpretive rubric ... of all the historical approaches to come out of the 1970s', when it was seen and presented, he said, 'as an autonomous religious outlook, at once ancient and of the people, a set of indigenous sacred practices overtly or covertly resistant to the christianizing forces of the elite'. Phenomena such as superstition and heresy emerged, Van Engen continued, as central to understanding medieval religion and culture, 'sometimes an alternative way into an alternative religious past, sometimes a way of getting at the "people" rather than the "prelates"'.[9] Spirituality, on the other hand, is not autonomous or alternative. In the middle ages it was usually orthodox and in many respects cut across class lines. St. Louis practised the same devotions, worshipped in the same manner, and was inspired by the same ideals as his humblest subject, as indeed did St. Thomas Aquinas, aside from the fact that as a priest he also celebrated mass. It is not my purpose in this paper to study popular religion, except to stress the interaction between lay and monastic spirituality in the late middle ages and early modern period, when practices previously found primarily in religious communities spread into secular society. Many of these, such as frequent communion, praying in private chambers, devotion to the Virgin, and the art of death, were studied by Henri Bremond in his *Histoire littéraire du sentiment religieux en France.*

In the study of medieval spirituality the name of one scholar stands out, Jean Leclercq, whose career covered the second half of the twentieth century. Himself a Benedictine monk, his influence spread far outside the walls of his monastery, or perhaps I should say monasteries, since he was a mighty traveller. Taking up in many respects where André Wilmart left off, Leclercq was an interpreter as well as an editor of texts. He wrote dozens of books

---

[9] J. Van Engen, 'The future of medieval church history', *Church History*, lxxi (2002), 492–522, at p. 498.

and hundreds of articles which, though of uneven quality, reached a wide audience and of which a number were translated into English. Among his many influential contributions was the distinction between the theologies found in monasteries and in universities. Wilmart and Leclercq, together with Marie-Dominique Chenu, whose *Théologie au douzième siècle* was published in 1957 and appeared in English in 1968, changed the face of the study of medieval spirituality. They emphasized in particular the importance of the twelfth century, when there was a fundamental change in the way people saw themselves in relation to God and the church and which marked the beginning, they said, of modern religion.[10]

This included a redefinition of the *vita apostolica*, which no longer involved withdrawal from the world but came in the course of the eleventh and twelfth centuries to include an active apostolate, and which was central for Francis of Assisi and the mendicants, for whom it was not enough to be individually poor in possessions and in spirit, which was equivalent to being humble, without also being collectively poor. The established ideals of withdrawal, asceticism and contempt for the world did not disappear and were combined with a stress on physical labour, which had a special significance particularly for the Cistercians and members of the reformed orders, and also on human values, such as friendship, the importance of which in religious circles has been emphasized in recent studies. These ideals increasingly spread outside religious communities into lay society, and by the end of the middle ages many men and women shared the austere standard of behaviour that had previously characterized formal religious life and included practices and devotions which governed the smallest details of everyday life, such as the arrangement of the crumbs left on a table after a meal.

In addition to these outward marks of piety there was a stress on spiritual inwardness. People believed that their eternal salvation depended on their personal relations to God as much or more than on their behaviour or on the intervention of the clergy. This stress on inwardness led in its extreme forms, through self-knowledge and love of God, to a withdrawal into self-denial, nothingness and ultimately union with the Godhead in such a way, as Grundmann put it, that 'the religious experience supersedes all questions of ethics and morals' and that the perfection of individual believers exceeds the merits and claims of the saint.[11] For these people the ideal of the imitation

---

[10] A. Wilmart, *Auteurs spirituels et textes dévots du moyen âge latin* (Paris, 1932), pp. 59, 62–3; M.–D. Chenu, *La théologie au douzième siècle* (Etudes de philosophie médiévale, xlv, Paris, 1957), pp. 223–4, 239.

[11] H. Grundmann, *Religiöse Bewegungen im Mittelalter* (Historische Studien, cclxvii,

of Christ involved not only following the example of His life on earth but also identifying with Him as the suffering Son of God. This approaches the limits of orthodoxy, though at that time the boundaries between orthodoxy and heresy were less fixed than they became later.

In this and other ways the developments in medieval religious life and thought prepared the way for the modern world. There has been a growing awareness among scholars of the importance of medieval religious institutions for modern society, including political democracy (*maior et senior pars*), prisons ('cell' is a monastic term), the importance of clocks and time-keeping, and the organization of industry. The origins of sign language go back to the system of signs used in medieval monasteries. These are the subject of a different paper, however, and I mention them here only to emphasize the range of the influence of religious institutions and the overlap of spirituality with popular culture.

Turning now to the history of religious life, I shall divide my discussion into three sections: first, the types of life led by religious men and women (*religiosi* and *religiosae*); second, their relations with secular society; and third, the effect on the study of religion of some of the new historical techniques and approaches. In conclusion I shall look briefly at the reasons for the current interest in medieval religion.

Among the most interesting developments with regard to the nature of medieval religious life has been the study of the common features of religious movements, rather than their differences, and the attention paid to groups and individuals who were not technically speaking monks and nuns, in particular to canons, hermits and recluses, and to lay religious, female as well as male. In spite of significant earlier work on canons, some of it dating from the eighteenth century, their status and importance were not widely recognized and are still not fully appreciated, partly in view of the variety of canons who existed in the middle ages. Some of them, known as regular canons, followed a rule and were barely distinguishable from monks; others resembled the clergy and were called secular canons; and yet others, as Alcuin already recognized in the ninth century, occupied a middle position between the two. Hermits and recluses, who were also known as anchorites, were less cut off from monastic, clerical and lay society than was once thought and than descriptions of their way of life suggest. Many people, including women, spent periods of time in hermitages and later took up other types of life. Even Cluny, which was famous for the strictness of its monastic regime, was surrounded by hermitages to which the monks, including the abbots, retreated from time to time. Several scholarly

Berlin, 1935; repr. 1961), pp. 181–2.

congresses have been devoted to the study of hermits and eremitism, but the subject is far from exhausted.

The same is true of people leading a life withdrawn from secular society, either in groups or sometimes in their own families, which has been called domestic monasticism. This way of life was in its nature ephemeral and has left few written records. In institutional terms it constituted a sort of half-way house between the laity and better-established forms of religious life, and it is sometimes described as semi-monastic. People of this type were recognized as occupying a distinct and occasionally suspect status, parallel to that of heretics, but not the same, since they were less concerned with unorthodox beliefs than with a religious way of life. It appealed particularly to women, concerning whose history the flood-gates of research have opened during the past generation, though they had never been fully closed. I have already referred to Eileen Power and Herbert Grundmann, to whom should be added Ernest McDonnell, whose *The Beguines and Beghards in Medieval Culture* appeared in 1954. Many aspects of the religious life and culture of women throughout the middle ages have been studied in recent years, including the openness of some of the reformers in the eleventh and twelfth centuries to the religious aspirations of women, who played a significant part in the institutional, spiritual and intellectual life of the period. In the late middle ages women had a distinctive spirituality, found in both literature and art, the nature and importance of which have been increasingly recognized.

The members of religious communities were bound together by a common way of life and often by adherence to a written rule or set of customs which formed the basis of what have been called textual communities. Many groups of religious men and women, however, including some of the most celebrated, had no written customs and were governed in the details of their daily life by oral traditions. Rules were sometimes adopted relatively late, and customs were written down when the founding members died, a daughter house was established or another community wanted to adopt a similar way of life. Written customaries can also be seen as a reaction to the threat of change, which if welcome in principle might be met with hostility in practice. Some customaries represented a conservative effort to preserve existing practices, and their evidence must be taken with a grain of salt, because they tend to reflect an ideal rather than a reality. Very few if any religious houses adhered to every detail of a written document. Even the Rule of Benedict was modified in countless ways. There is no means of recovering now all the unwritten customs of a community, which were preserved in the minds of its members. Religious life was not an unchanging monolith, and there has been a growing recognition by scholars of the rapidity and occasional violence of change – or reform, as it was commonly called – which could uproot long-established customs and traditions, as it did in universities in the nineteen-sixties and seventies.

The study of rules and customs was a fertile area of research in the second half of the twentieth century. One of the pioneers was Kassius Hallinger, whose learned though controversial book entitled *Gorze-Kluny* stimulated other work on the similarities and differences between religious houses and congregations from the tenth to the twelfth centuries. Hallinger founded the *Corpus Consuetudinum Monasticarum*, which when complete will include new editions of all known customaries. It is paralleled for Greek monasticism by the corpus of Byzantine monastic typica, which has opened the way for comparative study of religious life in the Latin west and Greek east. The new edition of the *Carta Caritatis* and other early Cistercian documents has shown that they were probably written later than was once thought and has led to a reassessment of the beginning and early years of the order of Cîteaux.

The organization of most religious houses and the daily life of their members were governed by an elaborate system of rites and ceremonies, both within the church – the liturgy – and outside. Rites are of interest to sociologists and anthropologists as well as to students of religion and history, who have emphasized the importance of ritual as an expression of religious ideology and feelings. It involves not only what was said and done but also what was sung and seen, since observers participated in ceremonies no less than performers and responded to images and buildings. Rites were adapted to meet the institutional and social as well as the physical needs of religious life. The old contrast between rites and reason, which were traditionally regarded almost as opposites, has thus been broken down. Ritual is a way of looking behind the texts into the hidden world of attitudes and emotions. The application of psychology to history has also helped to deepen our understanding of the religious needs of contemplatives and has inspired a greater sympathy for the visions and miracles that played such an important part in the inner life of monks and nuns.

Religious men and women were also involved with life outside their enclosures. Even those who never left their communities had spiritual ties with the lay world which were none the less important for being invisible. The prayers, masses and blessings of monks and nuns benefited society as well as themselves. The names of innumerable lay benefactors and so-called co-brothers and co-sisters were listed, together with the names of former members of a community and of the communities with which it was affiliated, in the *libri vitae*, necrologies and books of commemoration and confraternity; and prayers, masses and alms were offered on the anniversaries of their deaths. These works have been known for many years, and some were published, mostly as undifferentiated lists of names, but they were regarded as of little use to historians. Their detailed study and publication, both in facsimile and in a form as close as possible to the originals, showing the placement and grouping of names, has been the special work of scholars at the University of Münster, whose greatest single achievement has been the reconstruction of the lost necrology of Cluny, which contains thousands of names and shows the wide range of Cluny's influence. Another relatively little-used source on the associations between religious houses are the mortuary rolls which were carried from house to house after the death of an individual for whom prayers and liturgical commemoration were solicited. A new edition of these rolls, of which the third volume has just appeared, is in preparation. Each house that was visited made an entry on the roll, which is often of interest as evidence not only of the value placed on liturgical intercession but also of the level of literacy and writing skills in the community, including houses of women about whom very little is otherwise known. The study of *scriptoria* and of library catalogues has likewise contributed to the somewhat meagre knowledge of the intellectual life of monks and nuns.

The spiritual links between religious houses and outside society were paralleled by political, social and economic ties, which can be described collectively as the regional ecology of a community. Most older works on monastic exemption, immunity and advocacy, though still not fully replaced, were written from a legalistic point of view and did not take fully into account the religious character of the institutions. Economic historians in particular tended to take an aggressively secular view. Marc Bloch criticized André Déléage for citing so many monasteries, and readers of Georges Duby's influential book on society in the Mâconnais in the eleventh and twelfth centuries, which appeared in 1953, would hardly know how heavily its conclusions were based on monastic sources and that they concerned religious as well as secular life. Duby later acknowledged that were he to rewrite the book he would pay more attention to the monastic framework from which his sources came. The lands of religious and lay proprietors were frequently contiguous and interlocking, and lay proprietors in the area of Cluny, down to the lowest levels of society, were referred to as neighbours of St. Peter, from whom they derived protection and prestige. The development of monastic priories and granges paralleled that of secular estates, and many towns grew up around religious houses that needed the services of lay dependents. Research on proprietary monasteries, or *Eigenklöster*, over which outside lords exercised a measure of control, has taken a flexible approach and emphasized the elaborate framework of personal relationships between religious houses and local magnates. Monasteries were *foci* of political and economic power and sometimes became centres of regional principalities.

This brings me to the effect on the study of medieval religion of the historical approaches and techniques that have developed over the past fifty years. Quantitative techniques in particular have been applied to necrologies and mortuary rolls, which I mentioned above, and to charters, which contain enough names, unlike most medieval sources, to be analysed for prosopographical evidence and for the social structure and membership of religious houses, about which comparatively little is known. Statistical studies have been done on religious texts, such as the *Dialogues* of Gregory the Great and the letters of Heloise and Abelard. Some of my own work would have been different if I had made word-counts. The existing resources privilege certain texts, especially those in the *Patrologia Latina*. Many types of sources, such as charters, letters and sermons, have not been statistically analysed. Indeed in some respects computer techniques have oriented research away from the study of integral original texts. The term 'secondary sources' is now sometimes used for works derived by computers from primary sources.

The study of medieval religion has also benefited from ancillary historical disciplines. I am thinking both of the traditional *Hilfswissenschaften* – palaeography, diplomatic, numismatics, sigillography – of which the contribution to religious history, as has been seen, goes back to the seventeenth century, and of literature, art and architecture, which have long been an almost intrinsic part of the history of religious life and spirituality. Albert Lenoir's *Architecture monastique* is still useful, though it appeared more than a century and a half ago, and Viollet-Le-Duc's great compendia contain information on medieval religion not easily found elsewhere. The setting of religious life, the images seen and adored by monks and nuns, the processions in which they participated, and the hymns and chants they sung were all part of medieval religion. In recent years there has been a particular interest in sacred spaces, both within and outside monasteries, the relationship to each other of the various buildings in a monastic enclosure, and their effect on the lives of the inhabitants. Churches were symbolic spaces: the image of paradise and the heavenly Jerusalem. Cemeteries were par excellence the sacred spaces of the dead. Archaeological findings have thrown doubts on the written sources, forcing historians to reconsider established views of the nature of religious life and the 'myths of origins' embodied in medieval foundation histories. Dendrochronology – the study of tree rings – and geology have presented new material on the dating and techniques of medieval building, and the analysis of bones and pollen have shed light on the diet, health and age of monks and nuns. Geography, toponymy and aerial photography, which developed in the period between the two world wars, have contributed to the study of the siting, foundation and ground-plans of religious houses, some of which have entirely vanished from above ground.

Aside from their architecture and decoration, however, only a start has been made on the study of the physical aspects of medieval religious houses and of the recruitment, social origins and numbers of their members, particularly in the so-called reformed houses of the eleventh and twelfth centuries. In the early middle ages many monks were offered (*oblati*) by their parents and were nourished (*nutriti*) in the monastery. Others converted to the religious life as adults and were known as *conversi* and *conversae*, a term which was used (somewhat confusingly) both for full members of the community who entered as adults and for lay-brothers and lay-sisters who performed manual labour and occupied a subordinate position. Some laymen became monks when they were dying, or thought to be dying, in order to enter the next world clad in the monastic habit. Others bought the right to bed and board in a community, known as a corrody, or only board, and yet other types of hangers-on are found. Jacques Dubois said that 'Ancient monasteries accepted to have living in their orbit a crowd of people who served God in their own way and who, since they refused during their lifetimes to enter into any defined category, cannot be put into one posthumously'.[12] The confusion of the past challenges the clarities imposed upon it by the present, and this, like other aspects of medieval and early modern monasticism, remains to a great extent *terra incognita*. The same is true of comparative monasticism, both within the Christian tradition and in other faiths, which will doubtless shed important light on the nature of the religious life.

It remains to say a few words in conclusion about the reasons for the current interest in the study of medieval religion. Three factors come to mind. First is the importance of religion in world affairs today. I hesitate to call this, as some scholars do, a 'return' of religion.[13] A 're-emergence' would be better, since religion has always been there, though hidden and below the surface, at least in some countries, and certainly in the view of scholars whose prejudice against religion has tended to obscure its importance. Their interests reflect the concerns of the present, however, and religion is no exception. Over the

[12] J. Dubois, 'Quelques problèmes de l'histoire de l'ordre des chartreux à propos de livres récents', *Revue d'histoire ecclésiastique*, lxiii (1968), 47.
[13] See Lamin Sanneh in the *Times Literary Supplement*, 13 Oct. 2006, pp. 13–14, where within the scope of a brief article the term 'return' is used seven times and 'comeback', 'reconstruction', 'awakening' and 'resurgence' once each.

past fifty years there has been a loss of confidence in the political, economic and social ideologies which dominated historical studies in the first half of the twentieth century, and a recognition of the importance of religion, like it or not, has emerged. There has been at the same time – and this is my second point – a realization of the close relation between religion and politics, especially nationalism, the origins of which go back to the middle ages. There is no inherent contradiction between studying religion and secular history. The spread of Islam, the split between the Latin and Greek churches, and the divisions within western Christianity which culminated in the Reformation – all medieval phenomena – paralleled political developments and created many of the problems to which the modern world is heir. It is often hard to distinguish religion from nationalism. Edmund Burke cited Cicero when he said that 'We know, and what is better, we feel inwardly that religion is the basis of civil society and the source of all good and of all comfort'.[14] Third, and perhaps most important for our purpose today, is a shift in historical thinking, partly under the influence of anthropology and sociology, that accepts that what people believe and think, as well as their material interests, influence their behaviour. A case in point is the crusades, which were long regarded as a predominantly secular movement masquerading under a religious cover. To argue the reverse was regarded as naive. They are now increasingly seen as a religious movement with political, social and economic overtones. It is no accident that Erdmann's groundbreaking book was not translated until the nineteen-seventies. It is a case not of either/or but of both/and. The study of medieval religion, as Christopher Brooke has shown in so many of his works, thus enriches our understanding of all aspects of the middle ages.

[14] Edmund Burke, *Reflections on the Revolution in France* (Harvard Classics, xxiv, New York, 1909), p. 238.

Medieval history and generic expansiveness: some thoughts from near Stratford-on-Avon

Paul Binski

> Not far from Stratford-on-Avon there is a spot where, owing to the extreme confusion of county boundaries, four shires meet. My purpose is to pursue a line of thought, a string of problems; they are problems on the boundaries of five fields of study, of liturgy, theology, literature, archaeology and *Kunstgeschichte*, and it would be absurd to pretend to have solved these.
>
> (Christopher Brooke, 'Religious sentiment and church design in the later middle ages', in *Medieval Church and Society: Collected Essays* (London, 1971), p. 163.)

I have before me two of Christopher Brooke's books which I read as a budding medievalist in the nineteen-seventies: what eye-openers they were, and still are, in every sense! One is *The Twelfth Century Renaissance* (1969). It is difficult to convey how, to a schoolboy and later Caius College history undergraduate hopelessly buried beneath the (to my mind, rather blank) writings on English political and constitutional history, this swift and elegant book brought to my mind the fresh reality, the ever-presentness, of that most important of centuries. The other book is the set of essays published as *Medieval Church and Society* (1971), particularly that lucid and true paper 'Religious sentiment and church design in the late middle ages' from which I borrow my epigraph. A scholar's early mental preparation counts for all; as a medievalist, mine had begun at Cambridge only a few years before the return of Christopher Brooke as a Fellow of Caius, in, I think, 1977. I recall my first undergraduate question to him after he presented a Caius History Society paper on cities and churches not long after his return – it was about the parish churches of London. It was a silly Betjemanesque question; rightly, he looked stumped, or at least bemused in a way which will be familiar to his many friends and pupils. He cannot have known that my early mental preparation was already taking on some of his

P. Binski, 'Medieval history and generic expansiveness: some thoughts from near Stratford-on-Avon', in *European Religious Cultures: Essays offered to Christopher Brooke on the occasion of his eightieth birthday*, ed. M. Rubin (London, 2020), pp. 17–33. License: CC-BY-NC-ND 4.0.

key ideas. He had already validated what I was soon to become as a research student. *The Twelfth Century Renaissance* had pictures in it. I liked, and still like, such books; indeed I like them so much that I myself now write them. But pictures were never left to speak for themselves, nor should they be. The book's aim, as its author sets out in its preface, was 'to give an insight into the cultural movements of the twelfth century by combining copious pictures and questions with an attempt to interpret them'.[1] The voice is that of an imaginative teacher; for me, it also formed an agenda (though I hope not a rigid one) for research.

We learn from Christopher Brooke that to think historically is not just to *use* images where they can help; it is to think imaginatively – to *form* images. Such images may open out vistas, perspectives which enable us to reach beyond the compartments of specialism to a wider horizon of medieval study. Perhaps high academic training can shape such vistas and encourage such visions, though much (perhaps more) depends too on schooling, family, general education and a willingness to be an 'amateur in many studies'. Just as scholarly tradition may be sapped by a process of authoritarian mummification which precludes change and questioning, so historical imagination necessarily requires risk, the educated leap of faith, the open-minded encounter with the unfamiliar. Christopher's work in the nineteen-sixties was positioned between scientific specialism and something inherently more liberal and of its time: the 'grand narrative' of church history was, in his view, also obliged to take into account the twelfth- and thirteenth-century counter-cultures of heresy, of the Franciscans, of images, of spiritual interiority or sentiment, of the popular. People and ideas could no longer be set aside.

This new humane, inclusive and liberal vision has been tremendously successful. It has not left my specialism, the history of art, untouched: far from it. Recently, I delivered the first set of Slade Lectures at the University of Oxford devoted to Gothic art and architecture in England in the thirteenth and fourteenth centuries. They were delivered in a chamber first spoken in by John Ruskin. I chose the theme in the knowledge that I would have to begin the series by offering some general intellectual framework for my subject, or at least for the way in which I intended to discuss it. My field is one which has for the most part been dominated by specialists and specialisms; but I believe very firmly (and for reasons that will now be obvious) that, despite this, it falls to the art historians to show why English Gothic art and architecture in this period might matter at all in general ways. Here, too, I belong to a tradition. The English have always enjoyed the process of lying back and being analysed

---

[1]   C. Brooke, *The Twelfth-Century Renaissance* (1969), p. 7.

by foreigners, or at least people of foreign extraction with Continental-sounding names. Hence perhaps the success of George Mikes's *How to be an Alien* with its lapidary and yet (almost) unfailingly accurate insight that 'In England everything is the other way round'. In the case of England in the later thirteenth and fourteenth century the debt to scholars of European training is immense: Otto Pächt, Nikolaus Pevsner and Jean Bony. Pächt showed how English manuscript illumination of the fourteenth century had something more general to show about the diffusion, albeit episodic, of the arts of *trecento* Italy in western Europe more generally; Pevsner placed English sculpture in the context of learned thought in the universities of northern Europe about man's relation to nature, seeing it as part of the onward march of science and English empiricism; Jean Bony created an eloquent case for seeing English Decorated architecture as the vanguard of late medieval Gothic in Europe as a whole.[2] The vision of these scholars was not necessarily 'interdisciplinary'; yet nor was it bound by the romantic nationalism of English scholarship of John Harvey and his generation.[3] If anything, it challenged such romanticism by insisting both on the wider vista of ideas and international relations, and on the proximity of England's culture to Europe's.

These were endeavours of enduring importance, shaped by a new post-war spirit of internationalism, and of course by the dominant concerns of the practice of art history itself at the time. My own field – let us say England and northern Europe between the twelfth and fifteenth centuries – has in the last half century witnessed a remarkable level of continuity as well as change, though the winds of change have started in the last two decades or so to blow more forcefully and to greater effect, just as they have within my discipline as a whole. The task of providing some Olympian summary of what has been going on in English Gothic for the last two or three generations is hopeless, but something at least must be said, if only because it shows why much has yet to be done. Experience teaches caution, and I might once have believed that in my chosen field the questions fell into two categories: easy ones and difficult ones. Now they all seem difficult.

English art history has been extraordinarily multi-stranded. But we tend to be coy about the way academic practice is determined, or at least shaped, by the intellectual and institutional structures of the academy. The

[2] O. Pächt, 'A Giottesque episode in English mediaeval art', *Journal of the Warburg and Courtauld Institutes*, vi (1943), 51–70; N. Pevsner, *The Leaves of Southwell* (London and New York, 1945) and *The Englishness of English Art* (repr. Harmondsworth, 1976); J. Bony, *The English Decorated Style: Gothic Architecture Transformed 1250–1350* (Oxford, 1979).

[3] J. Harvey, *Gothic England: a Survey of National Culture 1300–1450* (1947) and *The Perpendicular Style* (1978).

study of English medieval art in our universities is still shaped powerfully by two patterns of institutionalized thought: a tradition of positivistic, empiricist enquiry developed in the nineteenth century; and the science of art history, *Kunstgeschichte*. A third institutional manifestation is 'media-based specialization'.

In particular the methods propounded by Robert Willis (1800–75) are still with us. Willis was a Cambridge don, Jacksonian Professor of natural and experimental philosophy, and a formidable dissector of the masonry and structure of England's cathedral churches. His anatomy of Gothic architecture remains unshakable, not only in the sense that what Willis said has been shown in subsequent study to be almost invariably correct, but also in the sense that his way of doing things is still done.[4] Though a member of the Camden Society, he was obviously a Christian writer, but he was not an 'ideas' man so much as an empiricist who investigated the material foundations of architecture. Willis in effect invented what became the usual methods of building investigation used to the present day: close reading of the masonry, and equally close reading of the documentary sources which helped to account for its salient features, and which the Victorians had for the first time done so much to publish. The pages of the *Journal of the British Archaeological Association* and its *Conference Transactions* remain (with some significant exceptions) his most impressive monument.

It is in the light of this tradition that the impact in England of Pevsner's art history must be understood. Pevsner was both a formalist and an ideas man in the Germanic tradition of *Kunstwissenschaft*. We forget at our peril that it was Pevsner who, in the nineteen-forties, began to analyse such concepts as the identity of the architect, the debt of sculptors to Aristotelian natural philosophy and the thought of such men as Albertus Magnus (I think of his famous little book *The Leaves of Southwell* published in 1945), and the formal impact of the English Decorated style in Europe, rather before Erwin Panofsky's work in similar vein exploded in the field in the nineteen-fifties. In his preface to Joan Evans's volume on *English Art 1307–1461* which appeared in 1949 in the Oxford History of English Art series, Tom Boase reflected on the then current parochialism of English study as follows:

> Art history, a clumsy but useful term, does not hold in this country the position that has been given to *Kunstgeschichte* on the Continent . . . Our tradition of connoisseurship, the detailed study of works of art and objects of antiquity in order to decide their date and provenance, is, it is true, well established . . .

---

[4] R. Willis, *Architectural History of Some English Cathedrals* (2 pts., Chicheley, 1972).

This resolute objectivity has been the complete antithesis of the exuberance of *Stilkritik*.

Boase was right. And yet, though *Kunstgeschichte* as a set of practices and beliefs brought England into line with Europe, it raised another and rather more challenging question. It was interested in art and ideas. But which ideas? *Kunstwissenschaft* had already had the effect of elevating the value-free analysis of the development of form, of style, to hitherto unknown levels of academic respectability. It had become acceptable to relate art to ideas; and yet its language was by nature essentialist, collectivist, secularist and impersonal. This had two important consequences which are still with us, and which have to be addressed. Because it was essentialist and collectivist, it sidelined or only paid lip service to human agency, to the actuality of situations of human choice which produced art works. And because it was secularist in tone it sidelined almost completely the issue of religion. As late as 1979, Jean Bony's brilliant critique of English Decorated architecture provided a dazzling showcase of ideas undoubtedly rooted in nineteenth-century French rationalism, and which was scarcely at all a history of the human making, use and understanding of buildings: patrons, architects and users seem not to enter the equation; nor, needless to say, does religion (oddly, castles were omitted too).

The question of the historical actuality of human thoughts, choices and motives, to say nothing of the question of their beliefs, remains with us in the face of the new forms of art historical enquiry of the last few decades. These have wrestled both with positivism and one aspect of the old *Kunstgeschichte* especially: its unshakable conviction in the analytical and pedagogic value of formal analysis. Connoisseurship came to be seen as an unpleasant but necessary phase that thinking art historians had to grow out of, like adolescence: it was a bourgeois illusion, masking the ideological character of art production and reception. I myself started as a practitioner of *Kunstgeschichte* and still consider it essential at the pedagogic level to teach students about history and about style. These are, after all, techniques, means not ends, which establish the specialist basis for the wider vista. Art history at its best, it may fairly be claimed, has always been interdisciplinary. My sympathy for some of the methods of the (now not so new) new art history lies partly in its renewed challenge to the old disciplinary boundaries – our county boundaries near Stratford-on-Avon – policed so carefully in regard to 'media-based specialization', which meant in effect that more advanced students could be parcelled out into specialisms such as architecture, sculpture, book illumination, wall painting, decorative arts, and so on, and could continue throughout their professional lives to exist in a sort of tolerant co-existence with their neighbours over the wall, without asking whether this division of the field was necessary or helpful, except as a defence of the vested interest of specialization itself. Indeed it seems to me that many, if not most, of the really engaging and transformative ideas in my discipline have entered it from outside.

The key difficulty in relation to the intellectual health of the discipline posed by media-based specialization was that each medium had its own traditions of practice, critical language, object domain and its own canon of great works. But the boundaries of practice acted in effect as an inhibition, because they created an implicit legitimacy of practice. To look beyond what was considered the normal range of sources and concepts that might be brought into relation to a building or art object became not just questionable, but in some way *unprofessional*. It was actively hostile to the idea that the imaginative historian is necessarily an 'amateur in many studies'. And it was this self-denying ordinance that the new art histories, with their implicit questioning of the concept of the canon mounted from outside the discipline, effectively challenged. The counter-culturalism of the nineteen-sixties had, by the end of the nineteen-nineties, become a sort of philosophical multiculturalism: with the triumph of 'theory', the primacy of old-fashioned skills was challenged, and broad patterns of development dissolved. An (apparently) more sophisticated perspective on texts and sources emerged. In dealing with the ideas invested in written sources, for example, could there actually be such things as respectable, utterly reliable, value-free, 'official' writings or 'straight historical material'; might 'bad' art as well as 'good' art not be considered; were these pre-ordained structures of thought not rather elitist and exclusionary?

Not all these developments were necessarily as healthy or liberal as they might seem, and I concede immediately that my remarks are themselves precisely instances of the legacy of empiricism, formulating generalized opinion in such a way as to eliminate bias and diversity of outlook. But I want to persist with this theme by looking at current architectural history in which, as I have suggested, the Willis paradigm is still extraordinarily tenacious in the English-speaking world. English architectural history even at its best (and most 'professional') remains cautious about ideas. Consider the rather rough handling Panofsky's reading of the treatises of Abbot Suger of St.-Denis has recently had at the hands of more empirically-minded architectural writers such as Peter Kidson.[5] Suger's writings of the eleven-thirties to eleven-forties have long enjoyed something like canonical status

---

[5] P. Kidson, 'Panofsky, Suger, and St.-Denis', *Journal of the Warburg and Courtauld Institutes*, l (1987), 1–17.

as a foundation text for the explanation of the origins of Gothic in Paris. They were dragged into art historical discourse by Erwin Panofsky, who edited them as if they were chapters on art history rather like Jex-Blake's *The Elder Pliny's Chapters on the History of Art*, which of course they are not: they belong to a literary genre, the abbatial history or *Gesta Abbatum*, and so concern many other things as well, which Panofsky simply left out.[6] Art history produced its own 'canonical' texts by permitting a certain brutalization of their form and possibly meaning. It has been pointed out that Suger's writings were either of nugatory importance because they were not circulated outside St.-Denis (which is undeniable, though whether the circulation of a text is a sole guide to its eventual interest or importance is questionable)[7] or that they were anyway conventional in tone, and hence stood in a loose relationship to the real preoccupations of historians of Gothic.

Or take a well-known English text, the *Metrical Life* of St. Hugh of Lincoln, written in Latin *c.*1220 at around the time of St. Hugh's canonization, which contains an astonishing section on the new choir which Hugh himself built at Lincoln cathedral in the eleven-nineties.[8] As with Panofsky on Suger, there is always the risk of conscripting texts to the service of answering questions they were not designed to answer; questions framed by us, not them. One distinguished architectural historian has recently dismissed outright the use and value to architectural historians of the *Metrical Life*.[9] He observes

as a document of the contemporary response to Gothic architecture this text is extremely disappointing since it is mostly couched in traditional symbolic-allegorical terms, with the occasional fanciful touches such as the likening of the high vaults to the wings of hovering birds. There is nothing to indicate that the writer realized or cared that he was in the presence of one of the strangest and most innovatory churches of his time. Indeed there is no sign that he possessed any kind of conceptual framework in which to situate the individual work of art. Like virtually all medieval writers who discuss buildings, the author of the Metrical Life was content to marvel.

But my interest in this text, on the contrary, is to see what it tells us precisely about the text's conventions and its audience, the commissioning class of

---

[6] *Abbot Suger on the Abbey Church of St. Denis and its Art Treasures*, ed. E. Panofsky (2nd edn., Princeton, N.J., 1979).

[7] C. Norton, 'Bernard, Suger and Henry I's crown jewels', *Gesta*, xlv (2006), 1–14.

[8] *The Metrical Life of Saint Hugh*, ed. and trans. C. Garton (Lincoln, 1986).

[9] C. Wilson, *The Gothic Cathedral* (1990), p. 10.

canons at Lincoln, as much as about the building. In regard to the quoted passage, I have a particularly important reservation about *convention*. It seems to me that we cannot simultaneously argue that a text is framed in 'traditional symbolic-allegorical terms' and that it possesses no 'conceptual framework'. An *a priori* norm is surely concealed in such judgements: we recognize as authentic or useful only those texts which contain something apparently free of convention, or familiar to us. The norm is, of course, that of the modern rationalist or empiricist, sceptical about 'mere' rhetoric as representing flapdoodle, as in the 'fanciful' 'wings of birds' passage in the *Life*. Fanciful to whom? Presumably not the readers of psalms 54, 83 or 138, or those many medieval writers familiar with the common analogy of rapture to being carried aloft, experienced in the presence of great buildings. A text of this order could make successful claims if, and only if, it construed innovation, including innovation in architecture, in terms which were seen as traditional or legitimate by its audience. The terms selected are indicative of normative beliefs located in the community, not in the will of the author or the modern art historian expecting *Kunstgeschichte* to drip from the medieval pen. I do not see any harm in suggesting that Gothic architecture in the twelfth century was in part the product of a very sophisticated game in the production of meaning, played between highly intelligent masons and clerical interpreters. The fastidious control of truth beloved of empiricism is, however, unlikely to be sympathetic to such exchanges.

In contrast to this positivistic hierarchy of genre and media-based specialization, I proceed from the assumption that what has been called 'generic expansiveness' – the admission of a wider range of objects and texts into the discussion, in more unorthodox combinations and relations – is intrinsically healthy.[10] I do not think one can write a history of the arts in Gothic England without studying all the arts, and any texts that may be helpful regardless of their canonicity: historical writings, hagiography, texts on the regulation of conduct, works of pastoral instruction, encomiastic poetry, ecumenical and diocesan legislation, visitation records, curricular literature, secular literature, religious literature, polemical rants and – in our period especially – sermons. These texts must be read carefully and as far as is possible on their own terms – but they must be read and understood, because they pose any historian the question of what exactly it is that we count as evidence.

---

[10] For 'generic expansiveness' I am indebted to M. Goldie, 'The context of the foundations', in *Rethinking the Foundations of Modern Political Thought*, ed. A. Brett, J. Tulley and H. Hamilton-Bleakley (Cambridge, 2006), pp. 3–19, at pp. 9–10.

Another important vehicle, which has gained hugely in importance in the public presentation of our subject, offers an opportunity to give these preoccupations shape and purpose: the exhibition. There will always be disagreement about the use and value of public exhibitions: for academics, aside from stressing the importance of what they do in a wider arena, they may offer valuable professional opportunities to up-and-coming scholars; they may act to summarize the state of the discipline, of study, or come into being in order to motivate or even galvanize further work. Certainly the catalogued 'show' has become the great *summa* of our time. In the mid nineteen-eighties Jonathan Alexander offered me the incomparable opportunity of assisting him with the catalogue of the exhibition *Age of Chivalry: Art in Plantagenet England 1200–1400*, held at the Royal Academy, London, in 1987–8. Since (as a co-editor of the catalogue) I am partly to blame, I see no reason not to take this opportunity to issue in some well-intended criticisms of what was in many ways the largest and most spectacularly successful exhibition of its type ever mounted. *Age of Chivalry* had been preceded by exhibitions of English Romanesque art and Anglo-Saxon art at the Heywood Gallery and British Museum in 1984. It offered a snapshot of the results of the veritable explosion of specialized studies which have dominated the field as we understand it at present. It was shaped by a progressive interest in the patronage, social history and function of art in the whole period 1200–1400, taking far greater account of various social groups and reflecting a far more inclusive notion of 'visual culture' than would have been conceivable in the nineteen-forties or fifties. With the benefit of twenty years' hindsight one only has to look at the lead essays in the catalogue to see the direction things were taking: the common use of the word 'image', not 'art'; essays on written sources of the more generically expansive kind, and on language itself; and on women. These topics were introduced, it must be said, in a polemical spirit of righting past wrongs, of rebalancing the field in a more socially responsible way. Quotidian art appeared with high art; the mighty buttresses of the edifice of scientific certainty were being consciously subverted from the margins.

But other things were steered around as if they were obstacles, or simply vanished over the horizon. For instance, the issue of the representation of power and patronage at the centre rather than at the margins was taken on tangentially, as if political theory and practice were already beyond serious discussion; there was therefore no satisfying discussion of monarchy or political principle and practice in art. The tendency, by no means wrong in itself, was to look in to the centre, not out from it. Over the horizon it went. Worse, and I think most problematically, there must be some doubt as to whether *Age of Chivalry* dealt adequately with religion and the institutionalized framework of religious belief. In its choice and balance of expository essays especially, religion's importance was taken for granted, not scrutinized. I think this was more than the product of a commercial fear of 'churchiness' as a poor selling-point for the public at large, though that may have been a consideration. The sub-Marxist social bent of *Age of Chivalry* had contrived, paradoxically, to align it with the positivistic tradition which so much of the exhibition was attacking, in disclosing scepticism about religious belief as anything more than mere 'ideology' and the church as anything more than an agent of social and economic control. There was no lead chapter about the *constitutive* role that religious belief, knowledge, sentiment and practice had in medieval England. One might never have guessed from it that this was the era of St. Francis, St. Dominic, St. Thomas of Canterbury, St. Edmund of Abingdon, St. Thomas Aquinas, St. Albertus Magnus, to say nothing of Richard Rolle or Wyclif, the legislation of the Fourth Lateran Council, the emergence of Purgatory and so on: for it is one thing to mention these people and things *en passant*, another to appreciate to the full their gravity, force and sheer diversity of outcome. This issue of balance was highlighted only a few years later by the publication of Eamon Duffy's *The Stripping of the Altars* (1992) which is a text precisely about the constitutive social role of religion as a fundamental ordering principle: the superstructures of belief shaped the substructure of economy and society. Whatever one's views about Professor Duffy's influential book and its particular stance, it served almost immediately to wrong-foot the types of assumption that I am pinpointing in *Age of Chivalry*.

The much greater role played by religion in the catalogue of the sequel exhibition held at the Victoria and Albert Museum, London, in 2003, *Gothic: Art for England 1400–1547,* reminds us that recent thinking has seen a more general revision of this systematic and professional flight from religion, one brought about at least in part by the human science of anthropology, a discipline that has been especially influential in the sphere of medieval studies (Hans Belting's *Bild-Anthropologie*, Caroline Walker Bynum's work on religious culture). Giles Constable writes about this theme elsewhere in this volume. It has been at least partly through anthropology that the wider importance of the religious domain has been rediscovered. Indeed with this re-emergence has come a challenge to what one might call the secular theories of modernity. These theories had promoted formalism in art-historical analysis: and it now became possible to see that formalism was itself an aspect, of not an outright strategy, of secularization. This insight helps place in due perspective not only the formalist techniques of art history, but also the 'new historicist' movement in medieval studies since the nineteen-eighties and nineteen-nineties, whose founding ideas were not merely secularist, but at times positively anticlerical: I think of the brilliantly engaging, but also consciously troubling, work of Michael Camille. According to this history-as-power school of thought, religious practices and artefacts are essentially ideological constructs ripe for demystification, rather than being owed recognition and understanding on something like their own terms. Historical 'sympathy' is a reactionary affliction.

It perhaps goes without saying that the unsentimental and (I do not think the word is too strong) anticlerical tenor of the new historicist writings – for instance the work of R. I. Moore on the origins of racial and other types of persecution – has gone hand in hand with scepticism about moral systems of thought in general. In my view, *Age of Chivalry* marginalized religion; but it also set aside the history of ethics. To understand why this matters, we might start with the very title *Age of Chivalry*, a topic which, again, finds no commentary within the catalogue on the importance of chivalry as something which became codified by the early thirteenth century as a formal discourse of nobility. As it happens, when planned the show was going to be called something like 'The great Gothic show'. But then two things happened in Thatcher's London. First, 'Gothic' was appropriated fashionably as a post-Punk style of dress and so at the time was not medieval, just transgressive. The Royal Academy was not the place for a weird fashion statement. Second, Lloyds Bank, late in the day, agreed to sponsor the show. The Bank's logo was a prancing horse, so horses had somehow to be worked in, and pretty quick: no room for commissioning new articles and rejigging the show's contents. Hence 'chivalry', floating free of much actually in the show, became part of the title. So there was an excuse (of sorts). But I mention chivalry as but one aspect of the ethical-religious question in the art of the middle ages which again seemed for a while to drop out, and then drop back in, to serious discussion. We recall that it was the practitioners of *Kunstgeschichte* who were interested in art and ideas. Erwin Panofsky laid the foundations for much speculation in 1951 when he published his ambitious *Gothic Architecture and Scholasticism* on the art-ideas nexus. Pevsner's *Leaves of Southwell* appeared even earlier. But somehow between 1951 and the mid nineteen-eighties this type of high-minded art-ideas relation was pushed out of the picture. In *Age of Chivalry*, once again, we learn little about the schools or universities, about the relation of learned or intellectual culture to society at large, and as itself an agent of change; nothing about scholasticism or law, or science. The reasons for this lie, again, in a mindset which has tended to demote the importance of elite intellectual culture and practice, except as a negative exemplification of certain sorts of grasping social ambition and supercilious social intolerance and privilege. The targets are of course the clerks, the young men trained in the episcopal households and universities of medieval Europe who entered government or the lucrative arts, law, medicine and who rose to high office: the men who, in effect, governed. In contrast to them, popular culture might well come to seem innocent and virtuous.

I think the importance of this clerical class is really twofold: as a point of origination of ethical practice and theory; and as an instance of that institutionalized intellectualism which Alexander Murray identified in his remarkable book *Reason and Society in the Middle Ages*. In recent work I have adopted the position that to understand Gothic art we have to face up to a fact that by its nature seems to draw one into the politics of class: that this art was not only frequently religious in its means and ends, but that its tenor, its ethos, was essentially aristocratic.[11] My reasons for adopting this nakedly revisionist stance will perhaps be becoming clearer in the light of what I have said about my field so far. But I could claim serious philosophical sanction for my general approach in Clifford Geertz's statement in his paper 'Religion as a cultural system' (1966):

> let us begin with a paradigm: viz. that sacred symbols function to synthesise a people's ethos – the tone, character and quality of their life, its moral and aesthetic style and mood – and their world-view – the picture they have of the way things in sheer actuality actually are, their most comprehensive ideas of order.[12]

In short I wanted to reclaim the domain of the aesthetic, of form perceivable to the senses, from its post-Kantian dead end in modern times. I hoped to understand how form might embody value, without wishing to insinuate that form could only be understood morally. This is not a matter of 'ethicism', that is, the legitimization of actual ethical judgement of art; it is merely the recognition of the pervasive character of ethical thought and practice in the aesthetic domain more generally. So, I asked if there were any common features in the systems of ethical and aesthetic inhibition developed by men professionally attached to the church and the universities – legislative aesthetics as it were – which might link, say, architecture, conduct, dress, church furnishing, music and the inner regulation of the moral self. The question is of course inherently 'generically expansive'. My answer was that there were and there weren't: it is the case, for instance, that the medieval church in its

---

[11] I will, I hope, be excused for mentioning *Becket's Crown: Art and Imagination in Gothic England 1170–1300* (New Haven and London, 2004).

[12] C. Geertz, 'Religion as a cultural system', in *Anthropological Approaches to the Study of Religion*, ed. M. Banton (1966), pp. 1–46.

very makeup of liturgy, sacraments and so on, had a didactic element as a sign of divine order, as did the *Lives* of the saints as exemplifications of what we can be. But the moral case could not be argued universally. The link between the moral and the aesthetic in the middle ages was strong but not automatic. The question at least allowed us to continue to take an interest in appearances without falling into the trap of an intellectually bankrupt formalism.

My recent debt to such American thinkers as Geertz and C. Stephen Jaeger will perhaps be evident. Jaeger's work on courtliness was a particular stimulus, and it showed me how my own work was preoccupied with Norbert Elias's 'civilizing process'.[13] Could we dare to argue that the clerical class itself was involved in the development of what became known as courtliness, courtesy, and in the legitimation of that code of conduct known as chivalry; and could we admit too, that these codes were actually derived from the ethical philosophies and practices of pre-Christian Rome? Was chivalry actually a neoclassical institution? Jaeger sees civility as a practical accomplishment of the cathedral schools of Ottonian Germany. The eminent and very amusing art historian Christopher Hohler once observed that good manners had been invented by the French with the sole purpose of annoying the Germans. Jaeger argued that this was the wrong way round: courtesy in its French guise was actually a Romano-German invention based on Ciceronian precepts, which became romanticized and textualized in the twelfth and thirteenth centuries as it ceased actually to be practised. It lived on in formal courtesy books for the secular nobility and clerical tags like William of Wykeham's 'Manners makyth man'. What it left western Europe with was a versatile concept of nobility of behaviour founded on virtues such as temperance: as Alexander Murray observed in 1978, 'The equation of nobility with virtue was a widespread idea. Exactly who believed it and in what sense cannot be gauged, certainly not as medieval studies now stand'.[14] Jaeger has since tried to gauge exactly this.

The tendency to detach the ethical institution of chivalry from Christian roots is also marked to an extent in the work of Maurice Keen, or at least so we are told in David Crouch's recent study *The Birth of Nobility* (2005). But one sign of the importance of churchmen and literate clerks seems to be indicated precisely by the anticlerical tenor of the history-as-power school of thought. Anticlericalism (medieval or modern) serves the useful purpose of underlining precisely the constitutive power of the clerical class's

---

[13] I refer especially to C. S. Jaeger, *The Origins of Courtliness: Civilizing Trends and the Formation of Courtly Ideals 939–1210* (Philadelphia, Pa., 1985) and *The Envy of Angels: Cathedral Schools and Social Ideals in Medieval Europe, 950–1200* (Philadelphia, Pa., 1994).

[14] A. Murray, *Reason and Society in the Middle Ages* (Oxford, 1978), p. 272.

thinking which I myself have drawn upon. Alexander Murray showed how the rise of rational culture of mathematics and learning, the 'Upward thrust of mind', was both a positive and negative force, something against which reaction occurred. Building on this case, R. I. Moore indicated the ways in which intellectual culture did not naturalistically reflect society, but was *constitutive* of its ideas and prejudices.[15] It defined 'types' in terms of which it itself was to be defined: heretics, homosexuals, sinners, but also saints, in the creation of which it held a new monopoly through the agency of the papacy. As a regime it was powerful. It invented the Inquisition. It largely formed the bureaucracies of power trained in Latin which were emerging in the monarchical states of England, France and the papacy. In the universities it sought the defence of private law, the *privilegium*, of freedom in the schools from the coercive actions of public and diocesan power. These clerks subscribed to the ethics of nobility but were themselves frequently worldly social upstarts, natural meritocrats. They evinced the replacement of warriors by literate clerks as the agents of government. One of their symbolic types was the ambitious, Faust-like clerk Theophilus, who sold his soul to the devil but who was redeemed by the Virgin Mary. Such men's ambition stood in opposition to blood and land, to hereditary right, nobility of the flesh; they also stood aside from the calm, reflective virtues of monasticism. In regard to them it may be interesting to consider to what extent noble and monastic patronage in England felt a certain mutual sympathy. It is tempting to think of Whigs and Tories, for in cultural life, as in literature (as Northrop Frye suggested) there are only so many stories to tell.

In *Becket's Crown* I hoped to show why, to my mind, this class mattered in regard to the landscape of English art and architecture. On the positive side we have the issues which Panofsky, among others, spotted: the rise of a rational intellectualist culture was associated with the rise of the 'expert', the technocrat, who might in cathedral building demonstrate superior science in regard to geometry, mathematics, logistical planning, man-management, and so on. Here was the basis for a sociology of the professions which has since exploded onto the scene. On the negative side, again in relation to architectural history, we can see how attitudes to the clerks were of formative importance. The history of patronage at Canterbury cathedral was manifestly affected, as the monk Gervase of Canterbury tells us towards 1200, by the appalling relations between the archbishops' secular clerks, the young bureaucrats in their households, and the conservative and privilege-minded monks of the priory. Were it not for Pope Innocent III who blocked

---

[15] R. I. Moore, *The Formation of a Persecuting Society* (Oxford, 1987).

the plan, the metropolitan church might under Archbishop Hubert Walter have been built anew at Lambeth. London would have been the primatial see, and a third giant Gothic church would have risen on the banks of the Thames along with Westminster abbey and St. Paul's.[16] This did not happen; but it might have, because the clerks wanted an independent electoral college for the archbishop, perhaps on the lines of the college of cardinals in Rome, and free of monastic influence, as at Canterbury. Again, this powerful class of religious administrators was enclosing itself behind fortified walls in the fourteenth century as relations between the cities and the great ecclesiastical corporations degenerated: indeed, as Charles Coulson has suggested in his study of crenellation – the fortifying in appearance or effect of cathedral precincts – this was not simply a virtuous defensive battening down of the hatches in face of windy urban populaces but a positive 'will' which could issue from the aggressive, supercilious clerical class itself as an aspect, among other things, of class ambition.[17]

In this relationship, this creative friction, between the new rational culture and the old social orders may lie the possibility of a different type of history of the visual arts in the thirteenth and fourteenth century in England. In framing such a history, the work of earlier generations of historians will play a vital part. It was Edmund Bishop's remarkable chapter on the history of the Christian altar published in *Liturgica Historica* (1918) which provided the starting point for the essay by Christopher Brooke on 'Religious sentiment and church design in the later middle ages' I mentioned earlier. The theme was an important one which provided the perfect context for that balance between different fields of study which constitutes imaginative history. By the thirteenth and especially the fourteenth century the clerical corporations were not just enclosing themselves and adopting a siege mentality in regard to the 'windy' urban populaces: they were parcelling out the interiors of their churches into equally screened and contained safe places for the enclosure of relics and especially the reserved sacrament. The compartmentalized early medieval church interior gave way to the tremendous unified Romanesque vista, only to return as the great churches' interiors were screened and enclosed in the interests of religious sentiment, or what Bishop called 'feeling'. Christopher Brooke rightly understood that this process of screening was not just aesthetically significant, even though no-one would doubt the sheer visual impact of the giant reredos screens that were to rise between 1300 and the Reformation behind the

[16] See T. Tatton-Brown, *Lambeth Palace* (2000), pp. 19–28.
[17] C. Coulson, 'Hierarchism in conventual crenellation. An essay in the sociology and metaphysics of medieval fortification', *Medieval Archaeology*, xxvi (1982), 69–100.

high altars of many major cathedrals and cathedral priories in England. The significance lay in the way that the screen form, the enclosure, the creation of the elite domain, was itself a form symbolic of something deeper and more complex, located within the development of private religious sentiment and the relation of the soul to God, as expressed in the Eucharist and the sacraments. Considerations of actual form, style, were (indeed are) in a sense less important than the strategies of life-arrangement implicit in these enclosed spaces, that is, 'style' in a much more general sense. The aim was not to explore the 'privatization' of the religion and class structure of medieval England as an aspect of the aetiology of the Reformation. It was rather to suggest a new agenda for the study of selfhood and religion in the pre-Reformation period. No claim was made that this notion of sentiment or feeling was simple in make up and origin. The point is that something fundamental was obtained by deploying, within the Victorian spirit of enquiry, a humanity and precision suited also to modern times.

I conclude with a final thought: for the present writer, much indebted to this style of enquiry, the approach of Christopher Brooke's prescient essay lies precisely in its 'generic expansiveness' – the idea that we cannot limit our understanding of English medieval art or history to the insights afforded by a set range of canonical texts or by the constraints of conventional disciplinary boundaries created by university curricula. The canon changes: and I might perhaps be allowed a final reflection on how things seem to change at the same time, in the same way, but for different reasons. In the early nineteen-eighties as a young research student and then Fellow at Caius, Christopher lent me great support in my study of the so-called Painted Chamber at Westminster, the royal bedchamber in the medieval palace covered lavishly in wall paintings in the reigns of Henry III and Edward I which, though copied and documented, vanished almost entirely in the great palace fire of 1834. Before my work was published in 1986 the Painted Chamber scarcely existed as a 'canonical' work. My starting-point was of course from within the English empiricist and antiquarian tradition. Yet I found myself creating a book (and indeed, in a sense, a work of art) which has since re-entered the broader historical reassessment of the reigns of Henry and his son. Indeed in the nineteen-eighties, as I was later to discover, a new perception was arising that public or semi-public wall paintings could embody ideas as more than mere epiphenomena, but rather as actual transforming and constitutive ideologies: paintings worked to do something, as well as embodying ideas. They could be admitted responsibly to the canon of the history of ideas more generally. I cite the work, also published in 1986, by Professor Quentin Skinner – a noted contextualist incidentally – on the fourteenth-century frescos of good and bad government by Ambrogio Lorenzetti in the

Palazzo Pubblico in Siena, in which Skinner took issue with the idea that their discourse was Aristotelian rather than pre-humanistic, that is, Greek rather than Roman.[18] The Westminster images were themselves not wholly unrelated to thought about the legitimacy and illegitimacy of certain styles of governance, expressed not in abstract personification as at Siena, but in practical narrative example from the universal text, the Bible. Recently Professor Skinner has argued that the virtue of taking wall paintings and other cultural productions seriously is that doing so challenges the notion of a distinct 'history of political theory'. He continues 'We need to replace [this notion] … with a more general form of intellectual history in which, even if we continue to centre on 'political' texts, we allow the principle of generic expansiveness the freest reign'.[19] It will be obvious that I concur: my aim has been to celebrate Christopher Brooke's part in the growing recognition that made these sentiments possible.

---

[18] Q. Skinner, 'Ambrogio Lorenzetti: the artist as political philosopher', in *Proceedings of the British Academy*, lxxii (1986), 1–56. My study was published as *The Painted Chamber at Westminster* (1986).

[19] Skinner, Brett, Tully and Hamilton-Bleakley, p. 244.

II

Life-cycle and vocation

Ninth-century vocations of persons of mature years

Janet L. Nelson

In 1970, Christopher Brooke published two papers that for this reader at least were intellectually life-changing: in one, on 'Historical writing in England between 850 and 1150', he pointed out, *inter alia*, the dependence of Asser's biography of Alfred on the *Lives* of Louis the Pious by Thegan and the Astronomer; in the other, his presidential lecture to the Ecclesiastical History Society on 'The missionary at home: the church in the towns 1000–1250', Christopher compared the 'worker priests', that is, the secular clergy, in late Anglo-Saxon towns with the early friars, alike engaged in the work of conversion 'by infiltration and example'.[1] In 1989, Christopher published *The Medieval Idea of Marriage* which has ever since been a mainstay of my M.A. teaching on medieval religion and medieval women.[2] That book was dedicated, with exquisite aptness, to Rosalind. And I cannot resist mentioning another mainstay-book which Christopher and Rosalind wrote together: *Popular Religion in the Middle Ages: Western Europe 1000–1300*.[3] Note the time-spans covered in all those works – here you can see confident traversing of the divides between laypeople and professional religious and between earlier and central medieval periods. In deciding to talk this morning about a variant of conversion in the ninth century, I was encouraged by the thought that no medieval age, nor form of conversion, is alien to Christopher. I confess I was encouraged too by the vice-chancellor's words yesterday about actuarial calculations of academic longevity; and also by Giles Constable's acknowledgement of the varieties of religious

---

[1] C. N. L. Brooke, 'Historical writing in England between 850 and 1150', in *La storiografia altomedievale* (Settimane di Studio del Centro Italiano di Studi sull'Alto Medioevo, xvii, 1970), pp. 233–47; C. N. L. Brooke, 'The missionary at home: the church in the towns 1000–1250', *Studies in Church History*, vi (1970), 59–83.

[2] C. N. L. Brooke, *The Medieval Idea of Marriage* (Oxford, 1989).

[3] C. N. L. and R. Brooke, *Popular Religion in the Middle Ages: Western Europe, 1000–1300* (London, 1984).

J. L. Nelson, 'Ninth-century vocations of persons of mature years', in *European Religious Cultures: Essays offered to Christopher Brooke on the occasion of his eightieth birthday*, ed. M. Rubin (London, 2020), pp. 37–46. License: CC-BY-NC-ND 4.0.

life and the range of people serving God in their own way who could be embraced under the term *conversi*.[4] Renouncing the world in mature years is a pan-medieval phenomenon.

But my paper for Christopher is about the ninth century – where some interesting conjunctures become visible. I begin with a reference in an unexpected place, and I explore the secular contexts for such renunciations. Then I turn to religious contexts, and discuss those gendered female. Finally I bring secular and religious together by extending the picture to include male renunciation.

First then, the reference:

> If any one of our faithful men after our death and pierced by love for God and for us (*Dei et nostro amore compunctus*), wishes to renounce the world (*seculo renuntiare*), and has a son or kinsman who can be of service to the state (*qui reipublicae prodesse valeat*), let him be able to pass on his office(s) in a lawful assembly (*suos honores ... ei valeat placitare*), as he thinks fit. And if he wants to live quietly on his own property (*si in alode suo quiete vivere voluerit*), let no-one [i.e., no state official] presume to put any obstacle in his way, nor require anything from him, except only this, that he go to the defence of the fatherland.[5]

This is Charles the Bald, king and emperor, about to set off from Francia for Italy in June 877, making arrangements for the welfare of the *res publica* in chapter 10 of the Capitulary of Quierzy. The text is famous not for the chapter just quoted, but for the one just before it, chapter 9, which provides for succession to countships – allegedly symptomatic of the growing tendency towards the heritability of office that brought down the Carolingian empire, but in fact foreseeing special conditions (*si comes obierit* [sc. back in Francia] *cuius filius nobiscum* [sc. in Italy] *sit*), providing for interim measures to have been taken by the officers of the county and the bishop acting together, and reserving the right of the king, once informed of the situation, to give the county to whomsoever he pleased.[6] Chapters 9 and 10 belong together in the fairly obvious sense that they are both concerned with the transmission of office from one generation to the next. That theme in fact hovers over the whole capitulary: Charles the Bald, aged fifty-four, had the possibility of his own demise, and the succession to

---

4 See above, p. 43.

5 *Capitularia Regum Francorum*, ed. A. Boretius (2 vols., Monumenta Germaniae Historica, Leges, Hanover, 1883–93) (hereafter M.G.H. Capit.), ii, no. 281, c. 10, 358.

6 M.G.H. Capit., c. 9, 358. For the doom-laden reading, see Montesquieu, *The Spirit of the Laws*, pt. vi, bk. 31, chs. 25, 28–30, trans. A. M. Cohler, B. C. Miller and H. Stone (Cambridge, 1989), pp. 708–9, 712–15. For a contextualized reading, see J. L. Nelson, *Charles the Bald* (London, 1992), pp. 248–51.

his own office, very much in mind as he embarked on what was indeed to be his final journey to Italy, 877 the last summer of his life. In chapter 10, however, he envisages that his own death might impel some of his faithful men who have adult sons (or kinsmen) of their own to withdraw from the world into monastic life. It is this renunciation of the world on the part of a man of mature years, a decision termed *conversio* in other Carolingian texts, whose meaning I want to explore in this paper.

A number of ninth-century cases of projected or actual withdrawal from the world of persons of mature years can be set in the context of familial strategies. The earliest of the ninth-century cases – and I confess it is an atypical one, for reasons which will become clear – is that of Angilbert.[7] Born into the high Frankish aristocracy, probably just a few years younger than Charlemagne, and 'nurtured' in the palace 'almost from the rudiments of infancy', Angilbert prospered at court, in part thanks to his poetic talents: Alcuin, chief scholarly adviser and for a while Angilbert's teacher, nicknamed him Homer (or as Charlemagne called him, 'Homerianus puer'),[8] from which we can infer he had mastered the epic genre. Among Angilbert's early work has been claimed 'De conversione Saxonum' (777), which celebrated Charlemagne 'leading the new progeny of Christ into the palace'.[9] Angilbert also rendered services of a different kind in the seven-eighties by helping to establish the Carolingian regime in Italy as adviser to Charlemagne's young son, the sub-king Pippin, and then returning to Francia to advise Charlemagne himself (the king called him *manualis nostrae familiaritatis auricolarius*, 'our close and intimate counsellor'), serving as a cleric in the royal chapel, and as chief envoy to Rome in the seven-nineties. At more or less the same time, Angilbert's career at court progressed in two ways: he was given the abbacy of St.-Riquier, near Amiens, and became the lover of Charlemagne's favourite daughter, Bertha. These signs of royal favour might seem to pull in different directions only if you did not appreciate the peculiar character of Charlemagne's court. In the seven-nineties, Angilbert and Bertha produced two sons, one of them Nithard, the future historian of Carolingian dynastic wars, while Angilbert, wearing his abbatial hat, rebuilt the abbey-church on a splendid scale. He remained close to Charlemagne, and accompanied him to Rome in 800.

---

[7] For a thumb-nail sketch of his career, see J. L. Nelson, 'La cour impériale de Charlemagne', in *La royauté et les élites dans l'Europe carolingienne*, ed. R. Le Jan (Lille, 1998), pp. 177–91, at pp. 186–7, repr. in J. L. Nelson, *Rulers and Ruling Families in Early Medieval Europe* (Aldershot, 1999), ch. xiv.

[8] M.G.H. Epistolae, iv, no. 92 (dated 796), 136.

[9] S. Rabe, *Faith, Art and Politics at Saint-Riquier: the Symbolic Vision of Angilbert* (Philadelphia, Pa., 1995), pp. 54–81, at p. 65.

For Angilbert's life in Charlemagne's later years there is little evidence. He attested Charlemagne's will in 811, perhaps on a rare visit to Aachen. He is not otherwise mentioned as involved in court activity, there was no more poetry, and there were no more children. My guess is that he had decided on *conversio* and that his last decade or so (he died on 18 February 814, just three weeks after Charlemagne) was spent at St.-Riquier living the life of monastic *quies*, quietness. It suited his age and stage of life. Other men, a new generation (Einhard, Wala), took his place in the inner counsels of Charlemagne.

A second case was that of William, count of Toulouse. Unlike Angilbert, William was no cleric but a *palatinus* and a warrior. But in 806 he too relinquished the life of the world to live his last years in a monastery. Of what inner motives impelled him there is absolutely no evidence. But Alcuin's influence (804 was the year of his death) had encouraged laymen to practise daily private prayer, and thus, even while still *in vita activa*, to move towards a monastic life.[10] Further, the presence of influential monks at court – Benedict of Aniane, Adalard of Corbie – encouraged the interest of lay aristocrats in monastic patronage, even monastic foundation. Benedict's hagiographer wrote in the eight-twenties:

> Count William who was more distinguished than anyone at the emperor's court clung to the blessed Benedict with such affection of love that, despising the honours of the world he chose Benedict as his guide on the way to salvation . . . . After he received permission [from the emperor] to convert, he surrendered to Benedict with gifts of gold and silver and all kinds of precious clothing. Nor did he allow any delay in having himself tonsured on the feastday of the apostles Peter and Paul. He put off his clothing embroidered with gold thread, and assumed the habit (*habitus*) of the worshippers of heaven . . . At Gellone, where he had ordered a cell to be built while he was still placed in the honour of this world, he entrusted himself to the service of Christ. Born to noble parents, he was eager to become nobler by embracing the highest poverty of Christ. For Christ he gave up the honour attained through birth.[11]

The hagiographer did not add that William had amassed countships on both sides of the Pyrenees, and that when he 'converted', he divided these between his two eldest sons (by different wives).[12]

---

[10] See J. L. Nelson, 'Did Charlemagne have a private life?', in *Writing Medieval Biography, 750–1250: Essays in Honour of Frank Barlow*, ed. D. Bates, J. Crick and S. Hamilton (Woodbridge, 2006), pp. 15–28.

[11] Ardo, *Vita sancti Benedicti Anianensis,* c. 30, ed. G. Waitz (M.G.H. Scriptores, xv (i), Hanover, 1887), p. 211, trans. P. E. Dutton, *Carolingian Civilization: a Reader* (Peterborough, Oreg., 1993), p. 171 (I gratefully use Paul Dutton's translation, making only slight changes).

[12] M. Aurell, *Les noces du comte: mariage et pouvoir en Catalogne (785–1213)* (Paris, 1995), p. 35.

A third case was that of Unroch, another of Charlemagne's *palatini*, and an attester of his will, drawn up in 811.[13] A fourth case was that of Charlemagne himself. His will envisaged the possibility that he might decide on withdrawal from the world (*voluntaria saecularium rerum carentia*), at which point his testamentary disposition would come into immediate effect.[14] In the event, the emperor died in his Aachen palace, less than three years later.

One or two other ninth-century examples are worth mentioning: Louis the Pious was only forty when his first wife died, but had to be deterred by his counsellors from withdrawing from the world.[15] Louis's successor, the emperor Lothar I, did withdraw from the world, to the monastery of Prüm, disposed of his realm between his sons but died six days later: so, this was most likely the decision of a dying man rather than an aging one.[16] Charles the Fat suffered, or staged, a mental and physical crisis in 873 when he publicly declared his wish to withdraw from the world, but since he was only thirty-four, this was hardly the *conversio* of an aged man.[17] The episode's context, though, was one of very serious tension between Louis the German and his three sons. Louis and his wife Emma, who lived into their early seventies and early sixties respectively, may well have had good political reasons for letting it be understood that they were living out a chaste marriage in later life – once their sons had begun to cause serious difficulties by repeated rebellion, solo or as duo or trio, against their father.[18]

[13] Einhard, *Vita Karoli magni*, c. 33, ed. O. Holder-Egger (M.G.H. Scriptores rerum Germanicarum, xxv, Hanover-Leipzig, 1911) (hereafter M.G.H.S.R.G.), p. 41, lists Unroch at number five of the counts attesting Charlemagne's will; Unroch appears as the minder of a Saxon hostage in *Indiculus obsidum Saxonum* (M.G.H. Capit. i, no. 115, 233, and as a *missus* in the Ponthieu-Ternois-Flanders area in M.G.H. Capit., i, no. 85, 183. For Unroch and his descendants, see K. F. Werner, 'Bedeutende Adelsfamilien im Reich Karls des Grossen', in *Karl der Grosse. Idee und Wirklichkeit*, ed. W. Braunfels (5 vols., Düsseldorf, 1965–6), i. 83–142, at pp. 133–7 ('Exkurs I, Die Unruochinger'); and for Unroch's retirement from the world, see K. H. Krüger, 'Sithiu/Saint-Bertin als Grablege Childerichs III und der Grafen von Flandern', *Frühmittelalterliche Studien*, viii (1974), 71–80.

[14] Einhard, *Vita Karoli*, c. 33, 39. Cf. K. H. Krüger, 'Königskonversionen im 8. Jhdt', *Frühmittelalterliche Studien*, vii (1973), 169–222.

[15] Astronomer, *Vita Hludowici imperatoris*, c. 32, ed. E. Tremp (M.G.H.S.R.G., lxiv, Hanover, 1995), p. 392.

[16] *Annales Bertiniani*, s.a. 855, ed. F. Grat and others (Paris, 1964), p. 71.

[17] S. MacLean, 'Ritual, misunderstanding, and the contest for meaning', in *Representations of Power in Medieval Germany, 800–1500*, ed. B. Weiler and S. MacLean (Turnhout, 2006), pp. 97–120, at p. 118, points out that Charles fathered a son by a concubine not long after this event.

[18] E. J. Goldberg, '*Regina nitens sanctissima Hemma*: Queen Emma (827–876), Bishop Witgar of Augsburg, and the Witgar-Belt', in Weiler and MacLean, pp. 57–95, at pp. 78–85.

The point that emerges strongly from all the above is that the transmission across time of familial authority had an inbuilt tendency to cause intra-dynastic conflict. The ninth-century Carolingians, with so many territories to share out, presented a series of particularly fraught cases. There were structural reasons, therefore, why an aging father might wish to opt out, or whose sons were ready to enforce his monastic retirement. That actually happened in 833, to Louis the Pious – a very clear case of *carentia saecularium rerum involuntaria*.[19] Much less well recorded but likely to have produced similar conflicts were inter-generational tensions in aristocratic families. In the case of ninth-century elites, then, the developmental cycle of the domestic group (I borrow Jack Goody's very useful concept) brought both father-son conflict and fraternal rivalry, sometimes sequential, sometimes simultaneous.[20]

The aging process for men, in the context of that cycle, could result in more mundane scenarios. The eighth-century *Lex Bauiwariorum* included a section on the circumstances in which the rebellion of the duke's son against his father – an action normally repugnant in the law-maker's view – might be seen as justified:

> if [the father] could no longer argue a good case in a lawcourt, lead an army, judge the people, mount a horse in manly fashion (*viriliter*), wield his weapons vigorously (*vivaciter*), and, conversely, was troubled by deafness or poor sight.[21]

A little passage in the Royal Frankish Annals for 790 shows Charlemagne, aged only forty-two, but with four adult sons to think about, anxiously navigating up and down the river Saltz to avoid giving an appearance of slothfulness (*ne quasi per otium torpere videretur*).[22]

The case of Cozbert, a middle-ranking landowner in Alemannia in the early ninth century, could suggest an individual response to the developmental cycle, or, perhaps more probably, to aging itself (it is not clear that Cozbert had offspring), analogous to a corrody.[23] He granted

[19] See M. de Jong, 'Power and humility in Carolingian society: the penance of Louis the Pious', *Early Medieval Europe*, i (1992), pp. 29–52.

[20] Cf. J. L. Nelson, 'Charlemagne – *pater optimus?*', in *Am Vorabend der Kaiserkrönung*, ed. P. Godman, J. Jarnut and P. Johanek (Stuttgart, 2002), pp. 269–81.

[21] *Lex Baiuwariorum* II, 9, ed. E. von Schwind (M.G.H. Leges nationum Germanicarum v (i), Hanover, 1926), pp. 302–3.

[22] *Annales regni Francorum* (so-called revised version), ed. F. Kurze (M.G.H.S.R.G., vi, Hanover, 1895), p. 87.

[23] For a Catalan *conredium* in 878, see P. de Marca, *Marca Hispanica sive Limes Hispanicus* (Paris, 1688), col. 803, cited by J. F. Niermeyer, *Mediae Latinitatis Lexicon Minus* (Leiden, 1997), p. 252, s.v. 'conredium'. See now the evidence sensitively discussed by W. Davies, *Acts*

lands at three places, and a church, to the monastery of St.-Gall in May 816 on the following terms:

> first, while I wish to remain in the world (*cum in seculo manere voluero*), I am to receive every year between the feast of St. Gall (16 October) and the feast of St. Martin (11 November) 8 *solidi* in silver, clothing and certain livestock as seemed suitable to the monks, and at the same time I am to receive two servile workers, a boy and a girl. And if it happens that I have to go to the palace or to Italy, the [community's provosts responsible for managing three estates in the Bertholdsbaar] are to provide me with a horseman to serve me, and a well-loaded pack-horse. But when I want to convert to the monastery (*ad monasterium converti voluero*), then I shall have a room with a chimney assigned for my private use (*kaminata privatim deputata*) and I shall receive provender such as must be given to two monks (*et ut duobus monachis debetur provehendam accipiam*), and every year a woollen robe and two shirts and six [i.e., three pairs of] shoes and two gloves (*manices*) and one cape, and bedding, and every two years a jacket; and I shall have a suitable place in the inner court when I wish to give myself to the community (*me mancipare congregationi*).[24]

This seems very much like a two-stage personal pension policy, underwritten by the monastery. Cozbert sounds rather like a prudent corrodian – a word and thing to be found in ninth-century Catalonia as in later medieval England. Private accommodation sounds the antithesis of the Benedictine Rule. Yet Cozbert seems to use the term *ad monasterium converti* interchangeably with *me mancipare congregationi*. (It is just possible that two distinct stages of withdrawal are anticipated.) Pre-arranged and paid-for care for the relatively well-off elderly was just one of the many functions performed by earlier medieval monasticism. Conversely, an irresponsible abbot of Fulda – according to complaints made by that community in 812 – had been expelling elderly monks when they became too needy and consigning them to private accommodation managed by laymen.[25] There was some blurring of boundaries there.

of Giving: Individual, Community, and Church in Tenth-Century Christian Spain (Oxford, 2007), esp. pp. 139, 149–54. For corrodies in later medieval England, see B. Harvey, *Living and Dying in England 1100–1540* (Oxford, 1993), pp. 179–209, noting that the young as well as the old could be beneficiaries of such care (both were, after all, in a state of *inbecillitas*, according to the Rule of St. Benedict, c. 37); see also S. Shahar, *Growing Old in the Middle Ages* (London, 1997), p. 125.

[24] H. Wartmann, *Urkundenbuch der Abtei Sanct Gallen* (4 vols., Zurich, 1863–99), i. no. 221 (May, 816), 211. I am very grateful to Gesine Jordan of the University of Saarland for drawing this text to the attention of the Earlier Medieval Seminar at the Institute of Historical Research, University of London (25 Apr. 2007).

[25] *Supplex Libellus*, c. v, ed. J. Semmler, in *Corpus Consuetudinum Monasticarum*, ed. K.

All the above needs to be set in the broader context of Christian thinking about old age. Where did earlier medieval people get their ideas about old age from? Many, evidently, were derived from observation and experience, but there is curiously little material on this subject from the earlier middle ages.[26] As for learned tradition, despite a few spectacularly old people in the Old Testament, and some substantial passages in Proverbs, biblical history had little to offer on this subject compared with classical sources, moral and medical. The central theme was, and has since remained, ambiguity. E. M. Forster noted 'the seductive combination of increased wisdom and decaying powers'. Medical writers tended to stress the second. Cicero, on the other hand, had celebrated among the special joys of old age increased interest in agriculture and horticulture; also enjoyment of conversation and conviviality in the company of friends enhanced by now-natural moderation and abstemiousness in appetite for food and drink; but most of all growing pleasure in 'intellectual pursuits and the satisfactions of the mind', which in turn brought respect from juniors rather than contempt, provided that greater personal austerity was not accompanied by sourness or meanness, but like good wine, smoothed and matured by age.[27]

Hrabanus Maurus in the mid ninth century weighed up the good and bad: 'Old age brings with it many good things and many bad things. Good things: because it frees us from very powerful masters, places a limit on our lusts, breaks the force of desire, increases wisdom, and gives more mature counsels'. The bad things were summed up in two words: *debilitas* and *odium*, bodily weakness and social contempt. Hrabanus had more to say about those, and especially about infirmity.[28] Old age is relative: early medieval writers might rehearse the seven ages of man, but few had personal knowledge of persons of *senectus* in the strict classical sense of over-seventies. In practice anyone over fifty was old. In them, wisdom, mature counsel, a

Hallinger, i (Siegburg, 1963), 321–7, trans. J. L. Nelson, 'Medieval monasticism', in *The Medieval World*, ed. P. Linehan and J. L. Nelson (London, 2001), pp. 576–604, at p. 590.

[26] P. E. Dutton, 'Beyond the topos of senescence: the political problems of aged Carolingian rulers', in *Aging and the Aged in Medieval Europe*, ed. M. M. Sheehan (Toronto, 1990), pp. 75–94, repr. and retitled as 'A world grown old with poets and kings', in P. E. Dutton, *Charlemagne's Mustache and Other Cultural Clusters of a Dark Age* (London, 2004), pp. 151–68, indicates the limits of available source-material. Shahar, an excellent survey, is typical in focusing almost exclusively on the period from the twelfth century onwards.

[27] Cicero, *De senectute*, cc. iv and v, trans. M. Grant, *Cicero, Selected Writings* (Harmondsworth, 1960), pp. 228–38, at p. 233. I have snitched the Forster quotation from Grant's introduction to Cicero's text, p. 211.

[28] Hrabanus Maurus, *De rerum naturis*, in *Patrologia Latina*, ed. J. P. Migne (221 vols. Paris, 1844–1903), iii, cols. 185–6.

mind set on the next world, the weakening of lust and desire: all these were powerful assets, the last not least.

Women – *deo devotae* – were the first to see their chastity in mature years linked firmly with holiness and religious authority. Chaste widows were a separate *ordo* within the church, entitled to special respect, and protection. They wore a special habit and veil. Rich and well-born widows living in their own homes posed problems for bishops: in the end these women defied attempts at episcopal control.[29] With the bishop's approval, such women devoted themselves to prayer, and to pious works, especially the liturgical commemoration of their deceased husbands. Their old age was seen in positive terms. In one early ritual for veiling widows, the consecration-prayer asked God to 'grant them glory for their good works, reverence for their modesty, and sanctity for their chastity'.[30] Such widows were a firm fixture of various early medieval scenes, in Anglo-Saxon England, and on the Continent. They had, strictly speaking, no male equivalent. There was no word for widower. Nevertheless, my guess is that in the ninth century, as in the later middle ages in the view of Shulamith Shahar, the old body was seen 'as an opportunity and means of atonement [for sins]'.[31]

With all that in mind, I think we should revisit those earlier medieval renouncers of the world. They renounced in a spirit not of defeatism but of hope. Through devotion to prayer, kings or leading men hoped to benefit their subjects as well as themselves. In 877, King Charles had the converse idea: namely, that his faithful men, in choosing to live *quiete*, that is, to renounce the world (*quies* had become virtually a synonym for such religiously-motivated withdrawal), might benefit him. Further, the timing of the withdrawal from the world was to coincide with the availability of a son or kinsman – sc. of the younger generation – to continue the father's service to the state. Thus this clause, clause 10 of the Capitulary of Quierzy,

[29] J. L. Nelson, 'The wary widow', in *Property and Power in Early Medieval Europe*, ed. W. Davies and P. Fouracre (Cambridge, 1995), pp. 82–113, repr. in J. L. Nelson, *Courts, Elites and Gendered Power* (Aldershot, 2007), ch. ii.

[30] *The Claudius Pontificals*, ed. D. H. Turner (Henry Bradshaw Soc., xcvii, Chichester, 1971), Pontifical I (tenth-century, but with older material), p. 71. Cf. E. Palazzo, 'Les formules de bénédiction et de consécration des veuves au cours du haut moyen âge', in *Veuves et veuvage dans le haut Moyen Age*, ed. M. Parisse (Paris, 1993), pp. 31–6; for Anglo-Saxon evidence, see S. Foot, *Veiled Women* (2 vols., Aldershot, 2000), i, ch. 5, esp. pp. 127–34.

[31] Shahar, p. 54, with nn. 79 and 84, citing St. Bernard, who said explicitly that the old body brought a man nearer to God because it had become free of lust, and Dante, who imputed spiritual elevation to the old: 'calmly and gently, the ship lowers its sails as it approaches the harbour'. Hrabanus expressed a similar view less beautifully (cf. above, pp. 42–3).

was organically linked with clause 9, the one about the transmission of a countship if a count should die leaving a son or kinsman. Here, in other words, the king connected the transmission of high office across time with the senior man's withdrawal from the world: the problem of succession found its solution. Finally, the king imagined the older man's choice to withdraw from the world as motivated by love for God and the king – himself. Special love between the king and the closest of his *fideles* was a theme deeply embedded in what Stuart Airlie has called *un monde quasi-idéologique*, that embraced the ninth-century Carolingians and their aristocracies.[32] Serving the king was a major constituent of the aristocrat's sense of his identity. The king's liturgical commemoration of favoured nobles was to have its *quid pro quo* in the prayers volunteered by *fideles* who were the kingdom's senior citizens.

Charles the Bald's approach was nothing if not instrumental: he intended to create a cadre of devoted intercessors. But it was also shot through with idealism: his faithful bedesmen would do it for love. The very fact that the king could entertain such hopes suggests something about the power his dynasty had acquired over aristocratic imaginations. It evokes a broader world, too, of house-monasteries in which old men lived in quasi-monastic *quies,* analogous to the house-convents of high-born widows; and of men like Cozbert who planned in old age to attach themselves to monasteries by special 'private' arrangement. I am reminded of the twelfth-century scenario that Giles Constable divined by touch in the evidential dark:

> Very little is known about such relationships [between monasteries and laypeople], but they were presumably considered mutually beneficial, like those between religious, educational, and cultural institutions today and their benefactors, patrons and friends – the same old terms – who in return for donations receive prestige, invitations to dinners and receptions, and secular immortality on a bronze plaque, bench, or bookplate, or, if they give enough, a building.[33]

How should we situate that twelfth-century world vis-à-vis the ninth century? After re-reading Christopher Brooke on conversion by infiltration, and after focusing specifically on the needs and desires and aptitudes of ninth-century *conversi* of mature years, my own answer, borrowed from E. M. Forster, is: 'only connect'.

---

[32] S. Airlie, '*Semper fideles*? Loyauté envers les Carolingiens comme constituent de l'identité aristocratique', in Le Jan, pp. 129–43, at p. 131.

[33] G. Constable, *The Reformation of the Twelfth Century* (Cambridge, 1996), pp. 84–5.

William Wykeham's early ecclesiastical career

Virginia Davis

Modern writers have largely neglected William Wykeham, bishop of Winchester 1367–1404. His importance as a key figure in the circle around Edward III in the latter part of Edward's reign has been widely recognized.[1] His apparent greed in lapping up benefices until he was the most beneficed pluralist in Christendom by 1366 has been criticized. Wykeham's tenure of the see of Winchester for nearly forty years has been largely ignored and it is only his extensive activities in lay and ecclesiastical building projects and his foundation of the pioneering linked colleges of Winchester College and New College, Oxford which have been studied in depth.[2] Early biographers in the century after Wykeham's death provided short lives of the bishop which were somewhat hagiographical in tone.[3] More recent all-round studies of Wykeham's life and career were also the work of Wykehamists. In 1758 Robert Lowth published a biography of Wykeham which was based on extensive research in the Winchester College archives. Lowth, the son of a Winchester cathedral prebendary who had been a scholar at both Winchester College and New College was in 1764 a candidate for the wardenship of Winchester, although ultimately unsuccessful.[4] He was an accomplished poet and distinguished pamphleteer, and his biography of Wykeham has remained the most comprehensive archival-based study of the bishop's career. His work substantially influenced later writers and works, in particular the biography written by George Moberly, bishop of Salisbury.[5] In 1835 Moberly had been appointed headmaster of Winchester College,

---

[1] See, e.g., W. M. Ormrod, *The Reign of Edward III* (New Haven and London, 1990), pp. 90–4.

[2] Ormrod, *Reign of Edward III*, p. 90.

[3] The early lives by Robert Heete (d. 1433) and Thomas Aylward (d. 1413) are printed as appendices to G. H. Moberly, *Life of William of Wykeham* (1887).

[4] S. Mandelbrote, 'Lowth, Robert (1710–87)', *Oxford Dictionary of National Biography* (Oxford, 2004) <http://www.oxforddnb.com/view/article/17104> [accessed 31 Dec. 2007].

[5] R. Lowth, *The Life of William of Wykeham, Bishop of Winchester* (1758); Moberly.

V. Davis, 'William Wykeham's early ecclesiastical career', in *European Religious Cultures: Essays offered to Christopher Brooke on the occasion of his eightieth birthday*, ed. M. Rubin (London, 2020), pp. 47–62.
License: CC-BY-NC-ND 4.0.

a post which he held for thirty years and in which he was followed by his son in law George Ridding, one of the most influential of the nineteenth-century headmasters.[6] George Moberly's mid nineteenth-century work has remained the fullest biography; more recent books such as Hayter's *William of Wykeham, Patron of the Arts* have concentrated on particular aspects of Wykeham's career.[7] This article arises from research carried out for a new biography of Wykeham.[8] It will explore the circumstances surrounding Wykeham's change of career direction and its possible motivations and then proceed to examine his rapid acquisition of benefices in the early thirteen-sixties, before his elevation to the episcopate in 1366.

Wykeham's career was a dramatic 'rags to riches' story. The level of social mobility he achieved in his own lifetime would more typically have taken several generations. Born in Wickham in 1324, son of a Hampshire peasant villager, he rose – via royal service to King Edward III – to be bishop of Winchester, England's wealthiest episcopal see. On Wykeham's death in 1404, Pope Boniface IX translated John of Gaunt's legitimized son Henry Beaufort from the bishopric of Lincoln to Winchester.[9] The Hampshire peasant who had risen to become bishop of Winchester was succeeded by the king's half-brother. The contrast between the respective backgrounds of these two bishops of Winchester highlights Wykeham's enormous personal achievement.

Why did Wykeham enter the church? It has always been assumed that Wykeham was destined to become a cleric. His medieval biographers portray a pious, devout boy. They refer in particular to his early devotion to the Virgin Mary, to whom both of his educational foundations were later dedicated. Wykeham is depicted in close association with the Virgin in sculptures and stained glass at Winchester and New College and she appeared on his episcopal seal, reflecting his long-standing devotion to her.[10] Robert Heete, fellow of Winchester College, writing a decade or two after the bishop's death, provided an account of Wykeham's daily attendance at mass in Winchester cathedral while a schoolboy. Aylward's

[6] J. A. Hamilton, 'Moberly, George (1803–85)', rev. G. Rowell, *O.D.N.B.* (Oxford, 2004) <http://www.oxforddnb.com/view/article/18862> [accessed 31 Dec. 2007].

[7] W. Hayter, *William of Wykeham, Patron of the Arts* (1970).

[8] V. Davis, *William Wykeham* (2007).

[9] *Handbook of British Chronology*, ed. F. M Powicke and E. B. Fryde (2nd edn., 1961), p. 259.

[10] The image of the Virgin Mary can be found in many places within Wykeham's collegiate foundations. At Winchester College, for example, her statute can be found over the main entrance, while glass at New College depicts Wykeham robed as a bishop, gazing devoutly at the Virgin Mary.

biography claimed that every morning Wykeham used to kneel near an image of the Virgin Mary which stood against a column in the nave and listen to mass being said by one of the monks from St. Swithun's priory, Richard Pekis, which was 'vulgarly called Pekismass'.[11] Wykeham's early biographers certainly convey the impression that Wykeham was destined for an ecclesiastical career from an early age. Yet a close examination of the evidence surrounding his ordination to the priesthood and the timing of his early acquisition of benefices suggests otherwise.

Wykeham was well into medieval middle age when he finally became ordained acolyte in 1361. His advanced age (thirty-seven) at ordination as a priest was relative unusual in the mid fourteenth century. The minimum canonical age for being ordained acolyte was fourteen and the fact that Wykeham was thirty-seven when ordained acolyte and thirty-eight by the time he had attained the priesthood is in dramatic contrast to the majority of his contemporaries who became bishops. Bishop Buckingham (Lincoln, 1363–98) had been ordained acolyte aged twenty-four and was a priest by the time he was twenty-six; Archbishop Courtney (London, 1375–81) appears to have taken orders as soon as it was canonically permitted. Richard Scrope, later archbishop of York (1398–1405), was not an acolyte when appointed official to the bishop of Ely in 1375, but by the following year he had been ordained to the priesthood aged twenty-six.[12] There were other models for Wykeham's behaviour, however, for example his fellow royal servant, the successful lawyer-clerk and diplomat Michael Northborough, bishop of London (1354–61), who had been collecting benefices from the early thirteen-forties, but remained un-ordained until he was provided to the bishopric of London in 1354.[13]

That Wykeham had reached the age of thirty-eight before committing himself irrevocably to a career in the church clearly suggests that – even though he was to reach the pinnacle of the English church hierarchy – this was not part of his original career plan. His decision to enter the church marks a decisive change of career direction in middle age. Once his

---

[11] Moberly, p. 288.

[12] A. K. McHardy, 'Buckingham, John (c.1320–1399)', *O.D.N.B.* (Oxford, 2004) <http://www.oxforddnb.com/view/article/2786> [accessed 24 Feb. 2008]; R. N. Swanson, 'Courtenay, William (1341/2–1396)', *O.D.N.B.* (Oxford, 2004) <http://www.oxforddnb.com/view/article/6457> [accessed 24 Feb. 2008]; P. McNiven, 'Scrope, Richard (c.1350–1405)', *O.D.N.B.* (Oxford, 2004) <http://www.oxforddnb.com/view/article/24964> [accessed 24 Feb. 2008].

[13] R. M. Haines, 'Northburgh, Michael (c.1300–1361)', *O.D.N.B.* (Oxford, 2004) <http://www.oxforddnb.com/view/article/20324> [accessed 24 Feb. 2008]; *Calendar of Papal Letters 1342–62*, p. 522.

mind was made up, he acted with speed, proceeding rapidly to attain the status of priesthood within twelve months. This was despite the canonical injunction that a year should elapse between ordination as acolyte and as sub-deacon.[14]

Most boys undergoing formal education, as Wykeham did in Winchester in the thirteen-thirties,[15] received the first tonsure but this, usually taken at about the age of twelve, did not commit a boy to a lifetime of celibacy or becoming a priest. Having been tonsured, there were seven formal stages to ordination. These seven steps were divided into two parts: the minor orders comprised the first four – janitor, lector, exorcist and acolyte – and the major orders the remaining three, which were sub-deacon, deacon and finally priest.[16] It was not until a man reached the level of sub-deacon that he was firmly committed to a celibate career within the church. Indeed the first three steps – janitor, lector and exorcist – were clearly not regarded as particularly significant and were not usually a matter of record for episcopal registrars.[17] Bishops' registers most commonly note men's ordinations once they reached the level of acolyte, implying that this status was regarded as a significant and worthy of record. Even so, ordination as an acolyte did not yet require the abandonment of lay life and an acolyte was not yet irrevocably committed to a career in the church.

There is no evidence that Wykeham considered entering the church before the late thirteen-fifties; up to this point his working life had been pursued as a layman. Throughout his early career Wykeham moved in circles of laymen and clerics, working equally easily with senior churchmen such as Bishop Edington of Winchester and with aristocratic laymen such as the Foxley family, father and son. That Wykeham had not even been ordained as an acolyte by the late thirteen-fifties suggests that a career in the church was not what he was seeking. He was a clerk in royal service, not a cleric. There was nothing to stop him behaving as some other clerks in royal service did, remaining a layman and being paid for his services by grants and annuities. This, for example, was the case with his younger contemporary, the poet Thomas Hoccleve (d. 1426), who rose to become one of the senior clerks in the privy seal office. In his poem *The Regiment of Princes*, Hoccleve wrote that when he fell in love he abandoned plans to

---

[14] V. Davis, *Clergy in London in the Late Middle Ages* (2000), p. 12.

[15] No records of tonsures in the diocese of Winchester are recorded from this period.

[16] Davis, *Clergy in London*, pp. 5–8.

[17] Occasionally exorcists are recorded, for example they are quite frequently noted in late medieval registers of the bishops of Exeter. From the 1490s ordination as exorcist begins to be regularly recorded by London episcopal registrars (Davis, *Clergy in London*, p. 7).

enter the church and married instead.[18]

The early support obtained from his patron Bishop Edington was secular rather than ecclesiastical in nature; Wykeham was granted wardships rather than ecclesiastical benefices.[19] Had Wykeham been seeking to enter the church, it would not have been difficult for Bishop Edington to find him a benefice in the wake of the destruction wrought by the Black Death. Nearly half of all beneficed clergy died in the diocese of Winchester when the initial plague outbreak struck and in the months immediately after the worst of the plague had passed, Bishop Edington was anxiously seeking appropriate candidates to fill the many vacancies in his diocese. In 1349 he had over 300 vacancies to fill in the diocese, compared with twelve in 1348 and even in the early thirteen-fifties the numbers of vacancies remained above pre-plague levels.[20] In these circumstances, it would not have been difficult to present Wykeham to a benefice.

Wykeham's decision to enter the church was not a change of direction hastily undertaken; there was no 'road to Damascus' experience. Rather, in the late thirteen-fifties Wykeham must have come to realize that becoming a churchman was a wise move. From late 1357, Edward III's recognition of the valuable services which Wykeham was rendering to him is evident from the grants of ecclesiastical benefices which begin in November of that year. Such grants were a normal way for a king to reward clerks in his service but from Wykeham's personal perspective they moved him to consider his future. The timing of Wykeham's ordinations in 1361 reinforces the suggestion that even in the late thirteen-fifties, when Edward III was beginning to reward him with benefices in the royal gift, Wykeham was only cautiously exploring the idea of becoming a priest.

At the end of November 1357 Edward made his first presentation of a benefice to Wykeham, the Pulham rectory in Norfolk.[21] Interestingly, Pulham, worth £53 6s 8d, had earlier been held by Michael Northborough when he was Edward III's secretary and was clearly reguarded as a suitable

[18] J. A. Burrow, 'Hoccleve, Thomas (c.1367–1426)', O.D.N.B. (Oxford, 2004) <http://www.oxforddnb.com/view/article/13415> [accessed 20 Feb. 2007].

[19] Davis, Wykeham, ch. 2.

[20] The Register of William Edington, Bishop of Winchester, ed. S. F. Hockey (Hampshire Record ser., vii–viii, 2 vols., Winchester, 1986) (hereafter Edington Register), i. xii.

[21] Calendar of Patent Rolls 1354–8, p. 642; this presentation was in fulfilment of a royal grant made earlier that month whereby Wykeham had been granted an additional 1s a day from the exchequer pending suitable ecclesiastical preferment (Calendar of Patent Rolls 1354–8, p. 634). This was Wykeham's first benefice from the king; the 1349 presentation of a 'William de Wykeham, chaplain' by Edward III to the Norfolk parish of Irstead refers to a different William of Wykeham (Davis, Wykeham, p. 13).

benefice for a rising member of the royal circle.[22] However, Wykeham was never instituted at Pulham; owing to tension between king and pope, inflamed by the bitter dispute between Edward III and Thomas Lisle, bishop of Ely, who had fled to the papal court at Avignon in 1356, this presentation became the subject of litigation at the papal curia.[23] In April 1359 Wykeham was granted an annuity of £20 from King Edward III pending the successful resolution of the dispute.[24] Wykeham's ambivalence about becoming a churchman clearly remained since, while awaiting the outcome of the litigation, he still made no move towards ordination as a priest. Even in March 1359 when Edward III granted him the prebend of Flixton in Coventry and Lichfield cathedral, he did not proceed to become an acolyte.[25] This grant, too, fell foul of the tense relationship between king and pope, this time over a dispute as to whether the king's chaplain Robert Stretton was a suitable candidate to be bishop of Coventry and Lichfield. Although Wykeham's presentation to Flixton prebend was reiterated by the king in August 1360, he was left in limbo, the presentation ignored by the guardian of the spiritual property of Coventry and Lichfield diocese during the vacancy.[26] Only in the spring of 1361, by which time Robert Stretton was firmly in place as bishop, was Wykeham successfully installed in this prebend. He did not go to Lichfield cathedral for the installation in person, but sent instead a proxy, Nicholas Ivinghoe.[27] While this may reflect the fact that Wykeham was an exceedingly busy man, actively concerned with a range of royal business, it also suggests that he remained ambivalent about a career in the church, though this is clearly conjecture.

A third early preferment, and the first one which Wykeham actually obtained, was the grant on Tuesday 5 May 1360 of the deanery of St. Martin le Grand, London.[28] St. Martin le Grand, a royal free chapel, was situated in the City of London very close to St. Paul's cathedral. By the fourteenth century, the majority of the eleven men who held prebends in the free chapel were active royal servants, so Wykeham was not unusual among them. However, he may also have been attracted by the position because St. Martin le Grand

---

[22] *Calendar of Papal Registers 1342–62*, pp. 394, 419; Haines.

[23] On Lisle, see J. Aberth, 'Crime and justice under Edward III: the case of Thomas de Lisle', *English Historical Review*, cvii (1992), 283–30. For the litigation, see Davis, *Wykeham*, pp. 43–5; Moberly, pp. 36–9.

[24] *Calendar of Patent Rolls 1358–61*, p. 198.

[25] *Calendar of Patent Rolls 1358–61*, p. 182.

[26] *Calendar of Patent Rolls 1358–61*, p. 455.

[27] *Register of Robert de Stretton Coventry and Lichfield, 1358–85*, ed. R. A. Wilson (William Salt Archaeol. Soc., new ser., viii, 1905), p. 158.

[28] *Calendar of Patent Rolls 1358–61*, p. 353.

was urgently in need of major building works to restore this prestigious free chapel to its former glory, a task which Wykeham began immediately.[29]

Wykeham hesitated to embrace the idea that his future career lay in the church. Even in the late thirteen-fifties he was reluctant to make a move in this direction despite the evident opportunities for wealth and advancement which it offered. The year 1361 was marked by a momentous change of direction in career terms. By now being referred to in administrative documents as 'the king's beloved clerk',[30] he was an increasingly valued figure in the circle of men surrounding the king at court.[31] By mid 1361 royal writs were being issued with the subscription, 'By the King on the information of William of Wykeham', while the first description of Wykeham as the king's secretary is found in August 1361.[32] It was not, however, just in terms of his growing influence within the royal circle that 1361 was important for Wykeham; this was also the year in which he finally made a decisive and significant alteration in his career. In December 1361, after a period of hovering on the edge of becoming a churchman, Wykeham took the final step. In a small ceremony held during mass on Sunday 5 December in Bishop Edington's private chapel at Southwark palace, he was ordained acolyte.[33] He was aged thirty-seven. Wykeham then moved rapidly through the levels of ordination to achieve priestly status within six months, being ordained as priest by Edington in Southwark manor chapel on 12 June 1362.[34] Henceforth Wykeham's rise in the church hierarchy was nothing short of dazzling. Within five years he was bishop of Winchester, the wealthiest diocese in the English church and one of the richest in Christendom.

What brought about this change of mind, this shift in career direction from a resolutely secular career in royal service to a high-flying ecclesiastical career? As indicated above, there was no sudden moment of conversion. One influence may have been the return of a virulent outbreak of the plague in 1361. While the overall effect of this outbreak was not as drastic as that of 1348–9, observed by Wykeham while in the service of Bishop Edington early in his career, nonetheless mortality rates were high – mortality among the clergy in Lincolnshire, for example, was about three times higher than

---

[29] Davis, *Wykeham*, pp. 29–30.

[30] *Calendar of Close Rolls 1354–60*, p. 371.

[31] Davis, *Wykeham*, pp. 25–7.

[32] Davis, *Wykeham*, pp. 30–1, nn. 47, 51.

[33] *Edington Register*, ii. 192.

[34] He was ordained subdeacon in Southwark manor chapel on 12 March 1262 (*Edington Register*, ii. 195); priest (*Edington Register*, ii. 197). Wykeham must have been ordained deacon between March and June but the details do not survive.

normal.[35] Contemporary moralists such as the chronicler John of Reading regarded the plague as being God's vengeance on an unworthy people.[36] Among the people whom Wykeham knew and worked with, a number of important figures died of the plague, including perhaps Henry Grosmont, duke of Lancaster.[37] Other wealthy figures were also victims. Henry Pycard, ex-mayor of London and royal office-holder who memorably had recently hosted a lavish dinner in Coldharbour Mansion for four kings – Edward III of England, Jean I of France, David of Scotland and Peter of Cyprus – had died by early July.[38] Edward's own daughter Princess Margaret, who had recently married Wykeham's ward John Hastings, the thirteenth earl of Pembroke, died late that year.[39] Clearly, entering the church was no protection against the plague since no fewer than three English and Welsh prelates died of its effects in 1361, as did Richard Kilvington, dean of St. Paul's cathedral.[40] Nonetheless the high levels of mortality to be seen in London and throughout England in 1361 would certainly have focused Wykeham's attention on thoughts of the afterlife.

In the absence of autobiographical writings it is impossible to know about possible changes in personal circumstances which might have occasioned Wykeham's change in attitude towards a career in the church. Rather than a sudden religious conversion, however, it is more likely that Wykeham embraced an ecclesiastical career in the early thirteen-sixties because of his increasing conviction that riches and opportunities were likely to be very much more accessible as a churchman than as a layman from a peasant background. Without the backing of family resources Wykeham was dependent on royal largesse or membership of a noble affinity. He did not, for example, enjoy the privileges of his near-contemporary Geoffrey Chaucer, who was to follow in Wykeham's footsteps as clerk of the king's works in the thirteen-nineties.[41]

[35] Mortality among the clergy in Lincolnshire was about three times higher than normal (see J. Saltmarsh, 'Plague and economic decline in England in the later middle ages', *Cambridge Historical Journal*, vii (1941), 23–41).

[36] *Chronica Johannis de Reading et Anonymi Cantuariensis, 1346–67*, ed. J. Tait (Manchester, 1914), p. 150.

[37] W. M. Ormrod, 'Henry of Lancaster, first duke of Lancaster (*c*.1310–1361)', *O.D.N.B.* (Oxford, 2004) <http://www.oxforddnb.com/view/article/12960> [accessed 6 Nov. 2007].

[38] R. L. Axworthy, 'Picard, Henry (d. 1361)', *O.D.N.B.* (Oxford, 2004) <http://www.oxforddnb.com/view/article/52213> [accessed 6 Nov. 2007].

[39] R. I. Jack, 'Hastings, John, 13th earl of Pembroke (1347–75)', *O.D.N.B.* (Oxford, 2004) <http://www.oxforddnb.com/view/article/12580> [accessed 6 Nov. 2007].

[40] Thomas Fastolf, bishop of St. David's, died in June 1361; Thomas Lisle, bishop of Ely, also died that month while Bishop Michael Northburgh of London died in Sept. 1361.

[41] G. L. Harriss, 'Mulso family (*per. c*.1350–1460)', *O.D.N.B.* (Oxford, 2004) <http://www.oxforddnb.com/view/article/52789> [accessed 20 Feb. 2007].

Chaucer had been born into a wealthy London merchant family, and had money behind him which offered him some freedom of action, even within the bounds of royal service, and left him free to marry.[42] Wykeham's case was different. Elevation to the deanship of St. Martin le Grand where Wykeham's talents as a building project manager could be utilized to the full may have influenced his decision, increasing the realization that many of his passions and interests could be carried forward within the framework of the English church hierarchy.

What was remarkable about Wykeham and the benefices he held was not just the huge income he derived from them, but also the short period within which he acquired them. With the exception of the East Anglian rectory of Pulham to which the king had tried to appoint him in 1357, all the other benefices for which dates of acquisition are known were acquired between May 1360 and the end of 1363. During this period thirty-two benefices passed through his hands, eighteen of them being acquired (and in some cases disposed of) in 1361 alone. All of the benefices were granted by Edward III, often while he was in temporary control of the right to present due to vacancies of bishoprics or abbeys. Wykeham was not in breach of contemporary canon law in amassing this portfolio of benefices. In 1366, when the papacy required declaration of all pluralists' holdings, Wykeham only held a single benefice with cure of souls, the archdeaconry of Lincoln, although in addition he held eleven benefices without cure, all of which were prebends in cathedral chapters or in other collegiate churches.

Edward III began to shower his trusted royal servant with benefices from early July 1361.[43] In the second half of 1361 the king granted Wykeham no fewer than fifteen benefices, some of which he only retained for a few weeks before exchanging them for others. There is no doubt that he was high in royal favour at this period. This flood of benefices predated Wykeham's ordination as acolyte in early December 1361. It is perhaps surprising, since he must now have had his sights set firmly on an ecclesiastical career, that he delayed even beginning to be ordained until December of that year. However, the explanation may simply be that the opportunity did not present itself. Bishop Edington held no general ordination ceremonies on the stipulated ember days in February, May or September 1361, perhaps because of the dangers from the plague.[44] The loss of the London register

---

[42] D. Gray, 'Chaucer, Geoffrey (*c.*1340–1400)', *O.D.N.B.* (Oxford, 2004) <http://www.oxforddnb.com/view/article/5191> [accessed 24 Feb. 2008].

[43] In addition this is discussed in Moberly, pp. 45–51, though not all the material cited there is accurate.

[44] There were no general ordination ceremonies held in the diocese of Winchester between

of Michael Northburgh (1355–61) means it is not known if there were other ceremonies held during this period in London which Wykeham could have attended with permission from his diocesan bishop, Edington.[45] It would also have been possible for Wykeham to be ordained at a private ceremony by the bishop, had he been keen to do so; in January 1361 Bishop Edington had ordained a single acolyte in Farnham castle chapel.[46] Even now, however, he was clearly not yet prepared to take the final step of committing himself to a clerical career; had he been ready, Wykeham could have taken the opportunity to ordained as a subdeacon at the same time as acolyte, a not-uncommon process.

On Saturday 10 July at Westminster, Edward, who had perhaps just received the news from Avignon of the death of the controversial Bishop Thomas Lisle on 23 June from plague, regranted the disputed rectory of Pulham to Wykeham.[47] King Edward followed this two days later with a grant of the prebend of Church Withington in Hereford cathedral worth £7 1s 4d.[48] This was in the king's gift because Hereford diocese was vacant. On Friday 16 July 1361, Edward, now at his favoured manor of Henley and with Wykeham likely to have been present in his household, took advantage of the fact that the recent death from the plague of bishop Thomas Fastolf of St. David's offered him further opportunities to dispose of ecclesiastical patronage. The king therefore granted two Welsh prebends to Wykeham. These were Treffelegh prebend in the collegiate church of Llanddewi Brewi in Cardiganshire in the diocese of St. David and the prebend of Trathelan in the collegiate church of Abergwili in the same diocese.[49] Eight days later, on Saturday 24 July 1361, Edward presented Wykeham to a vacant Hereford prebend in Bromyard collegiate church worth £20.[50] His interests were also being promoted by royal officials at the papal curia. In February 1361, a joint petition from the kings of England and France (John II, who knew Wykeham well as a result of his lengthy period as a French hostage at Edward's court in the thirteen-fifties), asked the pope for a prebend in Lincoln cathedral for Wykeham.[51] In the end Wykeham did not obtain a prebend in Lincoln cathedral until the late summer of 1362 but on 1 August 1361 Pope Innocent

May 1360 and Dec. 1361 (*Edington Register*, ii).

[45] D. M. Smith, *Guide to Bishop's Registers of England and Wales* (1981), p. 136, n. 3.

[46] *Edington Register*, ii. 190.

[47] *Calendar of Patent Rolls 1361–4*, p. 42.

[48] *Calendar of Patent Rolls 1361–4*, p. 42.

[49] *Calendar of Patent Rolls 1361–4*, pp. 43, 112.

[50] *Calendar of Patent Rolls 1361–4*, p. 46. This grant was made by a 'letter of the secret seal'. The see of Hereford was vacant because of Bishop Charlton's death Nov. 1360.

[51] *Calendar of Papal Registers 1342–1419*, p. 363.

VI provided him to a prebend in St. Andrew's collegiate church in Bishop's Auckland in Durham diocese.[52] However, Pope Innocent VI commissioned Wykeham's fellow royal clerk, Adam Houghton, bishop-elect of St. David's, directing him to examine Wykeham and if he was found fit to allow him to take this prebend. At this point Wykeham decided not to pursue the issue further, as he explained in his 1366 pluralism return.[53]

On Monday 16 August, Wykeham was granted the prebend of Yetminster Prima in Salisbury cathedral.[54] By this time he had resigned the controversial rectory of Pulham, of which he had been trying to get possession since November 1357.[55] By now he may have felt that the range of other benefices which he had acquired in recent months adequately compensated for the potential loss of income from Pulham rectory, which was worth at least £20 a year. However, divesting himself of Pulham would have been convenient, because it was the one benefice Wykeham held which entailed the care of souls; a care that he was not in a position to exercise since he had yet to be ordained. He was thus in an awkward position vis-à-vis the church authorities. Concerns had already been expressed by Pope Innocent VI as to his suitability to be presented to the Bishop's Auckland prebend. In the light of these queries and his meteoric rise both in royal favour and in ecclesiastical circles it is not surprising that he was attracting some hostile criticism.

There was no slowing down, however, in Wykeham's gathering of benefices without the cure of souls throughout the autumn of 1361. On 24 September 1361, Edward granted Wykeham the prebend of the Altar of St. Mary in Beverley collegiate church, worth £16, while on 1 October, with more ecclesiastical patronage in the royal gift because of the recent death from plague of the bishop of London, Michael Northborough, Wykeham was presented to Oxgate prebend in St. Paul's cathedral in London.[56] This was the first of several prebends Wykeham was to hold in St. Paul's cathedral, although the

---

[52] *Calendar of Patent Rolls 1361–4*, p. 244 (re. Sutton). *Calendar of Papal Registers 1342–1419*, p. 320. Edward's request to the curia had been made earlier that year (*Calendar of Papal Registers 1342–1419*, p. 373).

[53] *Registrum Simonis de Sudbiria diocesis Londoniensis, A.D. 1362–75*, ed. R. C. Fowler and C. Jenkins (2 vols., Canterbury and York Soc., xxxiv, xxxviii, 1927–38), ii. 164–5.

[54] 'Prebendaries: Yetminster Prima', *Fasti Ecclesiae Anglicanae 1300–1541*, iii: *Salisbury Diocese* (1962), pp. 100–1 <http://www.british-history.ac.uk/report. aspx?compid=32371> [accessed 6 Nov. 2007].

[55] There is no record of the date of Wykeham's resignation, but on 20 Aug. 1361, a royal grant of Pulham was made to Andrew Stratford (*Calendar of Patent Rolls 1361–4*, p. 44).

[56] *Calendar of Patent Rolls 1361–4*, p. 79; *Calendar of Patent Rolls 1361–4*, p. 79; the grant was repeated on 1 Nov. 1361 (*Calendar of Patent Rolls 1361–4*, p. 107).

rationale for the exchanges he made within the cathedral is unclear. However, he consistently held a prebend in St. Paul's until he resigned all his benefices upon becoming bishop in 1367.[57]

By the autumn of 1361, then, Wykeham had a clutch of benefices and he began to play the market with exchanges, although he also continued to acquire additional benefices from Edward III. The reasoning behind all of Wykeham's exchanges is unclear at this point and it is apparent that complex negotiations were involved as Wykeham sought to rationalize his mass of benefices.[58] Thus, for example, he resigned his prebend in Bromyard collegiate church on 23 October 1361 and it was subsequently granted to the well-connected civil lawyer John de Waltham, nephew of archbishop Thoresby, archbishop of York (1353–73).[59] This resignation and grant are likely to be connected with that which took place three days later on 26 October when Wykeham and John de Waltham exchanged other benefices. Wykeham exchanged his Coventry and Litchfield prebend of Flixton (worth £4 13s 4d) for John de Waltham's Southwell collegiate church prebend of Dunham, worth £36 13s 4d.[60]

After late 1361 the pace at which Wykeham acquired benefices slowed and he largely concentrated on acquiring a smaller number of very well-endowed benefices. These included the Lincoln cathedral prebend of Sutton which was described as worth 260 marks in 1366 (£173 6s 8d in

---

[57] There is particular confusion with Wykeham's holding of the prebend of Totenhall for which he exchanged Oxgate in Nov. 1361. Wykeham resigned Totenhall by Dec. 1362 and it went to John de Blewbury. However, Wykeham regained it in Apr. 1363 when he exchanged his prebend in St. Stephen's Westminster with Blewbury, returning as prebendary of Totenhall, which he was still holding in 1366 ('Prebendaries: Totenhall', *Fasti Ecclesiae Anglicanae 1300–1541*, v: *St. Paul's, London* (1963), pp. 62–4 <http://www.british-history. ac.uk/report.aspx?compid=32412> [accessed 6 Nov. 2007].

[58] Complex exchanges of benefices were sometimes facilitated by brokers which were nicknamed 'chop-churches'. Their activities were condemned by the bishops, as can be seen in 1391 when Archbishop Courtenay issued his *Litera missa omnibus Episcopis suffraganeis Domini contra Choppe-Churches* (H. Spelman, *Concilia Decreta, Leges, Constitutiones in re Ecclesiarum Orbis Britannici* (2 vols., London, 1654), ii. 641–4). On the market in benefices, see R. N. Swanson, *Church and Society in Late Medieval England* (1989), pp. 55–6; R. L. Storey 'Ecclesiastical causes in chancery', in *The Study of Medieval Records: Essays in Honour of Kathleen Major*, ed. R. L. Storey and D. A. Bullough (Oxford, 1971), pp. 236–59; A. H. Thompson, *The English Clergy and their Organisation in the Later Middle Ages* (Oxford, 1927), pp. 107–9; L. F. Salzman, '"Chopchurches" in Sussex', *Sussex Archaeological Collections*, c (1962), 137–41.

[59] *Calendar of Patent Rolls 1361–4*, p. 90.

[60] *Biographical Register of the University of Oxford* (1973). The values of benefices are taken from the online Taxatio Database developed from *Taxatio Ecclesiastica Angliae et Walliae Auctoritate Papae Nicholai IV* (Record Commission, 1802) (see <http://www.hrionline. ac.uk/taxatio/index.html> [accessed 22 Feb. 2008]).

Taxatio) and Laughton Prebend (£73 6s 8d) in York minster.[61] Five benefices were exchanged for Crowhurst in Sussex, the prebendal church of the royal free chapel at Hastings.[62] In addition, Wykeham's desires to have a prebend in the important cathedral of Lincoln were fulfilled in April 1363 when he became archdeacon of Northampton; he resigned this a month later to take up the wealthier and more prestigious archdeaconry of Lincoln.[63] Wykeham was inducted as archdeacon in person on 12 September 1363 and henceforth he was an active defender of the rights of the archdeaconry.[64] The archdeaconry, unlike his other benefices, did carry responsibility for the cure of souls. Wykeham also acquired (at an unknown date) the Cornish parochial benefice of Menheniot, just outside Liskeard. This too carried responsibility for cure of souls; Wykeham must have catered for the spiritual needs of the parishioners of Menheniot by providing a vicar to act in his stead. In 1366, he stated that he had apostolic dispensation to hold Menheniot but at this point he had resigned it, faced with papal hostility to the holding of multiple incompatible benefices.[65]

This concentration of benefices in a short period catapulted Wykeham rapidly into the upper ranks of non-episcopal churchmen's income. It also attracted hostile criticism both from English contemporaries and at the papal court. In this Wykeham was a victim of the timing of his rise in the English church. Fewer hostile comments would have been made a decade earlier but Wykeham's accumulation of benefices in the early thirteen-sixties took place in the decade during which the papacy launched a radical attack on pluralism. Successive generations of popes had sought to control pluralism through a range of decrees, beginning in 1317 with Pope John XXII's decree *Execrabilis* which was concerned with pluralism when it involved the cure of souls.[66] Benefices without cure of souls – literally *sine cura* – such as appointment to a cathedral chapter or as a canon in a secular cathedral, were of much less concern to the papacy before the time of Pope Urban V (1362–70). Multiple holding of such posts by a single individual did not

---

[61] *Calendar of Patent Rolls 1361–4*, p. 244; 'Prebendaries: Laughton', *Fasti Ecclesiae Anglicanae 1300–1541*, vi: *Northern Province* (1963), p. 64.

[62] *Calendar of Patent Rolls 1361–4*, pp. 167–8; the benefices concerned were an unnamed prebend in St David's diocese; the prebend of Ruyl in Aberwilly collegiate church; the prebend of Triffelegh in Landowybry collegiate church; the prebend of Church Withington in Hereford cathedral and the prebend of Warminster in Wells cathedral.

[63] *Calendar of Patent Rolls 1361–4*, pp. 319, 345.

[64] Davis, *Wykeham*, pp. 48–9.

[65] *Registrum Simonis de Sudbiria*, ii. 164–5.

[66] A. Hamilton Thompson, 'Pluralism in the medieval church', *Associated Architectural Societies Reports and Papers*, xxxiii (1915), 61–4.

imperil people's souls. Wykeham was not in breach of contemporary canon law in amassing this portfolio of benefices.

By 1366, when Pope Urban V demanded details of the extent of English pluralism, Wykeham's income from his benefices placed him firmly at the top of the list. His total annual revenue from benefices was £873 6s 8d, an astonishing amount which was more than three times the income of the next person on the English list whose benefices totalled £270 a year.[67] In amassing such an extensive portfolio of benefices Wykeham was to attract the hostility of Pope Urban V, who from the outset of his pontificate in 1362 aimed to enhance the educational standards of the clergy throughout Christendom. To achieve this ambition Urban V embarked on reforms to the benefice system which were intended to reduce the concentration of rich prebends in the hands of a few men. Instead he aimed to 'distribute the wealth of the church more widely among the lettered clergy'.[68] The resources freed in this manner were intended to support clergy seeking higher education in the universities. It is likely that Urban was thinking of men such as Wykeham when he complained in his bull *Horribilis et detestabilis,* in the spring of 1363, about the greed 'of those reprobate clerks, quite incapable of study themselves, who nevertheless hold an excess of benefices, while innumerable prudent, wise and learned men, studying in the schools and elsewhere, have no benefice at all'.[69] Edward III's response was to protest to a cardinal at Avignon that Wykeham was a man 'of all the kindness, knowledge, loyalty, honesty and sufficiency of his person'.[70]

Wykeham, always conscious of his rights and keen to defend them, was equally careful to remain within the letter of canon law with regard to his benefices. Despite the hostile criticism sparked by his huge portfolio of benefices, he was not actually in breach of the letter of contemporary canon law in amassing it. In 1366, when the papacy required declaration of all pluralists' holdings, Wykeham only held a single benefice with cure of souls, the archdeaconry of Lincoln, in addition to the eleven without cure, all of which were prebends in cathedral chapters or in other collegiate churches. In the return in archbishop Langham's register it is stated that he has only one benefice with cure of souls – which was the valuable archdeaconry of Lincoln – and eleven other benefices without cure, and that following the

---

[67] For more details, see Davis, *Wykeham*, pp. 41–3.

[68] J. J. N. Palmer and A. P. Wells, 'Ecclesiastical reform and the politics of the Hundred Years' War during the pontificate of Urban V (1362–70)', in *War, Literature and Politics in the Late Middle Ages*, ed. C. T. Allmand (Liverpool, 1976), pp. 169–89.

[69] Allmand, p. 171.

[70] Cited in J. R. L. Highfield, 'The promotion of William of Wickham to the see of Winchester', *Journal of Ecclesiastical History*, iv (1953), 44–5.

publication of the papal's bull on pluralities issued on 5 May 1365, he had resigned the Cornish living of Menheniot which he had been holding as an additional benefice with cure.[71]

The death of William Edington, bishop of Winchester, in early October 1366 provided the opportunity for Wykeham's final and most impressive promotion. On 13 October 1366 King Edward III issued a licence permitting the monks of St. Swithun's cathedral to proceed to elect a replacement for Edington, recommending as he did so that Wykeham was a suitable candidate, a recommendation which the monks duly followed.[72] Papal approval was also needed since Pope Urban V had reserved the see in Edington's lifetime for papal provision. It is clear that the pope was extremely reluctant to bend to Edward's request that he provide Wykeham to the see. Edward III was forced to launch a major diplomatic offensive at Avignon to guarantee his ultimate success, working to ensure that cardinals and other influential members of the papal court would intercede on Wykeham's behalf. Finally, in July 1367, Urban relented and provided Wykeham to England's most valuable benefice.[73]

The decade between 1356 and 1366 was a crucial one in the development of William Wykeham's career. These years saw his swift rise within the royal circle, to the point where he was indispensable to the king. As the keeper of the king's signet seal he was privy to Edward's thoughts and actions at the earliest moment. Contemporaries were aware of his growing influence. In addition to these rapid developments within his career, he had taken a decisive step in finally deciding to become a priest. Consideration as to whether or not to take this step must have dominated Wykeham's private thoughts for much of this period. Having proceeded to ordination, he had cut off opportunities for marriage, parenthood and carrying on his family name, although the fact that his sister Alice had married and produced nephews may have made this of less importance. It is ironic that his subsequent actions in founding Winchester College and New College, Oxford, made possible only because of the wealth of the see of Winchester, were to perpetuate his name far more effectively than fathering a family would have done.

Wykeham's promotion as bishop of Winchester provoked hostile remarks from contemporary commentators. John of Reading complained that

[71] *Registrum Simonis de Sudbiria*, ii. 164–5.
[72] *Calendar of Patent Rolls 1364–7*, p. 324.
[73] Davis, *Wykeham*, pp. 50–1; full details of the circumstances surrounding Wykeham's promotion and the complex interrelationship between individual promotion and international politics are discussed in Highfield, pp. 37–54.

'the mammon of iniquity raises the unworthy to be prelates'.[74] Wykeham's pluralism and relatively recent promotion to the priesthood made him an easy and obvious target for critics. Although he lacked pastoral experience when he became bishop of Winchester he was far from being unique in this among the episcopate. Hostility arose primarily from the speed of his ascent within the church hierarchy; he had only been ordained as a priest five years before his elevation to the episcopate. It arose too because his elevation had been to the wealthiest and one of the most powerful of the English dioceses. His successor – Henry Beaufort – was half-brother to the reigning monarch and was to become a cardinal. Already powerful as confidant of King Edward III and as keeper of the privy seal, this elevation as bishop would reinforce Wykeham's position in the upper ranks of English political society.

What sort of bishop did Wykeham turn out to be? There is no doubt that – throughout his episcopate – he was both concerned for and involved with his diocese. It was, of course, easier for a bishop of Winchester to be simultaneously politically involved and resident and active in his diocese than it would be for those whose dioceses were further from London. Nonetheless, Wykeham's engagement with his diocese was not merely a matter of geography. There is clear evidence of his active concern for the welfare of both people and buildings assigned to his care.[75] Much daily administration was the responsibility of his episcopal administrators but Wykeham oversaw them carefully. It was not his style merely to appoint commissions to carry out visitations or deal with other matters and to feel that in doing so he had discharged his duty. His episcopate saw magnificent redevelopment in Winchester cathedral and the rebuilding and refurbishment of key episcopal palaces, but also concern for the physical fabric of parish churches and for the pastoral care of their parishioners. Edward III had been right when he had assured the pope nearly forty years earlier that Wykeham would be an excellent bishop. Wykeham may have made a belated decision to enter the church, but as with everything he did, once he had embraced the decision he was committed to it.

[74] *Chronica Johannis de Reading*, p. 178.
[75] Davis, *Wykeham*, ch. 9.

III

Performance and ritual

Religious symbols and practices: monastic spirituality, pilgrimage and crusade*

William J. Purkis

In an article published in 1985 Christopher Brooke described the increasingly diverse nature of professed religious life in the central middle ages with the following words:

> The religious life and religious aspirations [of the eleventh and twelfth centuries] resembled a spectrum, with many subtle shades of colour – many slight differences adding up in the end to major divisions. And these were often shifting, and all subject to the many winds which blew. The patron who wished to found a religious house or the aspirant who sought his vocation might often be inspired with a dazzling vision; but each must equally often have been confused and blinded by the profusion of indistinguishable goods laid out in the shop for his choice.[1]

In this memorable passage of prose Professor Brooke captured the essence of what scholars often refer to as the 'reformation' of the twelfth century, when the previously predominant position of Benedictine monasticism became challenged by the emergence of new forms of professed religious life and the proliferation of a variety of new religious orders.[2] The relatively sudden emergence of a multiplicity of paths available to those wishing to pursue

---

* This is an extended and adapted version of the paper I gave in London on 19 June 2007. I am extremely grateful to Miri Rubin for giving me the opportunity to speak at the colloquium and for inviting me to contribute to this volume, and to Andrew Jotischky for reading and commenting on the revised version of the text.

[1] C. N. L. Brooke, 'Monk and canon: some patterns in the religious life of the twelfth century', *Monks, Hermits and the Ascetic Tradition*, ed. W. J. Sheils, *Studies in Church History*, xxii (Oxford, 1985), 129.

[2] See, e.g., B. M. Bolton, *The Medieval Reformation* (1983); H. Leyser, *Hermits and the New Monasticism: a Study of Religious Communities in Western Europe, 1000–1150* (New York, 1984); G. Constable, *The Reformation of the Twelfth Century* (Cambridge, 1996).

W. J. Purkis, 'Religious symbols and practices: monastic spirituality, pilgrimage and crusade', in *European Religious Cultures: Essays offered to Christopher Brooke on the occasion of his eightieth birthday*, ed. M. Rubin (London, 2020), pp. 65–85. License: CC-BY-NC-ND 4.0.

a religious vocation was, of course, also recognized by contemporaries. In his *Historia Ecclesiastica*, for example, Orderic Vitalis described the changes that were taking place in the first half of the twelfth century with a mixture of admiration and cynicism:

> See, though evil abounds in the world, the devotion of the faithful in cloisters grows more abundant and bears fruit a hundredfold in the Lord's field. Monasteries are founded everywhere in mountain valleys and plains, observing new rites and wearing different habits; the swarm of cowled monks spreads all over the world . . . In my opinion voluntary poverty, contempt for the world, and true religion inspire many of them, but many hypocrites and plausible counterfeiters are mixed with them, as tares with wheat.[3]

Orderic's concentration here was on those who withdrew from the world completely to follow one form of cenobitic life or another, but other contemporary writers recognized that the range of activities that could be undertaken by those who had sworn religious vows was becoming increasingly varied. In the eleven-forties, for example, Otto of Freising, who was a Cistercian by profession, commemorated the transformations of his era by including a 'description (*descriptio*) of the diverse religious orders' in his *Chronica sive Historia de Duabus Civitatibus*. He wrote of the different ways in which a twelfth-century religious might pursue his vocation, which might entail an engagement with the world rather than a withdrawal from it:

> Some of these [religious], dwelling in cities, in castles, in villages and in the countryside, impart to their neighbours by word and by example the rule of right living; others – not, indeed, avoiding intercourse with men but rather making provision for their own peace – shun crowds, and, devoting themselves to God alone, withdraw to retreats in the woods and in secluded places.[4]

---

[3] Orderic Vitalis, *Historia Ecclesiastica*, ed. and trans. M. Chibnall (6 vols., Oxford, 1968–80), iv. 310–13: *En abundante iniquitate in mundo, uberius crescit fidelium in religione deuotio, et multiplicata seges in agro surgit dominico. In saltibus et campestribus passim construuntur cenobia, nouisque ritibus uariisque scematibus trabeata, peragrant orbem cucullatorum examina . . . Voluntaria paupertas mundique contemptus ut opinor in plerisque feruet ac uera religio, sed plures eis hipocritae seductoriique simulatores permiscentur ut lolium tritico.*

[4] Otto of Freising, *Chronica sive Historia de Duabus Civitatibus*, ed. A. Hofmeister and W. Lammers (Berlin, 1960) (hereafter Otto of Freising), p. 560: *Quorum alii in urbibus, castellis et vicis et agris commorantes proximis normam recte vivendi verbo et exemplo tribuunt; alii non quidem commanentiam hominum asperantes, sed quieti suae amplius providentes frequentiam fugiunt solique Deo vacantes ad silvarum abditorumque locorum latibula se conferunt* (translation from C. C. Mierow, *The Two Cities: a Chronicle of Universal History to the Year 1146 A.D., by Otto, Bishop of Freising* (New York, 2002), p. 446).

Crucially, however, Otto ascribed to these groups and individuals common customs and practices, and in so doing recognized that there could be a degree of unity in the evident diversity that characterized his times. He noted, for example, that all religious abstained from eating meat, and that all were sworn to celibacy and renounced any contact with women.[5] Most importantly, though, Otto believed that the religious of the world were united by two fundamental and related aspirations: first, the imitation of Christ;[6] and second, the pursuit of the common life of the *vita apostolica*.[7] In this respect, Otto's description of 'the various bands of saints' provides a good example of the spiritual rhetoric that was applied by contemporaries to the reforming monastic movements of the eleventh and twelfth centuries:

> All [religious] alike spend their lives on earth in purity of living and conscience, and in chastity like that of the angels in heaven. Having but *one heart and mind* they dwell as one in monasteries or churches; they sleep at the same time, they rise with one mind for prayer, they take food together in one house, [and] they devote themselves to prayer, to reading, and to work by day and night with inexhaustible vigilance . . . Renouncing their desires, their possessions and even their parents in accordance with the command of the Gospel, [they] continually bear the cross for the mortification of the flesh and, being filled with heavenly longings, follow Christ.[8]

At around the same time that Otto was working on his *Chronica*, a cleric from Liège was composing a more detailed study of the 'diverse orders and professions that are in the Church' (*Libellus de Diversis Ordinibus et*

---

[5] Otto of Freising, p. 562.

[6] For the context, see especially G. Constable, 'The ideal of the imitation of Christ', in G. Constable, *Three Studies in Medieval Religious and Social Thought* (Cambridge, 1995), pp. 143–248.

[7] For the context, see especially M.-D. Chenu, 'Monks, canons, and laymen in search of the apostolic life', in *Nature, Man and Society in the Twelfth Century: Essays on New Theological Perspectives in the Latin West*, ed. and trans. J. Taylor and L. K. Little (Toronto, 1968), pp. 202–38; H. Grundmann, *Religious Movements in the Middle Ages*, trans. S. Rowan (Notre Dame, Ind., 1995).

[8] Otto of Freising, p. 560: *diversa sunt sanctorum agmina, qui propriis desideriis, facultatibus, parentibus iuxta mandatum evangelicum abrenuntiantes crucemque per mortificationem carnis iugiter portantes caelesti desiderio pleni Christum secuntur . . . Eque tamen omnes vitae et conscientiae puritate ac sanctimonia caelesti et angelica in terris vita degunt. Commanent autem 'cor unum et animam unam' habentes in unum in cenobiis vel ecclesiis, somnum simul capiunt, unanimiter ad orationem surgunt, in una domo pariter reficiuntur, orationi, lectioni, operi die noctuque ita indefessa incumbunt vigilantia* (citation from Acts 4:32). For a full translation of this passage, see Mierow, pp. 445–6.

Professionibus qui sunt in Ecclesia).[9] The writer in question, who was probably an Augustinian canon,[10] produced an account that bears comparison with Otto of Freising's *descriptio*. Like Otto, the author of the *Libellus* recognized the range of vocations available to those who wished to take up a religious life, and categorized them according to their proximity to the secular world. He wrote of hermits, 'who usually live alone or with a few others', and drew distinctions between three types of monk (those 'who live close to men, such as the Cluniacs and the like', those 'who remove themselves far from men, such as the Cistercians and the like', and those 'who are called seculars, who ignore their profession'), and between three types of canon (those 'who establish themselves far from men, such as the Premonstratensians and the canons of Saint-Josse', those 'who have their houses near the activities of men, such as the canons of St. Quentin in the field and of St. Victor', and, finally, those 'who live among men of the world and are called seculars').[11] The *Libellus*'s text also suggested that there was to be a supplementary discussion of other more nebulous forms of religious life, but this section was either unwritten or has been lost.[12]

A further similarity between the *Libellus* and Otto's *descriptio* was that both recognized that the establishment in the twelfth century of a variety of forms of religious life was a positive rather than a negative development.[13] The *Libellus*'s text was prefaced with a statement that acknowledged that it was perfectly proper for those who followed the 'way of God' (*uia Dei*) for 'some [to] walk one way and others another'.[14] In a subsequent section the *Libellus*'s author provided a musical metaphor to illustrate this point further. Responding to potential criticisms of the differing ways in which individuals might approach the pursuit of an eremitical life, he wrote that:

> If it still displeases you that all men of this calling do not live in the same way, look at the creation fashioned by the good Creator in various ways, and how

[9] *Libellus de Diversis Ordinibus et Professionibus qui sunt in Ecclesia*, ed. and trans. G. Constable and B. S. Smith (rev. edn., Oxford, 2003) (hereafter *Libellus*).

[10] For the authorship of the *Libellus*, see *Libellus*, pp. xv–xviii.

[11] *Libellus*, pp. 4–5, 16–17, 38–9, 50–1, 66–7, 86–7.

[12] *Libellus*, pp. 4–5, where it is stated that the *Libellus*'s analysis would include those who were *nec canonici nec monachi nec heremitae nec inclusi sed deicolae uel licoisi*, as well as a consideration of the religious opportunities available to women.

[13] For the context, see especially G. Constable, 'The diversity of religious life and acceptance of social pluralism in the twelfth century', in *History, Society and the Churches: Essays in Honour of Owen Chadwick*, ed. D. Beales and G. Best (Cambridge, 1985), pp. 29–47.

[14] *Libellus*, pp. 2–3: *Dilectissimo fratri suo .R. unica dilectione sibi coniunctus frater .R. uiam Dei bene ac fidenter ut coepit tenere, in qua alius sic, alius sic ambulat.*

a harmony has been achieved from different chords, so that the heavens are placed above, the earth below, water made heavier, air lighter, man wiser than the beasts, one above and another below, and you will not wonder if even in God's service different things are preferred, for according to the Gospel: *In my Father's house there are many mansions.*[15]

But in many ways the most significant parallel between the work of Otto of Freising and that of the author of the *Libellus* was their shared perception of the spiritual ideals that were at the heart of the foundations of new forms of twelfth-century religious life. For the author of the *Libellus*, like Otto, sought to demonstrate how all of the new religious orders of his age were modelled on ideals of *imitatio Christi* (and, in some cases, *vita apostolica*), and to illustrate how the brethren of those orders could find inspiration and justification for their ways of life in the writings of both the Old and New Testaments. In his discussion of hermits, for example, the *Libellus*'s author stated that he would 'consider whether perhaps we can find a likeness (*similitudo*) of these servants of God among the first men', and went on to show how Abel had lived in quasi-eremitical pastoral isolation (Genesis 4:2–4):

We find therefore a distinct likeness to hermits in the first age, when we find the just Abel living in the shade of trees and intent on grazing his sheep, having doubtless sought solitude, where he can both live without being disturbed and feed the sheep, which are the signs of his innocence, and then taking the offspring of these sheep make an offering to God.[16]

Perhaps more tangible though was the precedent that the *Libellus*'s author provided for hermits from the life of Christ. He described how he wished to 'see also whether our Jesus did anything that could be compared to this kind of life', before suggesting that Christ's withdrawal to the mountain (John 6:15) might offer a suitable parallel: 'Accept joyfully then my Lord Jesus, who fled into the mountain or the desert, and you will have before you examples you can imitate'.[17]

---

[15] *Libellus*, pp. 14–15: *Si autem adhuc tibi displicet quod omnes huius professionis homines non uno modo uiuunt, inspice facturam mundi a bono conditore diuerse dispositam, et de diuersis concordem effecisse armoniam, ut caelum superius, terra inferius, aqua grauior, aer leuior, homo belua sapientior, unum supra, alterum infra positum sit, et non miraberis si etiam in seruis Dei alter alteri preferatur, cum secundum euangelium 'in domo patris mansiones multae sint'* (citation from John 14:2).

[16] *Libellus*, pp. 4–9: *Habemus ergo in priori aetate heremitarum similitudinem expressam, ubi inuenimus Abel iustum in arborum umbra morantem et pascuis ouium intentum sine dubio solitudinem quaesisse, ubi et sine tumultu uiueret, et oues suae innocentiae indices nutriret, ac deinde de eisdem ouibus fructus capiens Domino offerret.*

[17] *Libellus*, pp. 10–13: *accipe etiam gratanter dominum meum Iesum in montem uel in desertum fugisse, et habebis ante te quos imitari possis.*

This methodology of justification through scriptural analysis was applied to all of the various forms of religious profession considered in the *Libellus* because, as the text's author put it, 'I see that Jesus demonstrated in himself the likeness (*similitudo*) of almost all the callings of the church, which we shall show in their place as well as we can'.[18] In this respect, the *Libellus*'s project was more focused and detailed than that of Otto of Freising's *descriptio*, but both texts' accounts of the increasingly diverse nature of twelfth-century religious vocations concentrated, understandably, on forms of asceticism that required individuals to commit to a lifetime of withdrawal from (or, in some cases, engagement with) the world. However, it is striking that at around the same time that writers such as Otto of Freising and the anonymous author of the *Libellus* were justifying innovations in professed religion by citing precedents from the Old and New Testaments, similar endeavours were taking place in relation to forms of devotional undertaking that required shorter, temporary votive obligations. In fact, there is a range of evidence to suggest that certain changes in the religious practices of the twelfth-century laity – namely developments in ideas of penitential pilgrimage and the emergence of the crusading ideal – ought also to be included in wider considerations of the 'reformation' of twelfth-century religious life.[19]

* * *

One of the most striking examples of the way ideas and rhetoric more normally associated with the spirituality of reformed monasticism influenced lay religious practices can be found with reference to the cult of St. James the Great. The pilgrimage to Santiago de Compostela was experiencing a period of significant growth in the eleventh and twelfth centuries,[20] and it is clear that as part of this process of expansion the cult's promoters were attempting to codify their institutional identity by redefining the hagiographical and iconographical representations of their saint.[21] The most significant output of this codification was the production in *c.*1140 of the

---

[18] *Libellus*, pp. 10–11: *Video etiam dominum Iesum pene omnium professionum aecclesiasticarum similitudinem in se ipso demonstrasse, quod etiam pro posse suis locis ostendemus, cum de aliis professionibus sermonem texuerimus.*

[19] As will be illustrated below, pilgrimage and crusading were devotional activities that were intended primarily for *bellatores* and *laboratores* rather than for *oratores*. For the context, see G. Constable, 'The orders of society', in Constable, *Three Studies*, pp. 249–360.

[20] J. Sumption, *Pilgrimage: an Image of Mediaeval Religion* (1975), p. 116, wrote that during this period the pilgrim road to Compostela became 'the busiest trunk road in Christendom'.

[21] For the context, see R. A. Fletcher, *St. James's Catapult: the Life and Times of Diego Gelmírez of Santiago de Compostela* (Oxford, 1984).

Liber Sancti Jacobi,[22] a compilation of five books that dealt with various aspects of the cult of St. James and the pilgrimage to Compostela, including a volume of liturgical materials, a collection of miracle stories, an account of the *translatio* of the saint's relics from the Holy Land to Iberia, and a guide for pilgrims who were en route to the Galician shrine.[23] The *Liber*'s opening volume of liturgy included a sermon known as *Veneranda Dies*,[24] which amounted to a lengthy exposition on the virtues of pilgrimage in general and on the merits of penitential journeys to Compostela in particular, and which contains important evidence for scholars interested in monastic influences on lay religious culture.

The *Veneranda Dies* sermon is a valuable source for a number of reasons. First, it provides a wealth of information about the practicalities and difficulties associated with twelfth-century pilgrimage; it included, for example, repeated condemnations of those sinful individuals who sought to hamper the pilgrim's progress, such as innkeepers (who are likened to 'the traitor Judas who betrayed the Lord by kissing him'),[25] prostitutes,[26] corrupt basilica guards,[27] moneychangers,[28] false pardoners ('as mild as sheep on the outside but rapacious wolves on the inside'),[29] 'crafty merchants'[30] and toll collectors.[31] Second, it gives testimony to the international profile of the saint's

---

[22] *Liber Sancti Jacobi: Codex Calixtinus*, ed. K. Herbers and M. Santos Noia (Santiago de Compostela, 1998). See also the *Historia Compostellana*, ed. E. Falque Rey (Corpus Christianorum: Continuatio Mediaeualis, lxx, Turnhout, 1988); and for comment, B. F. Reilly, 'The *Historia Compostelana*: the genesis and composition of a twelfth-century Spanish *Gesta*', *Speculum*, xliv (1969), 78–85.

[23] The *Liber* also included a Latin text of the *Historia Turpini*, which purported to be an eyewitness account of Charlemagne's eighth-century 'crusading' wars in the Iberian peninsula. For a discussion of the *Historia Turpini* and associations between St. James and Iberian crusading, see W. J. Purkis, *Crusading Spirituality in the Holy Land and Iberia, c.1095–c.1187* (Woodbridge, 2008), pp. 139–65, 175–8.

[24] For the Latin text of *Veneranda Dies* (hereafter *V.D.*), see *Liber Sancti Jacobi*, pp. 85–104. For a full English translation, see T. F. Coffey, L. K. Davidson and M. Dunn, *The Miracles of Saint James: Translations from the Liber Sancti Jacobi* (New York, 1996) (hereafter *M.S.J.*), pp. 8–56.

[25] *V.D.*, pp. 95–7; *M.S.J.*, pp. 34–8: *Cui illos similes dicam nisi Iude proditori qui Dominum tradidit osculando?*

[26] *V.D.*, p. 96; *M.S.J.*, p. 36.

[27] *V.D.*, p. 97; *M.S.J.*, p. 38.

[28] *V.D.*, pp. 97–9; *M.S.J.*, pp. 38–9, 41–3.

[29] *V.D.*, p. 98; *M.S.J.*, pp. 39–40.

[30] *V.D.*, p. 99; *M.S.J.*, pp. 43–4.

[31] *V.D.*, p. 101; *M.S.J.*, pp. 48–9. It is striking that these groups were largely condemned because of their engagement with the money economy, which was in direct contrast to the pilgrim's adoption of voluntary poverty. For the context, see L. K. Little, *Religious Poverty*

cult, claiming that pilgrims from no fewer than seventy-four different nations had recently venerated St. James's shrine,[32] and that the saint's miracles had been witnessed across the whole of western Christendom.[33] But perhaps most pertinently, the central part of the sermon consisted of a thorough discussion of the idea of pilgrimage itself, which included an analysis of the biblical models and precedents for the practice. In this respect, *Veneranda Dies* bears direct comparison with contemporaneous texts, such as the *Libellus de Diversis Ordinibus*, that were being composed to justify the variety of new forms of professed religious life that had emerged in the first half of the twelfth century.

Echoing the language used by the author of the *Libellus*, the sermon's analysis of the scriptural basis for pilgrimage began by explaining that it was necessary to show 'how the pilgrim road had its origins among the ancient fathers, and how it should be walked'.[34] The sermon then went on to illustrate how the practice of pilgrimage could be traced back to the very first book of the Old Testament:

> Adam is considered the first pilgrim, since because of his transgression of the commandment of God he was sent from paradise into the exile of this world . . . Similarly, the pilgrim is sent by his priest on a pilgrimage into a type of exile from his own region because of his transgressions, and if he has confessed properly and has completed his life after taking onto himself proper penitence, he is saved through the grace of Christ.[35]

Further Old Testament parallels were to be found in the lives of Abraham, '[who] was a pilgrim, since he went forth from his country to another as he was told by the Lord',[36] and of Jacob '[who] arose as a pilgrim, since, having gone out from his country, he travelled to Egypt and stayed'.[37] But a much greater proportion of the sermon's discussion dealt with the way

---

and the Profit Economy in Medieval Europe (1978).

[32] *V.D.*, p. 89; *M.S.J.*, p. 18.

[33] *V.D.*, p. 90; *M.S.J.*, p. 21.

[34] *V.D.*, p. 92; *M.S.J.*, p. 26: *Qualiter via peregrinalis a priscis patribus oriatur, et quomodo perambulari debeat, nobis est declarandum.*

[35] *V.D.*, p. 92; *M.S.J.*, pp. 26–7: *Primus peregrinus Adam habetur, quia ob transgressionem precepti Dei a paradiso egressus in huius mundi exilio mittitur, et per Christi sanguinem et gratiam ipsius salvatur. Similiter peregrinus a proprio loco digressus, in peregrinacione propter transgressiones suas a sacerdote suo quasi in exilio mittitur, et per gratiam Christi, si bene confessus fuerit et in penitencia sibi coniuncta propriam vitam finierit, salvatur.*

[36] *V.D.*, p. 92; *M.S.J.*, p. 27: *Abraham patriarcha peregrinus fuit, quia de patria sua in aliam profectus est, sicut illi a Domino dictum est.*

[37] *V.D.*, p. 92; *M.S.J.*, p. 27: *Item Iacob patriarcha peregrinus extitit, quia de patria sua egressus in Egipto peregrinatur et commoratur.*

the New Testament supplied *exempla* for pilgrims. Here, attention focused initially on the notion that pilgrimage was an act of Christo-mimesis and that by the very nature of their devotional undertaking pilgrims were imitators of Christ. The basis for this idea lay in an interpretation of Christ's post-Resurrection encounter with two of his followers on the road to Emmaus (Luke 24:13–35). According to *Veneranda Dies*, on this occasion 'Our Lord Jesus Christ himself, returning from Jerusalem, after he had risen from the dead, appeared first as a pilgrim, as the disciples meeting him said: *You alone are a pilgrim in Jerusalem*'.[38]

It seems unlikely that this reading of the Emmaus narrative would have been regarded as far-fetched by contemporaries; in a different context, the author of the *Libellus de Diversis Ordinibus* described how Christ's life could provide *exempla* for all manner of religious activities just as it was used to exemplify the grades of the ecclesiastical hierarchy:

> If therefore the Lord Jesus, as has often previously been said, was a lector by his reading of Isaiah in the synagogue, was a door-keeper by his driving the moneylenders from the temple, was an exorcist by casting out demons, was a candle-bearer by giving sight to the blind, was a subdeacon by ministering, a levite by preaching the Gospel of his reign, and a priest by offering himself, it will not be absurd to say that by withdrawing into the mountain or the desert, as is proper for hermits, he consecrated their life in himself.[39]

Indeed, the suggestion in the Gospel of St. Luke that Christ could be represented as a *peregrinus* was also taken up by the twelfth-century sculptors working at Santo Domingo de Silos, a monastery near Burgos, where he was depicted, in an adaptation of the road to Emmaus story, carrying a pilgrim's staff and a bag bearing the cockleshell – the traditional accoutrements of the

---

[38] *V.D.*, p. 93; *M.S.J.*, p. 27: *Ipse Dominus noster Ihesus Christus postquam suscitavit a mortuis a Iherosolimis rediens primus peregrinus extitit, ut discipuli obviantes illi dixerunt: 'Tu solus peregrinus es in Iherusalem'* (citation from Luke 24:18). From the context, it is clear enough that the *peregrinus* of the Vulgate ought to be translated here as 'pilgrim' rather than 'stranger', but the ambiguity in the sermon was almost certainly intentional.

[39] *Libellus*, pp. 10–11: *Si ergo dominus Iesus sicut et ante nos sepe dictum est legendo in libro Ysaiae intra sinagogam lector, et eliminando de templo nummularios hostiarius et eiciendo demones exorcista, et illuminando cecos ceroferarius, et ministrando subdiaconus, et predicando euangelium regni leuita, et se ipsum offerendo sacerdos, non erit absurdum si secedendo in montem uel in desertum quod heremitarum est proprium, uitam eorum in se ipso consecrasse dicatur.* For the broader context, see R. E. Reynolds, *The Ordinals of Christ from their Origins to the Twelfth Century* (Berlin and New York, 1978); for an Iberian perspective, R. E. Reynolds, 'An ordinal of Christ in medieval Catalan', *Harvard Theological Review*, xcix (2006), 103–10.

pilgrim travelling to Compostela.[40] Here, Christ was not only represented as a pilgrim, but a pilgrim of St. James, and it therefore seems possible that this image was intended to communicate the idea that those *peregrini* who followed in his footsteps to the north-west corner of the Iberian peninsula were to be regarded as virtuous *imitatores Christi*.

Such depictions of Christ-as-pilgrim are, of course, remarkable in themselves, but in many respects it was the final aspect of the *Veneranda Dies* sermon's biblical modelling for pilgrimage that was the most significant. For, having established that pilgrims were imitators of Christ, the sermon went on to show that the devotional undertaking of the pilgrim was also a kind of *vita apostolica*. What is more, pilgrims were portrayed in the sermon as not only living in accordance with the values of 'poverty and preaching' that Christ had enjoined on his disciples (and that were widely associated with the 'active' apostolic life);[41] they were also seen to be following a model of the communal life espoused by the brethren of the primitive church. According to *Veneranda Dies*:

> The apostles, therefore, whom the Lord sent out without money or footwear, were also pilgrims. Because of this it is in no way allowed for pilgrims to bring money, unless they expend this money on the needy. If he sent the apostles without money, what will become of those who now travel with gold and silver, eating and drinking to fulfilment and imparting nothing to the poor? Certainly they are not true pilgrims, but the thieves and bandits of God . . . [For] just as the multitude of believers had one heart and one soul and no one called something his own, but all held all in common, so must all things be held in common for all pilgrims: one heart and one soul.[42]

---

[40] For a brief discussion of this sculpture and its dating, see C. Hohler, 'The badge of St. James', *The Scallop: Studies of a Shell and its Influence on Humankind*, ed. I. Cox (1957), pp. 56–9. Hohler suggests a date of *c*.1130 on the basis that the depiction of Christ-as-pilgrim might be dependent on the *Veneranda Dies* sermon.

[41] Matthew 10:1–42. These ideas of mendicancy and apostolic activity are, of course, more normally associated by scholars with the devotions of the Franciscans, for which see R. B. Brooke, *The Coming of the Friars* (1975).

[42] *V.D.*, p. 93; *M.S.J.*, p. 28: *Et apostoli inde peregrini fuere, quos sine peccunia et calciamenta Dominus misit. Quapropter peccunia nullo modo peregrinantibus deferre conceditur, nisi cum egenis eandem peccuniam expendant. Si absque peccunia illos misit, quid erit ex illis qui nunc cum auro et argento pergunt, satis edentes et bibentes, et nichil egenis impertiunt. Profecto non sunt veri peregrini, sed fures et latrones Dei ... Sicut multitudini credencium olim erat cor unum et anima una, et nemo dicebat proprium, sed erant illis omnia communia, sic cunctis peregrinantibus debent esse omnia communia, cor unum et anima una* (citation from Acts 4:32).

These were striking images that were developed further by the provision of specific examples from the New Testament. Given the context, it is not surprising that the sermon focused on one apostle in particular, St. James the Great, to stress how pilgrimage to Compostela was a kind of active apostolate and how pilgrims ought to follow his blueprint for asceticism. 'If Blessed James went through the world as a pilgrim without money and footwear', the sermon questioned, 'why do pilgrims go to him oversupplied with diverse riches and paying out nothing to the needy?'[43] Indeed, although it should be stressed that St. James was not the only apostle to have had his credentials as a pilgrim emphasized in the sermon, it does seem possible that the equation in *Veneranda Dies* between pilgrimage and the apostolic life may have provided the inspiration for the idea that St. James could be portrayed in sculpture and other visual media as a pilgrim travelling to his own shrine – an image that was to become ubiquitous in the middle ages and beyond.[44]

In a context in which pilgrims were regarded as followers of Christ and his apostles, it is perhaps to be expected that throughout the *Veneranda Dies* sermon penitential pilgrimage was portrayed as a quasi-monastic devotional exercise. Like those who swore monastic vows, pilgrims were understood to be committing themselves to a form of religious poverty and were demonstrating their willingness to endure the austerity, hardship and suffering associated with their penitential undertaking. These themes were elucidated in the following words, which in some ways recall the language applied by contemporaries to the ascetic practices of the Carthusians or the Cistercians:

The pilgrim's way is the best way, but the most narrow. The way is, in fact, narrow that leads man to life, and wide and spacious that leads to death. The pilgrim's way is for the righteous: lack of vices, mortification of the body, restitution of virtues, remission of sins, penitence of the penitent, journey of the just, love of the saints, faith in the resurrection and remuneration of the blessed, distancing of the infernal, propitiation of the heavens. It reduces fat foods, it checks gluttony of the stomach, it tames lust, it suppresses carnal desires, which militate against the soul. It purifies the spirit, it provokes man towards contemplation, it humbles the lofty, it beatifies the humble. It loves

---

[43] *V.D.*, p. 93; *M.S.J.*, p. 29: *Si beatus Iacobus absque peccunia et calciamento per mundum peregrinus ivit, et tandem decollatus ad paradisum perrexit, cur ad eum peregrini diversis gazis refecti, nichil egenis erogantes tendunt?*

[44] Hohler, pp. 67–8, wrote that 'It would be tedious to attempt to review the innumerable versions of the theme of St. James as a pilgrim sculptured or drawn when, in the later middle ages, this type had become canonical'.

poverty; it hates the inventory that avarice keeps but that generosity loves when one dispenses it to the needy. It rewards those abstaining and working well, but it does not free those sinning and avaricious on it.[45]

It is not entirely clear why advocates for the cult of St. James felt the need to redefine the ideology of pilgrimage to Compostela in this manner; the nature of the devotional activity that they were promoting was certainly not revolutionary in the way that the observances of several of the new religious orders undoubtedly were.[46] It may be the case that the content of the *Veneranda Dies* sermon unconsciously reflected the character of twelfth-century religious discourse; equally, it is also possible that the sermon's anonymous writer[47] was attempting to tap into contemporary enthusiasm for ideals of *imitatio Christi* and *vita apostolica*, which were evidently of interest to ecclesiastics and laymen alike.[48] Either way, the material presented in the *Veneranda Dies* sermon marked a significant development in the history of ideas associated with the cult of St. James the Great and established an iconographical theme that would proliferate for hundreds of

---

[45] *V.D.*, p. 91; *M.S.J.*, p. 23: *Igitur via peregrinalis res est obtima sed angusta. Angusta enim est via que ducit hominem ad vitam, lata et spaciosa que ducit ad mortem. Peregrinalis via rectis est, defectio viciorum, mortificatio corporum, relevacio virtutum, remissio peccatorum, penitencia penitentum, iter iustorum, dilectio sanctorum, fides resurrectionis et remuneracionis beatorum, elongacio infernorum, propiciatio celorum. Cibaria pinguia extenuat, ventris ingluviem cohibet, libidinem domat, carnalia desideria que militant adversus animam comprimit, spiritum purificat, hominem ad contemplacionem provocat, sublimes humiliat, humiles beatificat, paupertatem diligit, censum quem observat avaricia odit, sed quem dispergit egenis largitas diligit, abstinentes et bene operantes remunerat, peccantes et avaros in se non liberat.* The reference at the beginning of this passage was to the 'Two Ways' of which Christ had spoken in Matthew 7:13–14. For medieval understandings of this text, see G. B. Ladner, 'Homo Viator: medieval ideas on alienation and order', *Speculum*, xlii (1967), 240–1.

[46] The most radical example of 'devotional novelty' was unquestionably that of the Order of the Temple. For contemporary attempts to legitimize the way of life of the Templars, see 'Un document sur les débuts des Templiers', ed. J. Leclercq, *Revue d'histoire ecclésiastique*, lii (1957), 81–91; Bernard of Clairvaux, 'Liber ad milites Templi de laude novae militiae', *Sancti Bernardi Opera*, ed. J. Leclercq and others (8 vols., Rome, 1957–77), iii. 205–39. For a modern discussion, see M. Barber, *The New Knighthood: a History of the Order of the Temple* (Cambridge, 1994). For the broader context, see B. Smalley, 'Ecclesiastical attitudes to novelty, c.1100–c.1250', in *Church, Society and Politics*, ed. D. Baker, *Studies in Church History*, xii (Oxford, 1975), 113–31.

[47] The sermon is ascribed in the *Liber Sancti Jacobi* to Pope Calixtus II (r. 1119–24), but it seems extremely unlikely that this attribution is accurate. For a recent consideration of the 'authorship' of the *Liber Sancti Jacobi*, see *The Pilgrim's Guide to Santiago de Compostela: a Critical Edition*, ed. A. Stones, J. Krochalis, P. Gerson and A. Shaver-Crandell (2 vols., 1998), i. 15–27.

[48] Chenu, *passim*.

years. But it is not only in texts and images that account for the spirituality of penitential pilgrimage to Compostela that monastic influences on eleventh- and twelfth-century lay devotional activities can be detected. Around forty years before the *Veneranda Dies* sermon was composed and the *Liber Sancti Jacobi* was compiled, thousands of armed pilgrims had set out from western Europe on the First Crusade with the intention of liberating Jerusalem and the Holy Land from the perceived tyranny of Islam, and it is clear from the many accounts of the crusade that survive that contemporaries understood participation in this expedition to be comparable to entry into professed religious life.[49] It is also clear that contemporaries believed that, like those who renounced their homes and possessions to pursue a religious vocation, the crusaders had taken the cross in imitation of Christ.[50]

* * *

The anonymous author of the *Gesta Francorum* opened his narrative of the First Crusade with the following words, and in so doing demonstrated how in touch he was with the spiritual *zeitgeist* of the late eleventh century:

> When now that time drew nigh, to which the Lord Jesus points out to his faithful every day, especially in the Gospel where he says *If any man will come after me, let him deny himself and take up his cross and follow me*, there was a great stirring throughout all the regions of Gaul, so that if anyone with a pure heart and mind zealously desired to follow God, and faithfully wished to bear the cross after him, he could make no delay in speedily taking the road to the Holy Sepulchre.[51]

---

[49] See especially Guibert of Nogent, 'Dei gesta per Francos', ed. R. B. C. Huygens, (Corpus Christianorum: Continuatio Mediaeualis, cxxvii A, Turnhout, 1996), p. 87: *instituit nostro tempore prelia sancta deus, ut ordo equestris et vulgus oberrans, qui vetustae paganitatis exemplo in mutuas versabantur cedes, novum repperirent salutis promerendae genus, ut nec funditus, electa, uti fieri assolet, monastica conversatione seu religiosa qualibet professione, seculum relinquere cogerentur, sed sub consueta licentia et habitu ex suo ipsorum officio dei aliquatenus gratiam consequerentur.*

[50] For a more detailed consideration of the themes discussed hereafter, see Purkis, *Crusading Spirituality*.

[51] *Gesta Francorum et aliorum Hierosolimitanorum*, ed. and trans. R. M. T. Hill (Edinburgh, 1962) (hereafter *Gesta Francorum*), p. 1: *Cum iam appropinquasset ille terminus quem dominus Iesus cotidie suis demonstrat fidelibus, specialiter in euangelio dicens: 'Si quis uult post me uenire, abneget semetipsum et tollat crucem suam et sequatur me', facta est igitur motio ualida per uniuersas Galliarum regiones, ut si aliquis Deum studiose puroque corde et mente sequi desideraret, atque post ipsum crucem fideliter baiulare uellet, non pigritaretur Sancti Sepulchri uiam celerius arripere* (citation from Matthew 16:24).

The *Gesta's* author went on to show that the crusade message of 1095–6 had obviously touched a nerve among contemporaries because, he wrote, after it had been widely disseminated, 'the Franks sewed crosses on their right shoulders, saying with one mind that they followed the footsteps of Christ'.[52] It is, of course, impossible to know how far ideas of *imitatio Christi* resonated with individual crusaders,[53] but it is striking nevertheless how many contemporary ecclesiastics described crusading using ideas and rhetoric that were borrowed from professed religion,[54] and how many emphasized the fact that the crusaders had set out 'to follow in the footsteps of the Gospel'.[55] One writer went so far as to present the crusade as the consummate act of Christo-mimesis:

> As the man errs who strives to hold back a wheel set in motion down a slope, when it gains speed, so errs the wretch who will not forsake the unclean world: he is ruined while he pursues what is doomed to ruin. And so let every man shake off hesitation, because the world is ours for but an hour, and seek that which no length of time eats away. Let no man's farm, his fine house, or the world hold him back from seeking the light by taking up his cross. Christ has gone before, and the victory has fallen to Christ: the cross he carried was our healing. Therefore let him who wishes to imitate Christ on equal terms bow his neck and take up the cross in his turn.[56]

[52] *Gesta Francorum*, p. 2: *Cumque iam hic sermo paulatim per uniuersas regiones ac Galliarum patrias coepisset crebrescere, Franci audientes talia protinus in dextra crucem suere scapula, dicentes sese Christi unanimiter sequi uestigia, quibus de manu erant redempti tartarea.*

[53] There are a handful of surviving references to ideas of Christo-mimesis in charters drawn up for crusaders before their departure and in letters written by crusaders on the march (see J. S. C. Riley-Smith, *The First Crusaders, 1095–1131* (Cambridge, 1997), pp. 62–3; see also Purkis, *Crusading Spirituality*, pp. 30–45, 57–8).

[54] See especially J. S. C. Riley-Smith, *The First Crusade and the Idea of Crusading* (1986), p. 2 and *passim*, who argued that some contemporaries perceived the crusade army to be 'a military monastery on the move'.

[55] See, e.g., the description of Tancred's response to the crusade message in Ralph of Caen, 'Gesta Tancredi', in *Recueil des historiens des croisades: historiens occidentaux*, ed. Académie des Inscriptions et Belles-Lettres (5 vols., Paris, 1844–95) (hereafter *R.H.C. Oc.*), iii. 606: *At postquam Urbani papae sententia universis Christianorum gentilia expugnaturis peccatorum omnium remissionem ascripsit, tunc demum quasi sopiti, prius experrecta est viri strenuitas, vires assumptae, oculi aperti, audacia geminata. Prius namque, ut praescriptum est, animus ejus in bivium secabatur, ambiguus utrius sequeretur vestigia, Evangelii, an mundi? Experientia vero armorum ad Christi obsequium revocata, supra credibile virum accendit militandi duplicata occasio.*

[56] Gilo of Paris, *Historie Vie Hierosolimitane*, ed. and trans. C. W. Grocock and J. E. Siberry (Oxford, 1997), pp. 68–71: *Errat ut ille rotam qui per decliuia motam / Nititur ut teneat cum rota missa ruat, / Sic miser inmundum qui non uult perdere mundum / Errat; dum sequitur quod ruit, obruitur. / Ergo quisque moram, quia mundus habetur ad horam, / Pellat, et hoc querat quod mora nulla terat. / Detineat fundus nullum, domus optima, mundus, / Quin querat*

As the *Gesta Francorum's* testimony indicates, the origins of these equations between crusading and the imitation of Christ can almost certainly be traced back to the papal preaching for the campaign, which had been initiated at the Council of Clermont in November 1095.[57] Various writers composed reports of the sermon delivered at Clermont by Pope Urban II; many of them included references to ideas of *imitatio Christi* in one form or another. Among the most important is the testimony of Robert of Rheims, who is likely to have witnessed the pope's preaching at first hand. According to his version of the sermon, Urban was said to have proclaimed that:

> Whoever therefore shall carry out this holy pilgrimage shall make a vow to God, and shall offer himself as a living sacrifice ... and he shall display the sign of the cross of the Lord on his front or on his chest. When, truly, he wishes to return from there having fulfilled his vow, let him place the cross between his shoulders; in fact, by this twofold action they will fulfil that precept of the Lord which he prescribed himself through the Gospel: *He that does not carry his cross and come after me is not worthy of me.*[58]

If Robert's testimony is accurate (and there is no real reason to think that on this point it is not), it would seem that Pope Urban was preaching the crusade as a Christo-mimetic devotional exercise, whose participants were supposed to show their commitment to the expedition, and to the idea of imitating Christ, by adopting the sign of the cross. In so doing, the crusaders were plainly seen to be fulfilling one of the principal injunctions on discipleship that Christ had given to his apostles, as recorded in Matthew 16:24 and its variants, and also to be following the example of selfless suffering that Christ had set during his Passion. This was certainly how one of Robert's contemporaries, Baldric of Bourgueil, saw it; he wrote that Pope Urban had

---

lucem suscipiendo crucem. / *Christus processit, Christo uictoria cessit:* / *Crux quam sustinuit nostra medela fuit:* / *Ergo lege pari qui Christum uult imitari* / *Subdat ceruicem, suscipiatque uicem.*

[57] See especially H. E. J. Cowdrey, 'Pope Urban II's preaching of the First Crusade', *History*, lv (1970), 177–88; Riley-Smith, *The First Crusade*, pp. 13–30; P. J. Cole, *The Preaching of the Crusades to the Holy Land, 1095–1270* (Cambridge, Mass., 1991), pp. 1–36; Riley-Smith, *First Crusaders*, pp. 53–66.

[58] Robert of Rheims, 'Historia Iherosolimitana', in *R.H.C. Oc.*, iii. 729–30: *Quicumque ergo hujus sanctae peregrinationis animum habuerit, et Deo sponsionem inde fecerit, eique se libaturum hostiam vivam, sanctam et bene placentem devoverit, signum Dominicae Crucis in fronte sua sive in pectore praeferat. Qui vero inde voti compos regredi voluerit, inter spatulas retro ponat; tales quippe bifaria operatione complebunt illud Domini praeceptum quod ipse jubet per Evangelium:* 'Qui non bajulat crucem suam et venit post me, non est me dignus' (citation from Matthew 10:38).

ordered potential crusaders to sew crosses onto their clothes 'because he had proclaimed the Lord to have said to his followers: *If anyone does not carry his cross and come after me, he cannot be my disciple*'.[59]

As the passage from Otto of Freising quoted above suggests, the idea of following Christ's example by bearing his cross was generally understood in the twelfth century in a figurative sense rather than a literal one; it is unlikely that the religious described by Otto in his *Chronica* 'took the cross' in the same way that the crusaders did. In this respect, Pope Urban's preaching at Clermont appears to have been pioneering,[60] because he succeeded in condensing the abstract theological ideal of *imitatio Christi* into a comprehensible package of image and gesture that could transcend linguistic, cultural and educational boundaries,[61] perhaps in much the same way that later advocates for the cult of St. James of Compostela may have hoped that presenting St. James as a pilgrim would cultivate the idea that penitential pilgrimage could be a form of the active apostolic life. The cross was a powerful symbol of *imitatio Christi* that was to be used time and again by future crusade preachers; in 1208, for example, Pope Innocent III drew a series of emotive connections between the badge worn by crusaders and the cross that Christ had carried to Calvary: 'You receive a soft and gentle cross', he wrote in a letter addressed to the crusader Duke Leopold VI of Austria, 'he bore one that was sharp and hard. You wear it superficially on your clothing; he endured it in the reality of his flesh. You sew yours on with linen and silk threads; he was nailed to his with iron and hard nails'.[62]

---

[59] Baldric of Bourgueil, 'Historia Jerosolimitana', in *R.H.C. Oc.*, iv. 16: *Digno itaque exercitui Dei invento primicerio praebuit assensum multitudo multa nobilium; et statim omnes in vestibus superamictis consuerunt sanctae Crucis vexillum. Sic etenim papa praeceperat; et ituris hoc signum facere complacuerat: quippe praedicaverat summus pontifex Dominum dixisse sequacibus suis: "Si quis non bajulat crucem suam et venit post me, non potest esse meus discipulus." Iccirco, inquit, debetis vobis crucem coaptare vestris in vestibus, quatinus et ex hoc tutiores incedatis, et his qui viderint et exemplum et incitamentum suggeratis'* (citation from Luke 14:27).

[60] C. Erdmann, *The Origin of the Idea of Crusade*, trans. M. W. Baldwin and W. Goffart (Princeton, N.J., 1977), p. 345, wrote that the crusaders' adoption of the sign of the cross was 'unquestionably an innovation'.

[61] See Riley-Smith, *The First Crusade*, p. 114, who noted that 'northern Europeans arriving in France on their way to the East and unable to make themselves understood would make the sign of the cross with their hands to signify that they were crusaders'.

[62] Innocent III, 'Opera omnia', in *Patrologia Latina*, ed. J. P. Migne (221 vols., Paris, 1844–1903), ccxv, col. 1340: *Tu enim crucem mollem suscipies et suavem, ille asperam subivit et duram: tu eam in vestis deferes superficie, ille in carnis pertulit veritate; tu ipsam assues tibi lineis filis aut sericis, ille in ea confixus est ferreis clavis et duris* (cited in J. S. C. Riley-Smith, 'Crusading as an act of love', *History*, lxv (1980), 180).

It would seem, therefore, that in his innovative delineation of a relationship between the crusade badge and the cross of the Crucifixion at Clermont in 1095, Pope Urban II was using ideas of *imitatio Christi* as a model for crusading and its rituals in much the same way that advocates for the new religious orders (and, indeed, for the pilgrimage to Compostela) found inspiration and legitimacy for their observances through the interpretation of scriptural texts pertaining to the life of Christ.

The contemporary reaction to Pope Urban's preaching gives some indication of the efficacy of the idea that 'taking the cross' ought to be perceived as an act of Christo-mimesis. The crusade badge was described variously as a 'sign of mortification'[63] and a '*stigma* of the Lord's Passion',[64] and in one account the crusaders were even compared to Simon of Cyrene,[65] who was, of course, an excellent scriptural blueprint for cross-bearing since he had literally 'carried the cross after Christ' on the march to Calvary.[66] Some responses to the crusade message were more extreme: a number of would-be crusaders were so eager to demonstrate their willingness to share in the sufferings of Christ that they burnt the sign of the cross onto their flesh using white-hot irons.[67] Remarkably, though, this self-mutilation was not restricted to a 'lunatic fringe' of uneducated crusaders; one of the individuals in question was Baldwin of Caesarea, an abbot who had left Europe as chaplain to one of the crusade's leaders and was to go on to become one of the most senior ecclesiastics in the Latin East. Guibert of Nogent offered a revealing account of this man's motives when he wrote that, although the branding had been unwise, Baldwin had simply been over-zealous in his desire 'to emulate God'.[68]

The equations between crusading and the imitation of Christ did not end with the symbol of the crusader's votive obligation, however. Like those whom the author of the *Libellus de Diversis Ordinibus* described as pursuing a monastic vocation, the crusaders were understood by many contemporaries to be following 'the way of God (*via Dei*)',[69] or, as the crusade was known

---

[63] Ekkehard of Aura, 'Hierosolymita', in *R.H.C. Oc.*, v. 19.

[64] Guibert of Nogent, p. 117.

[65] Ekkehard of Aura, p. 39.

[66] Matthew 27:32; Mark 15:21; Luke 23:26.

[67] For a more detailed discussion, see W. J. Purkis, 'Stigmata on the First Crusade', in *Signs, Wonders, Miracles: Representations of Divine Power in the Life of the Church*, ed. K. Cooper and J. Gregory, *Studies in Church History*, xli (Woodbridge, 2005), 99–108.

[68] Guibert of Nogent, p. 197: *Emulationem quippe dei habuerat, sed non secundum scientiam prorsus id egerat.*

[69] See, e.g., Baldric of Bourgueil, p. 21; Guibert of Nogent, p. 118; Ralph of Caen, pp. 678, 681; Orderic Vitalis, v. 36.

to others, 'the way of the Lord (*via Domini*)'[70] and 'the way of Christ (*via Christi*)'.[71] But in contrast to cloistered monks, whose purpose was to seek out the heavenly rather than the earthly Jerusalem,[72] the crusaders were quite literally walking and worshipping '*in the place where his feet have stood*',[73] and the physicality of their mimesis was stressed by a number of writers. In 1098, for instance, the Greek patriarch of Jerusalem wrote a letter to the West in which he called for fresh recruits to swell the ranks of the depleted crusader army; he implored the arms-bearers of Christendom 'to fight in the army of the Lord in the same place in which the Lord fought, in which Christ suffered for us, leaving you an example that you should follow in his footsteps'.[74] This phrase, which almost certainly referred to the call to discipleship promulgated in 1 Peter 2:21, is a particularly clear example of the way preachers used episodes from the life of Christ as *exempla* to inspire potential crusaders. Their efforts were certainly well received by those who wrote accounts of the campaign; the crusaders who reached Jerusalem in 1099, for example, were depicted as having an acute awareness of the parallels between the hardships they endured and the suffering that Christ had experienced during his Passion. During the final phase of the city's siege one combatant, Cono of Montaigu, was said to have reminded his comrades that 'our Lord Jesus Christ [also] suffered on a Friday in this very place'.[75] Similarly, those who lost their lives on the expedition were believed to have shown their willingness to die as martyrs for the Christian faith.[76] Baldric of Bourgueil wrote that it was 'beautiful' that the crusaders had been given an opportunity to die for Christ in the city in which he had died for them,[77] and he made reference to the text of John 15:13 as a

---

[70] See, e.g., Ekkehard of Aura, p. 39; *Gesta Francorum*, p. 1; Gilo of Paris, p. 52; Orderic Vitalis, v. 26.

[71] See, e.g., *Die Kreuzzugsbriefe aus den Jahren 1088–1100*, ed. H. Hagenmeyer (Innsbruck, 1901) (hereafter *Kreuzzugsbriefe*), p. 164; *Gesta Francorum*, p. 7.

[72] Bernard of Clairvaux, 'Epistolae', in *Sancti Bernardi Opera*, viii. 379–80.

[73] Psalm 131:7. For the appearance of this text in First Crusade narratives, see, e.g., Fulcher of Chartres, *Historia Hierosolymitana (1095–1127)*, ed. H. Hagenmeyer (Heidelberg, 1913), pp. 162, 331.

[74] *Kreuzzugsbriefe*, p. 148: *uenite ergo, oramus, militatum in militia Domini ad eundem locum, in quo Dominus militauit, in quo Christus passus est pro nobis, relinquens uobis exemplum, ut sequamini uestigia eius.*

[75] Orderic Vitalis, v. 168–9: *In nomine Domini nostri Ihesu Christi qui sexta feria hic passus est arma sumamus, et insigniter urbem aggredientes Domini sepulchrum hodie adeamus.*

[76] For an introduction to the issues surrounding the martyrdom of first crusaders, and references to the broader historiography, see now N. Housley, *Contesting the Crusades* (Oxford, 2006), pp. 41–2.

[77] Baldric of Bourgueil, p. 15: *Pulchrum sit vobis mori in illa civitate pro Christo, in qua Christus pro vobis mortuus est.*

source of inspiration for crusaders and their families: *Greater love has no man than this, that he lay down his life for his friends.*[78]

When the frequency and potency of these ideas of Christo-mimesis is taken into consideration, it is perhaps a little easier to understand why Pope Urban's crusade appeal stretched beyond the arms-bearing classes, who had of course been his target audience, to stimulate a positive response among a sector of society that he had certainly not intended to provoke to crusade: those who had already taken religious vows. The phenomenon of religious abandoning their monasteries and hermitages to undertake pilgrimages was not unprecedented in and of itself,[79] but the scale of the response in 1095–6 was clearly felt to be worthy of note by contemporary annalists and chroniclers. There are numerous references in the narrative sources for the First Crusade to the fact that 'abbots, monks and hermits' were deserting their lives of ascetic *stabilitas* and making for Jerusalem in response to Pope Urban's preaching, and a series of letters from the time give vivid testimony to the problems caused among the religious communities of the West by the crusade message.[80] Indeed, one of the few surviving missives directly concerning the crusade that Urban himself wrote amounts to an urgently-dispatched communication to the brethren of the congregation of Vallombrosa, instructing them that crusading was not suitable for 'those who have abandoned the world and vowed themselves to spiritual warfare'.[81] But such problems were not limited to the ten-nineties; some fifty years later, Bernard of Clairvaux, who had taken the primary responsibility for preaching the Second Crusade,[82] was forced to address a strongly-worded letter to the abbots of each and every Cistercian house in western Christendom, reminding them that in spite of its Christo-mimetic spiritual foundations the crusade was not a suitable devotional undertaking for monks:

[78] Baldric of Bourgueil, p. 15. On the use of this text by crusade propagandists, see especially Riley-Smith, 'Crusading as an act of love'.

[79] For the context, see G. Constable, 'Opposition to pilgrimage in the middle ages', *Studia Gratiana*, xix (1976), 123–46; G. Constable, 'Monachisme et pèlerinage au moyen âge', *Revue historique*, cclviii (1977), 3–27; A. Jotischky, *The Perfection of Solitude: Hermits and Monks in the Crusader States* (University Park, Pa., 1995), pp. 1–16.

[80] Geoffrey *Grossus*, 'Vita Bernardi Tironiensis', in *Patrologia Latina*, clxxii, col. 1378. For a full discussion, see Purkis, *Crusading Spirituality*, pp. 12–22, 27–9.

[81] 'Papsturkunden in Florenz', ed. W. Wiederhold, *Nachrichten von der Gesellschaft der Wissenschaften zu Götingen, Phil.-hist. Kl.* (1901), pp. 313–14.

[82] For Bernard's role in the preaching of the Second Crusade, see now J. P. Phillips, *The Second Crusade: Extending the Frontiers of Christendom* (New Haven and London, 2007), pp. 61–98.

Why do you seek the glory of the world when you have chosen to lie forgotten in the house of God? Why are you wandering through the countryside when you are professed to lead a life of solitude? Why do you sew the cross on your clothes, when you always carry it in your heart, if you keep the religious life?[83]

In this final phrase, Bernard was no doubt referring to the tension between monastic (or 'figurative') and secular (or 'literal') ideas of *imitatio Christi* that had arisen as a result of the emergence of a new strand of Christo-mimetic piety after Pope Urban's preaching at Clermont in 1095.

Why did these monks and hermits believe that crusading was a viable alternative to the religious professions to which they had already vowed themselves? An approach to answering this question conceivably lies in the words with which Professor Brooke opened his 1985 article, from which I have already quoted:

> If you were a religious of the 11th or 12th centuries choosing the order in which you were to find your vocation, how did you distinguish order from order, monk from canon? How did you determine gradations of the ascetic life? . . . At a time when asceticism and the religious orders flourished as never before, choice must have been bewildering.[84]

Ideals of *imitatio Christi*, however they might have been interpreted, were among the most significant stimuli to recruitment into religious life in the late eleventh and twelfth centuries.[85] In this context, it seems at least a possibility that the 'crusading monks' of the ten-nineties and eleven-forties may have believed that in responding to the preaching of Pope Urban II or Abbot Bernard of Clairvaux they were opting for a viable alternative to the cloister and, perhaps, choosing what they perceived to be a 'better' way to follow Christ.[86] If this was indeed the case, it would suggest that pilgrimage and crusading might have been understood (rightly or wrongly) to have offered religious of the eleventh and twelfth centuries even more choice

---

[83] Bernard of Clairvaux, 'Epistolae', viii. 511–12: *Quid mundi gloriam requiris, qui in domo Dei tui abiectus esse elegisti? Quid ad te regionum circuitus, qui in solitudine vitam ducere professus es? Quid crucem vestibus assuis, qui hanc corde tuo baiulare non cessas, si religionem conservas?*

[84] Brooke, 'Monk and canon', p. 109.

[85] Constable, *Reformation*, p. 125.

[86] The question of whether one form of religious life might be regarded as *melior* than another was considered by Hugh *Peccator* in his discussion of the Templars (*c.*1129) (see 'Un document sur les débuts des Templiers', pp. 88–9). For the context, see also C. W. Bynum, 'Did the twelfth century discover the individual?', in C. W. Bynum, *Jesus as Mother: Studies in the Spirituality of the High Middle Ages* (Berkeley, Los Angeles and London, 1982), pp. 82–109.

than they already had. It would also suggest that two further shades of colour could be added to Professor Brooke's 'spectrum' of twelfth-century religious life.

'The Devil made me do it': demonic intervention in the medieval monastic liturgy*

Susan Boynton

The manifold appearances of demons and the Devil are central themes in the monastic literature of the eleventh, twelfth and thirteenth centuries. Just as a more general fascination with the diabolical infuses medieval visual culture with grotesque or startling images,[1] a more specific instance of this preoccupation produced texts in which demonic interventions interfere and sometimes even intersect with the central activity of monastic life: the divine office. Of the eight daily services that comprised the liturgy of the hours, the one most often favoured with demonic visitations seems to have been matins, perhaps because it was performed in the very early hours of the morning, a time we would now consider the middle of the night.[2] The abundance of stories about the difficulty of rising for matins suggests that it could be a struggle just to get out of bed and to reach the church at all, not to speak of staying awake during the service. Somnolent monks might well have imagined dimly visible figures in the shadows of the choir, which were dispersed only by a few candles except on major feasts of the church year, when there was extra illumination.[3] In addition to a potentially

* I thank Giles Constable, Bryan Cuevas, Louis Hamilton and Elizabeth Teviotdale for their helpful comments on this study. The final version was prepared with support from the National Endowment for the Humanities and the Institute for Advanced Study, School of Historical Studies. Any views, findings, conclusions or recommendations expressed in this paper do not necessarily reflect those of the National Endowment for the Humanities.

[1] For a useful account of the role of the grotesque in monastic visual culture, see T. E. A. Dale, 'Monsters, corporeal deformities, and phantasms in the cloister of St-Michel-de-Cuxa', *Art Bulletin*, lxxxiii (2001), 402–36.

[2] Matins on Sundays and feast days could begin as early as 2.30 a.m.

[3] My own experience suggests that singing the office in a darkened church has a powerful effect on the imagination, and that the acoustical properties of medieval stone churches would only intensify the visual and aural perceptions discussed here.

causal relationship between the embodied experience of the monastic night office and the idea of diabolical influence, we should keep in mind the highly symbolic character of monastic discourse and of commentary on the liturgy, neither of which is ever purely descriptive. Even narratives with obvious implications can express concerns beyond the immediate matter at hand, bringing out latent conflicts in the community or more generally serving to reinforce the writer's underlying purpose.

To understand monastic texts about demonic intervention in the liturgy as more than just entertaining tales, then, one must seek out their underlying meanings. The night office not only provided ideal conditions for the creation of phantasms, but also functioned as the centre of gravity of the monastic liturgy, indeed its defining moment. Many of the texts and melodies of matins were distinctive, varying from church to church, making this office a particularly detailed reflection of a community's corporate identity.[4] In the eleventh and twelfth centuries, monastic reformers increasingly turned their attention to the divine office, stressing the proper execution of the readings and chants, and in some cases revising chant texts and melodies to make them conform to notions of authenticity.[5]

This historical context provides a useful framework for interpreting the longstanding topoi of angelic presence and demonic intervention in the monastic liturgy. These are common themes in medieval commentary on the liturgy, and by the central middle ages they had a long history in monastic writings going back to the Desert Fathers and to early western monasticism.[6] The monastic imaginary also created narratives about angelic presence in the divine office, forming a parallel to those about the threats from evil beings. For instance, the sixth-century Rule of the Master states that during prayer, frequent coughing, spitting and throat-clearing are manifestations of the Devil's attempts to impede prayers and psalmody. When blowing his nose, a monk should project the contents behind him on account of the angels that were arrayed invisibly in front of him. The Master then cites the beginning of psalm 137, 'In the sight of angels I will

---

[4] For a recent discussion of matins as indicative of a particular monastery's identity, see S. Boynton, *Shaping a Monastic Identity: Liturgy and History at the Imperial Abbey of Farfa, 1000–1125* (Ithaca, N.Y., 2006).

[5] A general discussion of liturgical reform in the twelfth century can be found in C. Waddell, 'The reform of the liturgy from a Renaissance perspective', in *Renaissance and Renewal in the Twelfth Century*, ed. R. L. Benson and G. Constable (Cambridge, Mass., 1982), pp. 88–109.

[6] For a recent discussion of the central role of demonology in early monasticism, see D. Brakke, *Demons and the Making of the Monk: Spiritual Combat in Early Christianity* (Cambridge, Mass. and London, 2006).

sing to you', concluding 'Therefore you see that we are shown as praying and singing before angels'. But the presence of angels is not enough. The Master continues that prayer should be brief to prevent dozing while lying on the ground (in the performance of psalmody described by the Rule of the Master, each psalm was followed by silent prayer performed in a completely prostrate position). The Devil could bring something extraneous before a monk's eyes or insinuate it into his heart.[7]

The Rule of Benedict's chapter on psalmody also affirms the presence of the divine: 'We believe that the divine presence is everywhere ... we should believe this to be especially true when we celebrate the divine office'. Like the Rule of the Master, the Rule of Benedict quotes the first verse of psalm 137, concluding 'Let us consider, then, how we ought to behave in the presence of God and his angels, and let us stand to sing the psalms in such a way that our minds are in harmony with our voices'.[8] As Giles Constable has pointed out, the correspondence between voice and mind in prayer was well established in Christian antiquity, also finding expression in the Rule of the Master's prescription to 'sing together in voice and in mind'.[9] While the Rule of Benedict and the Rule of the Master share this emphasis in their chapters on the discipline of psalmody, they differ in the extent to which they refer to demonic influence. The Rule of Benedict's exposition of psalmody makes no reference to the Devil. Indeed, Benedict hardly mentions the Devil, except in the chapter on entry into the monastery, where it is stated that a newly professed monk's lay clothing is taken away

[7] *La Règle du Maître*, ii, ed. and trans. A. de Vogüé (Sources chrétiennes, cvi, Paris, 1964), pp. 218–20: *Non frequens tussis, non excreatus adsiduus, non anelus abundet, quia haec omnia orationibus et psalmis ad inpedimentum a diabolo ministrantur. Nam illud, quod superius diximus, et in orationibus caueatur, ut qui orat, si uoluerit, expuere aut narium spurcitias iactare, non inante sed post se retro proiciat propter angelos inante stantes, demonstrante propheta ac dicente: 'In conspectu angelorum psallam tibi et adorabo ad templum sanctum tuum'. Ergo uides quia ante angelos ostendimur et orare et psallere. Nam ideo diximus breuem fieri orationem, ne per occasionem prolixae orationis obdormiat aut forte diu iacentibus diabolus eis ante oculos diuersa ingerat uel in corde aliud subministret.*

[8] *Regula Benedicti*, ch. 19, in *RB 1980: the Rule of St. Benedict in Latin and English with Notes*, ed. T. Fry (Collegeville, Minn., 1980) (hereafter *RB 1980*), pp. 214–16: *Ubique credimus divinam esse praesentiam et oculos Domini in omni loco speculari bonos et malos, maxime tamen hoc sine aliqua dubitatione credamus cum ad opus divinum assistimus. Ideo semper memores simus quod ait propheta: 'Servite Domino in timore', et iterum: 'Psallite sapienter, et: In conspectu angelorum psallam tibi'. Ergo consideremus qualiter oporteat in conspectu divinitatis et angelorum eius esse, et sic stemus ad psallendum ut mens nostra concordet voci nostrae.*

[9] G. Constable, 'The concern for sincerity and understanding in liturgical prayer, especially in the twelfth century', in *Classica et Mediaevalia: Studies in Honor of Joseph Szövérffy*, ed. I. Caslef and H. Buschhausen (Washington and Leiden, 1986), pp. 17–30, at p. 19.

from him and stored so that if he should ever agree to the Devil's suggestion to leave the monastery, he can reclaim his lay attire upon departure.[10]

These references to the Devil in the Rule of the Master and the Rule of Benedict draw upon the thematics of diabolical temptation that had already been established by late antique textual traditions such the lives and sayings of the Desert Fathers. The *Apophthegmata Patrum*, a fifth-century compilation of Greek aphorisms and anecdotes associated with the early monks of the Egyptian desert, contains numerous references to the ever-present threat of the Devil and demons, often in the form of temptation, such as pride, that the individual must vanquish through sincere humility. Since the earliest texts concern hermits who rarely gathered for worship, the *Apophthegmata Patrum* contains few allusions to communal liturgy. In one significant anecdote, however, the Devil attempts to prevent a monk from attending the Sunday synaxis by telling him that the bread and wine is not really the body and blood of Christ. When the deluded monk fails to appear in church, the other monks become concerned, seek him out, and set him straight, with the ultimate result that he overcomes the deception of the Devil and celebrates the Eucharist in community with the others.[11]

While some monastic writings of the central and high middle ages similarly invoke the Devil as a ubiquitous yet intangible threat, others contain vivid, even graphic descriptions of demons in all their diverse manifestations.[12] Some of the most prolix and precise visualizations depict demonic agency in the monastery, and particularly in the divine office, in terms that are as concrete as they are symbolic. Such anecdotes reify in narrative the longstanding belief in the constant threat of temptation and pride that was represented by the presence of evil influences in the monastery.

The eleventh-century monk Radulfus Glaber's *Histories* present a multitude of demons with differing appearances who act independently in various settings.[13] In the fifth book Radulfus describes three close encounters

---

[10] *Regula Benedicti*, ch. 58; (*RB 1980*, p. 270): *Illa autem vestimenta quibus exutus est reponantur in vestiario conservanda, ut si aliquando suadenti diabolo consenserit ut egrediatur de monasterio – quod absit – tunc exutus rebus monasterii proiciatur.*

[11] *Les Apophthegmes des Pères: Collection systematique*, 18.48.1–27, ed. and trans. J.-C. Guy (Sources chrétiennes, cdxcviii, Paris, 2005), pp. 112–15.

[12] On monastic texts presenting the Devil and demons as ever-present, see E. Langton, *Supernatural: the Doctrine of Spirits, Angels, and Demons, from the Middle Ages until the Present Time* (1934), pp. 160–74.

[13] R. Colliot, 'Rencontres du moine Raoul Glaber avec le diable d'après ses *Histoires*', in *Le Diable au Moyen Age: Doctrines, problèmes moraux, représentations* (Sénéfiance vi, Aix-en-

with a demon that occur in different locations but all around the hour of matins. These three anecdotes are linked mainly by the time of their occurrence and the fact that Radulfus himself is their protagonist. They are preceded by a pre-existing tale about a demon who appeared to a monk when the bell rang for matins and distracted him so much that the hapless monk missed the office altogether.[14] In the first of Radulfus's first-person narratives, he recounts that before matins, at St.-Léger de Champceaux, a small, ugly man spoke to him from the foot of his bed.[15] The second sighting was after matins, at dawn in the dormitory of Radulfus's own community, St. Bénigne at Dijon.[16] The third was in the priory of Moutiers-Sainte-Marie, when Radulfus failed to go to matins at the sound of the bell. Once the other monks had hastened to the church, the same creature ascended the dormitory stairs and paused, out of breath, declaring 'It is I, it is I who stay with those who remain'.[17]

Provence and Paris, 1979), pp. 117–32.

[14] *Rodulfi Glabri Historiarum Libri Quinque*, ed. J. France (Oxford, 1989), p. 216.

[15] *Rodulfi Glabri Historiarum Libri Quinque*, p. 218: *Nam dum aliquando in beati martyris Leodegarii monasterio, quod Capellis cognominatur, positus degrem, nocte quadam, ante matutinalem sinaxim, adstitit mihi ex parte pedum lectuli forma homunculi teterrimae speciei. Erat enim, quantum a me dignosci potuit, statura mediocris, collo gracili, facie macilenta, occulis nigerrimis, front rugosa et contracta, depressis naribus, os exporrectum, labellis tumentibus, mento subtracto ac perangusto, barba caprina, aureas irtas et praeacutas, capillis stantibus et incompositis, dentibus caninis, occipitio acuto, pectore tumido, dorso gibat, clunibus agitantibus, uestibus sordidis, conatus aestuans, ac toto corpore preceps; arripiensque summitatem strati in quo cubabam, totum terribiliter concussit lectulum, ac deinde infit: 'Non tu in hoc loco ultra manebis'. At ego territus euigilansque, sicuti repente fieri contingit, aspexi talem quem prescripsi. Ipse uero infrendens idemtidem aiebat: 'Non hic ultra manebis'. Ilico denique a lectulo exiliens cucurri in monasterium, atque ante altare sanctissimi patris Benedicti prostratus ac nimium pauefactus diutine decubui, cepique acerrime ad memoriam reducere quicquid ab ineunte aetate offensionum grauiumque peccaminum procaciter seu neglegenter commiseram.*

[16] *Rodulfi Glabri Historiarum Libri Quinque*, p. 220: *Post haec igitur, in monasterio sancti Benigni Diuionensis martyris locatus, non dispar, immo isdem mihi uisus est in dormitorio fratrum. Incipiente aurora diei, currens exiit a domo latrinarum taliter inclamanda: 'Meus bacallaris ubi est? meus bacallaris ubi est?' Sequenti quoque die, eadem fere hora, aufugiens abiit exinde quidam frater iuuenis, mente leuissimus, Theodericus nomine, reiecto habitu per aliquod temporis spacium seculariter uixit. Qui postmodum corde conpunctus ad propositum sacri ordinis rediit.*

[17] *Rodulfi Glabri Historiarum Libri Quinque*, pp. 220–2: *Tercio quoque, cum apud cenobium beatae semperque uirginis Mariae, cognomento Meleredense, demorare, una noctium dum matutinorum pulsaretur signum et ego labore quodam fessus, non, ut debueram, mox ut auditum fuerat exsurrexissem, mecumque aliqui remansissent, quos uidelicet praua consuetudo illexerat, ceteris ad ecclesiam concurrentibus, egrediens autem post fratrum uestigia hanelus ascendit gradum presignatus demon, ad dorsum manibus reductis, herensque parieti bis terque repetabat dicens: 'Ego sum, ego sum, qui sto cum illis qui remanent'. Qua uoce excitus caput eleuans, uidi*

Although none of these visitations takes place during the office, it is significant that they happen *around* the office. Radulfus's account is both deeply symbolic and oddly realistic, because his descriptions convey something of the everyday reality of the morning routine of rising for matins, interpreted in some monastic writings as signifying casting off sleep, and therefore sin, to espouse wakefulness, meaning salvation.[18] The demonic presence has an extraliturgical effect as well – following the last two appearances recounted by Glaber a monk fled the monastery to live briefly in the world before finally returning to the community.

Departure from the monastery at the instigation of the Devil, which was mentioned in the Rule of Benedict, also appears in a more overtly allegorical monastic text of the late twelfth century, Hildegard of Bingen's musical morality play, the *Ordo Virtutum*. Here a young soul, Anima, perhaps representing a novice or at least a younger member of a monastic community, starts out happy, but later desires to shed her garment, which could be interpreted as the monastic habit. The personification of Knowledge of God sings to Anima: 'Look at what you are wearing, daughter of salvation: be steadfast and you will never fall'. In response, Anima laments 'I don't know what to do or where to flee. Alas, I cannot fulfil what I am wearing. In fact, I want to cast it off'.[19] The Devil leads Anima astray, but she soon longs to return to the community, and Virtues welcome her back despite her intransigence, addressing her as a fugitive.[20] The soul laments her weakness and supplicates the help of the Virtues, who triumph over the Devil and return the lost soul to the fold. Both the Devil's role in this scenario and

---

recognoscens quem bis dudum iam uideram. Post diem uero tertium unus ex illis fratribus qui, ut dicimus, clancule cubitare soliti fuerant, procaciter a monasterio egressus, praefato demone instigante, sex dies extra monasterium cum secularibus tumultuose mansit. Septima tamen die correptus recipitur.

[18] Two instances of this idea appear in an anonymous gloss on a hymn for matins in three manuscripts from eleventh-century northern France (Amiens, Bibliothèque Louis Aragon (formerly Bibliothèque Municipale) 131 and Paris, Bibliothèque Nationale de France, MS. lat. 103 and 11550): *Qui ad celebrandum diuinum officium uel obsequium festinat, necesse est ut a se omnem somnolentiam et torporem repellat. Aliter dominum quem querit, inuenire non poterit*; Isidore of Seville's *Regula monachorum*, iii. 59–61, in *San Leandro, San Isidoro, San Fructuoso. Reglas monásticas de la España visigoda*, ed. J. Campos Ruiz and I. Roca Melia (Madrid, 1971), p. 93: *Torporem somni atque pigritiam fugiat, vigiliisque et orationibus sine intermissione intendat.*

[19] Wiesbaden, Hessische Landesbibliothek, MS. 2 fo. 479r: *Vide quid illud sit quo es induta filia saluationis et esto stabilis et numquam cades*; *O nescio quid faciam aut ubi fugiam oue michi non possum perficere hoc quod sum induta certe illud uolo abicere.*

[20] Wiesbaden, Hessische Landesbibliothek, MS. 2 fos. 480v–481r: *O fugitiue, ueni, ueni ad nos, et deus suscipiet te*; *O anima fugitiua, esto robusta et indue te arma lucis.*

the references to clothing recall the prescription in the Benedictine Rule regarding the change of clothing upon departure from the monastery at the instigation of the Devil. The Devil clearly represents the interference of the outside world in the life of the monastic community. He is the only character in the *Ordo Virtutum* who speaks instead of singing, with the result that his lines are the only ones in the manuscript of the play that lack musical notation.

The portrayal of the Devil as a being without music perfectly illustrates Hildegard's conception of the role of music in the monastic community as set forth in her epistle 23 to the clergy of Mainz, who had placed an interdict on the convent of Rupertsberg because of an excommunicate buried in its graveyard. For the period of the interdict, the nuns were forbidden to receive communion or sing the divine office.[21] Hildegard's letter refers to the Devil's schemes to disrupt musical praise of the divine, aptly yet subtly conveying the underlying point that the interdict furthered the work of the Devil.[22] As an explicit presentation of Hildegard's theology of music, this letter illuminates the meaning of the *Ordo Virtutum*. According to the letter, the life of a monastic community centres on singing the divine office, which the Devil seeks to impede; likewise, in the *Ordo Virtutum* the Devil temporarily interpolates his tuneless speech into the previously harmonious world of the monastery. When the choir of the Virtues overwhelms him, the community regains musical integrity and the symbolic order is restored. With Anima back in the fold, the voice without music is banished conclusively. The significance of singing in the *Ordo Virtutum* reflects both the lived experience of the daily liturgical round and Hildegard's ideal of the monastery as a sonic community.[23]

---

[21] On the letter, see also W. Flynn, '"The soul is symphonic": meditation on Luke 15:25 and Hildegard of Bingen's letter 23', in *Music and Theology: Essays in Honor of Robin A. Leaver*, ed. D. Zager (Lanham, Md., 2007), pp. 1–8.

[22] *Hildegardis Bingenis Epistolarium*, ed. L. van Acker (Corpus Christianorum: Continuatio Mediaeualis, xci, Turnhout, 1991), p. 64: *Cum autem deceptor eius, diabolus, audisset quod homo ex inspiratione Dei cantare cepisset, et per hoc ad recolendam suauitatem canticorum celestis patrie mutaretur, machinamenta calliditatis sue in irritum ire uidens, ita exterritus est, ut non minimum inde torqueretur, et multifariis nequitie sue commentis semper deinceps excogitare et exquirere satagit, ut non solum de corde hominis per malas suggestiones et immundas cogitationes seu diuersas occupationes, sed etiam de ore Ecclesie, ubicumque potest, per dissensiones et scandala uel iniustas depressiones, confessionem et pulchritudinem atque dulcedinem diuine laudis et spiritalium hymnorum perturbare uel auferre non desistit.*

[23] On the role of the *Ordo Virtutum* in Hildegard's monastic community, see M. Fassler, 'Composer and dramatist: "Melodious singing and the freshness of remorse"', in *Voice of the Living Light: Hildegard of Bingen and her World*, ed. B. Newman (Berkeley and Los Angeles, 1998), pp. 168–75.

Like Hildegard of Bingen, Peter the Venerable, abbot of Cluny, was a twelfth-century Benedictine deeply concerned with religious reform, and in this regard it is no coincidence that he also wrote vividly about the ways in which demons prevented monks from taking part in the liturgy. The first book of Peter's *De Miraculis* contains the story of a monk who customarily rang the bell for matins awakening one night with the impression that he has overslept because he can hear the sound of a bell. After finding no one in the church and then returning to his dormitory where all the other brothers are still asleep, he finally realizes that he has been deceived by demonic influence. Peter's commentary concluding this chapter notes that monks should not wander freely about the monastery at night, as they can be misled by demons in such a way that a disturbed sleep pattern causes them to miss the night office altogether.[24]

These texts by Radulfus Glaber, Hildegard of Bingen and Peter the Venerable all portray the exercise of free will undermined by demonic or diabolical influence. In the *Histories* and the *Ordo Virtutum*, agents of evil take a physical form to draw their objects away from monastic observance without taking part in the divine office. In other words, the Devil and demons interfere with the liturgy in various ways but do not appear to enter the discursive space of the church itself; their intervention in worship is indirect, mediated by the actions of monks, nuns and secular clergy. In the Cistercian *exemplum* collections of the early thirteenth century, however, demons gain full access to the monks' choir, in some cases becoming as much of a presence in the church as the angels who were thought to observe the services and occasionally to join in them. Cistercian narratives abound in colourful descriptions of the supernatural beings whose actions sometimes unfold in co-ordination with the divine office. Many stories depict demons witnessing and infiltrating the liturgical services they strive to disrupt. In several cases demons take on the role of an audience, appraising the performance verbally or expressing their approval of bad behaviour through enthusiastic cheers and applause.

Compilers of the *exemplum* collections were careful to frame these vivid stories with admonitions presenting the purpose and moral of each tale. The *exempla* are inherently didactic, employed in preaching and other forms of teaching.[25] While the potential applications of *exempla* were

---

[24] *Petri Cluniacensis Abbatis De Miraculis Libri Duo*, 1.17, ed. D. Bouthillier (Corpus Christianorum: Continuatio Mediaeualis, lxxxiii, Turnhout, 1987), pp. 53–4.

[25] For a useful discussion of the current state of research on Cistercian *exemplum* literature, see B. P. McGuire, 'Cistercian storytelling – a living tradition: surprises in the world of research', *Cistercian Studies Quarterly*, xxxix (2004), 281–309.

numerous, the intended audience of the Cistercian collections included the novices of the order. Caesarius of Heisterbach, author of the *Dialogus Miraculorum* (completed by 1223), was novicemaster in his convent of Heisterbach, although Brian Patrick McGuire has argued that Caesarius's travels and large literary output suggest that he did not hold the office continually.[26] Nevertheless, both the presentation of the collection as a dialogue (albeit an artificial one) between a novice and his teacher and the fact that many of the stories concern novices make the *Dialogus Miraculorum* particularly instructive for that sector of the Cistercian population.[27]

The *exempla* containing stories that unfold during the night office convey their messages in various ways; some seem intended to reinforce good behaviour while others deliver explicit warnings of the perils of common failings. An anecdote in the twelfth-century Cistercian *Collectaneum Exemplorum* is entitled 'How much care God and the Holy Angels have for those who take part in the offices purely'. In this *exemplum* a monk realizes that the unknown persons he saw in the choir one night sought to work mischief, because the following night he saw a terrifying demon enter the choir only to be expelled by an equally awesome angel.[28]

Many visions described in the *exempla* are far less reassuring. Another chapter in the *Collectaneum* relates that a monk saw the Devil in the guise of a monkey who enters the choir during the night office and ridicules sleeping monks by standing before them clapping his hands. The monk kept silent about his vision and witnessed it a second time, but it disappeared when he told others about it.[29] A chapter in Conrad of Eberbach's *Exordium Magnum*, a text from the beginning of the thirteenth century, begins by stating that the narrative illustrates the dangerous fantasies and illusions suffered by those monks who are so lukewarm in the service of God as to fall asleep in choir. The tale describes a monk who sees the angel of the Lord censing the choir and altar on Pentecost during the singing of the canticle at Lauds, *Benedicite Omnia Opera* (Daniel 3:57–88, 56). The angel

---

[26] B. P. McGuire, 'Friends and tales in the cloister: oral sources in Caesarius of Heisterbach's *Dialogus Miraculorum*', *Analecta Cisterciensia*, xxxvi (1980), 167–247, at p. 172.

[27] For analysis of the *Dialogus Miraculorum* and its sources, the fundamental studies remain McGuire, 'Friends and tales in the cloister'; B. P. McGuire, 'Written sources and Cistercian inspiration in Caesarius of Heisterbach', *Analecta Cisterciensia*, xxxv (1979), 227–82.

[28] *Collectaneum Exemplorum et Visionum Clarevallense*, 3.14, ed. O. Legendre (Corpus Christianorum: Continuatio Mediaeualis, ccviii, Turnhout, 2005), pp. 256–7.

[29] *Collectaneum Exemplorum*, 4.30, ed. Legendre, pp. 303–4. I am grateful to Martha Newman for referring me to this *exemplum*.

places a burning coal in the monk's mouth, causing him to fall ill and lie in the infirmary for three days as if dead. Recovered and back in the choir at matins, the monk witnesses a multitude of demons (invisible to the others) who seek to distract the other monks from worship, applauding those who are lazy or somnolent, and dumping filth on the sleepers so as to infuse their dreams with evil phantasms.[30]

In Cistercian *exempla*, demons not only seized upon the impulse to doze off during the night office but also symbolized other kinds of temptation, such as pride, continuing the tradition of diabolical incitement to pride seen in earlier monastic literature. Overweening pride in expert singing forms the central theme in a number of *exempla*. In the *Dialogus Miraculorum* of Caesarius of Heisterbach, one chapter in the *distinctio* on temptation describes a group of clerics in a secular church singing 'loudly, not piously, and lifting tumultuous voices on high'.[31] A *religiosus* who happens to be present sees a demon standing high up with a large sack that he filled with the voices of the singers, which he caught with his extended right hand. After the conclusion of the service, as the singers congratulated themselves upon their performance, the *religiosus*, who saw the demon, tells them: 'You have indeed sung well but you have sung a sack full'.[32] Although the story could be interpreted as privileging regular over secular clergy, the distinction between the singers and the *religiosus* is not made clear. More important is

---

[30] Conrad of Eberbach, *Exordium Magnum Cisterciense sive Narratio de Initio Cisterciensis Ordinis*, 5.18, ed. B. Griesser (Corpus Christianorum: Continuatio Mediaeualis, cxxxviii, Turnhout, 1994), pp. 375–7.

[31] Elizabeth Teviotdale very kindly pointed out to me a thirteenth-century Cistercian historiated initial depicting, in its upper register, the celebration of mass and, in the lower register, a group of monks singing from a choirbook inscribed with the text *Cantate fortiter*. This image, which would seem to attach a positive value to singing loudly, is suggestive in the context of *exempla* that mention loud singers. For a reproduction of the miniature with commentary, see *Buchmalerei der Zisterzienser: kulturelle Schätze aus sechs Jahrhunderten*, Katalog zur Ausstellung 'Libri Cistersienses' im Ordensmuseum Abtei Kamp, Nordrhein-Westfalen (Stuttgart, 1998), pp. 136–40 (I owe this reference to Elizabeth Teviotdale). Cistercian *exempla* concerning the mass are not discussed in the present study because they do not fit into the same distinctive pattern of demonic intervention seen in narratives about the Divine Office.

[32] Caesarius of Heisterbach, *Dialogus Miraculorum*, 5.9, ed. J. Strange (Cologne, 1851), i. 181: *Tempore quodam clericis quibusdam in ecclesia quadam saeculari fortiter, id est, clamose, non devote, cantantibus, et voces tumultuosas in sublime tollentibus, vidit homo quidam religiosus, qui forte tunc affuit, quendam daemonem in loco eminentiori stantem, saccum magnum et longum in sinistra manu tenere, qui cantantium voces dextera latius extensa capiebat, atque in eundem saccum mittebat. Illis exploeto cantu inter se gloriantibus, tanquam qui bene et fortiter Deum laudassent, respondit ille, qui viderat visionem: Bene quidem cantastis, sed saccum plenum cantastis.*

the striking description of the voices being captured and subverted to the demon's own purposes.

Caesarius explicitly links this story to the *distinctio* on demons, stating 'In the fifth chapter of the following distinction, you will hear how the raising of voices pleases [God]. There you will find how much demons rejoice if voices are lifted in psalmody without humility'.[33] This *exemplum* is just one of several texts from the twelfth and thirteenth centuries that condemn the excesses of virtuosic singing that aggrandized the performers, a form of pride that writers decried as an intrusion of the values of secular entertainment into the liturgy. One of the most detailed passages of this kind was written by the twelfth-century Cistercian Aelred of Rievaulx, who vividly described a kind of singing that made use of abundant embellishments, bodily display, histrionic gestures and a style of vocal production deemed more feminine than masculine (and therefore unnatural). Aelred does not link mannered performance explicitly to the Devil or to demons but denounces it as ludicrous minstrelsy that belongs outside the church.[34]

Cistercian *exempla* frequently invoke a direct causal connection between misbehaviour in the choir (including musical mischief) and the presence and even active involvement of demons. Just as Caesarius himself promises in the *Distinctio on Temptation*, a particularly remarkable concatenation of stories about demons in the monastic liturgy appears in the fifth chapter of the immediately following *Distinctio on Demons*, which recounts several demonic interventions during matins on feast days that fall in the month of November.[35] According to this narrative, a *conversus* at the abbey of Hemmenrode often saw demons running through the choir at night. Hermann, a monk in the community, prayed for and received the ability to

---

[33] *Dialogus Miraculorum: Quantum ei devota placeat vocum exaltatio, satis audies in sequenti distinctione capitulo quinto. Ibidem invenies, quantum ex hoc daemones laetentur, si sine humilitate in psalmodia voces exaltentur.*

[34] Aelred of Rievaulx, *De Speculo Caritatis*, 2.23, ed. C. H. Talbot, in *Aelredi Rievallensis Opera Omnia*, ed. A. Hoste and C. H. Talbot (Corpus Christianorum: Continuatio Mediaeualis, i, Turnhout, 1971), pp. 97–9. Another twelfth-century text denouncing ostentatious, 'womanly' singing in church is John of Salisbury's *Policraticus* (written in 1159) (see *Policraticus*, 1.6, ed. K. S. B. Keats-Rohan (Corpus Christianorum: Continuatio Mediaeualis, cxviii, Turnhout, 1993), p. 46).

[35] On the *distinctio* on demons as a treatise on demonology, see S. M. Barillari, *Cesario di Heisterbach, Sui demòni* (Alessandria, 1999), pp. 13–20. For a broader study of demons in the *Dialogus Miraculorum*, see S. M. Barillari, 'Dèmoni e demòni. Per una definizione della figura diabolica negli *exempla* di Cesario di Heisterbach', *Lingua e letteratura*, xviii (1992), pp. 73–82; and S. M. Barillari, '"Per gratiam Christi et ministerium diaboli". Rappresentazioni e funzioni del demoniaco negli *exempla* di Cesario di Heisterbach', *L'immagine riflessa*, new ser., ii (1993), 39–68.

see such visions.[36] During matins on the feast of St. Martin (11 November) he saw a demon in the form of a peasant enter next to the presbytery and stand in front of a novice. On the feast of St. Cunibert (12 November), Hermann saw two demons enter the presbytery and ascend the stall of the abbot between the choir of the monks and the novices. When they reached the corner, a third demon joined them, passing so close to Hermann that he could have touched them. The monk near whom the third demon had been standing is described as a lazy complainer who slept in the choir but sang grudgingly, happier to drink than to chant. Even the shorter night offices always seemed very long to him.[37] Here the ubiquitous condemnation of slothfulness in the choir combines with pithy and fantastical description.

The same chapter of the *Dialogus* contains two anecdotes that represent the height of demonic participation in the liturgy. On the feast of St. Columban (23 November), as the prior intoned the first psalm of matins, *Domine quid multiplicati sunt qui tribulant me*, the demons on that side of the choir multiplied so that the brothers there made mistakes in the psalmody. When the choir on the opposite side attempted to correct them, the demons flew across and disrupted their psalmody by mixing in with the monks so that they did not know what they were singing; the two choirs ended up shouting at one another. Discord in the choir is not only a choir leader's nightmare but also symbolizes a crisis in the internal order of the monastic community. The abbot and prior attempted in vain to remedy the situation but could not bring the singers back to the psalm tone or unite their dissonant voices. The Devil finally departed with his assistants and order returned to the choir.[38]

Demonic disruption of the choir was a serious threat because liturgical performance was a realization of the community's social structure and

---

[36] On the Cistercian understanding of this vision as a spiritual gift, see T. License, 'The gift of seeing demons in early Cistercian spirituality', *Cistercian Studies Quarterly*, xxxix (2004), 49–65 (specific reference to Herman at p. 53).

[37] Caesarius of Heisterbach, *Dialogus Miraculorum*, 5.5, ed. Strange, pp. 281–2.

[38] *Dialogus Miraculorum*, 5.5, ed. Strange, pp. 282–3: *Alio itidem tempore, in vigilia, ut puto, Sancti Columbani, tunc eo exsistente Priore, cum chorus Abbatis inciperet primum matutinarum Psalmum, scilicet 'Domine quid multiplicati sunt qui tribulant me?' daemones in choro adeo multiplicati sunt, ut ex illorum concursu et discursu mox in eodem psalmo fratres fallerentur. Quos cum chorus oppositus conaretur corrigere, daemones transvolaverunt et se illis miscentes ita eos turbaverunt, ut prorsus nescirent quid psallerent. Clamavit chorus contra chorum. Dominus Abbas Eustachius, et Prior Hermannus, qui haec vidit, a stallis suis semoti, cum stis ad hoc conarentur, non poterant illos ad viam psalmodiae reducere, neque vocum dissonantias unire. Tandem Psalmo illo modico et valde usitato, cum labore pariter atque confusione qualicunque modo expleto, diabolus, totius confusionis caput, cum suis satellitibus abcessit, et pax turbata psallentibus accessit.*

hierarchy. Successful psalmody depends on the singers' ability to listen to one another and to begin and end each phrase together. Even though medieval chant had no conductor in the modern sense and was sung in a more or less free rhythm, for those who perform chant often with the same people it is not difficult to maintain the integrity of the ensemble as long as everyone listens. Ambient darkness and imbalance among the voices can make it more difficult for singers to communicate effectively with one another, and are precisely the conditions that obtain in most of the Cistercian stories about demonic intervention.

In another anecdote within the same chapter of the *Distinctio* on demons, musical disorder seems to symbolize social disorder. One night at matins, the hebdomadarius (weekly cantor) sang the invitatory antiphon, and the monk near him then intoned the invitatory psalm 94, moderately – *voci mediocri* (probably signifying a combination of a moderate pitch and voice). As the choir of senior monks began to sing the psalm verse, a youth at the lower end of the choir found the intonation too low for his taste and sang the continuation of the psalm fully five tones higher, creating dissonance within his half of the choir (or possibly a form of parallel organum). The subprior resisted, but the youth persisted in raising the pitch of the choir on his side. When the other half of the choir sang the next verse, some followed the youth by singing at the same elevated pitch level, while others fell silent, scandalized. Then Hermann saw a demon move from the young monk to those in the opposite choir who had taken his part. Caesarius concludes this episode: 'a humble song (*humilis cantus*) with devotion of the heart pleases God more than voices lifted arrogantly to heaven'.[39]

The idea of humility and devotion in chant was important to the Cistercians, who expressed it in their writings more often than the Benedictines. This peculiarly Cistercian tenet of moderation or *mediocritas* in singing appears in statute 75 of the twelfth-century institutes of the general chapter at Cîteaux:

---

[39] *Dialogus Miraculorum*, 5.5, ed. Strange, pp. 283–4: *Cum nocte quadam hebdomadarius invitatorii antiphonam incipiere, et monachus ei proximus voce mediocri psalmum intonaret, Herwicus, tunc subprior, cum ceteris sernioribus eadem voce qua ille inceperat, psallere coepit. Stabat iuvenis quidam minus sapiens in inferiori pene parte chori, qui indigne ferens psalmum tam submisse inceptum, fere quinque tonis illum exaltavit. Subpriore ei resistente, ille cedere contemsit, et cum multa pertinacia ei resistente, ille cedere contemsit, et cum multa pertinacia victoriam obtinuit. Cuius partes in proximo versiculo quidam ex oppositio choro adiuverunt. Propter scandalum et dissonantiae vitium ceteri cesserunt. Mox is, qui supra, vidit daemonem de monacho sic triumphante quasi candens ferrum prosilientem et in oppositum chorum in eos, qui eius partem roboraverant, se transferentem. Ex quo colligitur, quod magis Deo placeat humilis cantus cum cordis devotione, quam voces etiam in coelum arroganter exaltatae.*

It is fitting for men to sing with a manly voice, not imitating the frivolity [or lasciviousness] of minstrels in a feminine manner with shrill or (as is commonly said) false voices. And therefore we have decreed that moderation (*mediocritas*), be preserved in chant, so that it may be redolent of seriousness, and that devotion may be preserved.[40]

Chrysogonus Waddell situates this statute around 1147 when the reformed Cistercian antiphoner was promulgated. The association of high pitch with frivolity or wantonness is frequently invoked in Cistercian texts. For instance, a chapter in the *Exordium Magnum* sets forth the negative example of a monk blessed with a beautiful voice who stayed silent during festal matins throughout the choral chants in order to save himself for his big solo, the verse of a great responsory which he sang 'extremely high, with his usual lasciviousness of voice'.[41] At the end of his virtuosic performance, the monk was applauded enthusiastically by a small, very dark demon. Both the narrative and Conrad of Eberbach's concluding comment borrow from the language of the statute of the general chapter stating that the moderation prescribed by the order and the authority of the rule teaches that monks must sing with humility both individually and together.[42]

In addition to the *exempla*, more practical writings on chant also illustrate the importance to the Cistercians of listening and singing together. Such pragmatic considerations form the substance of a short treatise written in the twelfth century and soon thereafter attributed to Bernard of Clairvaux. It begins with a passage echoing both the Rule of Benedict's chapter on psalmody and the liturgical theology of the Cistercians: 'Our venerable father Bernard, abbot of Clairvaux, ordered monks to maintain this manner of singing, affirming that it is pleasing to God and the angels'. The body of the text continues with admonitions for the technical execution of chant:

---

[40] *Viros decet virili voce cantare, et non more femineo tinnulis vel, ut vulgo dicitur, falsis vocibus histrionicam imitari lascivam. Et ideo constituimus mediocritatem servari in cantu, ut et gravitatem redoleat et devotio conservetur* ('Instituta generalis capituli apud Cistercium', in *Narrative and Legislative Texts from Early Cîteaux*, ed. C. Waddell (Cîteaux, 1999), pp. 360, 489–90).

[41] *Exordium Magnum*, 5.20, ed. Griesser, p. 382: ...*ut uersum responsorii sui non plane in grauibus, sed in acutis uel potius in acutissimis uocem quatiendo tinnulos que modulos flexibilitate uocis formando solita lasciuia decantaret.*

[42] *Exordium Magnum*, 5.20, ed. Griesser, p. 382: *Ideoque summopere nitendum est quatenus secundum mediocritatem, quam nobis sanctus ordo noster praescribit, necnon et secundum auctoritatem, qua regula, quam professi sumus, nos instruit et singuli specialiter et omnes in commune pariter cum grauitate, cum timore et tremore atque cum humilitate psallamus et cantemus Deo nostro.*

We should not draw out the psalmody too much, but we should sing with a round and full voice. We must start each half-verse and the end of each verse together and we must finish them together ... No one may presume to begin before the others and hasten too much, or to drag along after the others too much or to hold the final cadence. We must sing together, we must pause together, always listening.[43]

The remainder of the text explains how soloists and choirs should perform the intonations and repetitions of chants, as well as emphasizing the need for pauses between phrases.

This short treatise represents a useful complement to the collections of Caesarius of Heisterbach and Conrad of Eberbach and the statute of the general chapter mentioned above. All these writings concern the fitting performance of the office, which is essential to the proper functioning of the monastic community envisioned by the Rule of Benedict, as Bernard of Clairvaux himself emphasized in one of his sermons on the Song of Songs:

According to our rule, nothing may be put before the work of God, the name by which father Benedict called the rites of praise that we render to God daily in the oratory, showing by this more clearly that he wished us to be intent upon that task. Therefore I admonish you, dearly beloved, always to take part purely and vigorously in divine praises. Vigorously, so that just as you stand reverently, so also you stand briskly in chanting the praises of God, not lazy, not sleepy, not yawning, not saving your voices, not cutting off half the words, not jumping over them entirely, not with broken and slack voices sounding something stammering through the nose in a womanly fashion, but drawing out the words of the Holy Spirit with manly sound and disposition, as is fitting.[44]

[43] C. Waddell, 'A plea for the *Institutio Sancti Bernardi Quomodo Cantare et Psallere Debeamus*', in *Saint Bernard of Clairvaux: Studies Commemorating the Eighth Centenary of his Canonization*, ed. M. B. Pennington (Kalamazoo, Mich., 1977), p. 187: *Venerabilis pater noster beatus Bernardus abbatis clareuallis precepit monachis hanc formam canendi tenere, affirmans hoc deo et angelis placere, ita dicens: Psalmodiam non nimium protrahamus, sed rotonde et uiuia uoce cantemus. Metrum et finem uersus simul intonemus et simul dimittamus. Punctum nullus teneat, sed cito dimittat. Post metrum bonam pausam faciamus. Nullus ante alios incipere et nimis currere presumat, aut post alios nimium trahere uel punctum tenere. Simul cantemus, simul pausemus, semper auscultando.*

[44] Bernard of Clairvaux, Sermon 47 on the Song of Songs, *Patrologia Latina*, ed. J. P. Migne (221 vols., Paris, 1844–1903), clxxxiii, col. 1011C: *Ex regula namque nostra nihil operi Dei praeponere licet. Quo quidem nomine laudum solemnia, quae Deo in oratorio quotidie persoluuntur, pater Benedictus ideo voluit apellari, ut ex hoc clarius aperiret quam nos operi illi vellet esse intentos. Unde vos moneo, dilectissimi, pure semper ac strenue divinis interesse laudibus. Strenue quidem, ut sicut reverenter, ita et alacriter Domino assistatis: non pigri, non somnolenti, non oscitantes, non parcentes vocibus, non praecidentes verba dimidia, non integra transilientes, non fractis et remissis vocibus muliebre quiddam balba de nare sonantes; sed virili,*

This passage was quoted in full by Conrad of Eberbach at the beginning of the chapter on the vain singer in the *Exordium Magnum* (5.20, cited above), endowing it with the authority of a proof text. Bernard's own words on singing, and the notion that a particular form of chant performance constituted adherence to the Rule, pervade Cistercian writings on music. In the first half of the twelfth century the Cistercians reformed the chants of their antiphoner and hymnary in an attempt to restore what they considered authoritative versions of the chant so as to achieve an authentic observance of the Rule.[45]

The desire for a return to earlier traditions parallels the Cistercian renewal of the early monastic imaginary with its ever-present angels and demons. Giles Constable has situated Bernard of Clairvaux's statements regarding chant performance in the context of the Cistercian revision of the chant and he has also pointed out their relationship to an *exemplum*, extant in three different versions of the twelfth and thirteenth centuries, that recounts Bernard's vision of angels who were present among the monks of Clairvaux during matins recording each singer's degree of devotion in a different writing medium.[46] According to the *Collectaneum Exemplorum*, words performed purely for the love of God were recorded in gold, those sung on account of the saints in silver, those said out of habit or the enjoyment of singing were written in ink, and those produced complainingly by unwilling singers were recorded in water. The angels were altogether unable to write down the words emitted negligently or with levity of the mind.[47] The version in the

---

ut dignum est, et sonitu, et affectu voces sancti spiritus depromentes.

[45] The literature on the Cistercian chant reform is too extensive to be addressed in full here. A particularly useful exposition can be found in C. Waddell, 'The origin and early evolution of the Cistercian antiphonary: reflections on two Cistercian chant reforms', in *The Cistercian Spirit. A Symposium: in Memory of Thomas Merton*, ed. M. B. Pennington (Cistercian Studies, iii, 1970), pp. 190–223. Recent discussions of the exemplars used for the revision of the chant are M. P. Ferreira, 'La réforme cistercienne du chant liturgique revisitée', *Revue de musicologie*, lxxxix (2003), 47–56; introduction to *The Primitive Cistercian Breviary (Staatsbibliothek zu Berlin, Preussischer Kulturbesitz, Ms. Lat. Oct. 402), with Variants from the 'Bernardine' Cistercian Breviary*, ed. C. Waddell (Spicilegium Friburgense, xliv, Fribourg, 2007). Treatises on the revision of the chant repertory are 'Epistola S. Bernardi de revisione cantus Cisterciensis', and 'Tractatus Cantum quem Cisterciensis Ordinis ecclesiae cantare consueverant', both ed. F. J. Guentner (Corpus scriptorum de musica, xxiv, Rome, 1974), pp. 21–41; and the 'Regule de arte musica', ed. most recently in C. Maître, *La réforme cistercienne du plain-chant: étude d'un traité théorique* (Brecht, 1995). On the revision of the Cistercian hymn repertory, see the introduction to *The Twelfth-Century Cistercian Hymnal*, ed. C. Waddell (Trappist, Ky., 1984), i. 3–22.

[46] Constable, 'The concern for sincerity and understanding', p. 24.

[47] *Collectaneum Exemplorum*, 4.7, ed. Legendre, pp. 264–5.

Exordium Magnum states that the angels writing in gold signified the singers' fervour of devotion to the service of God and concentration on the text being sung. Writing in silver indicated the singers' lesser degree of passion, albeit still pure devotion. Writing in ink signalled the fact that they sang without much devotion but with good will, and writing in water expressed the defects of singers afflicted by somnolence or laziness or distracted by useless thoughts, whose hearts were not in concord with their voices. Those whose singing the angels did not record at all had developed a lamentable hardness of heart, had forgotten their profession and the fear of God.[48] These anecdotes reflect both the singers' varying degrees of participation and the belief in the presence of angels at the office, mentioned in the Rule of the Master and the Rule of Benedict.

An essential aspect of medieval monastic thought was the tenet that in the liturgy, heavenly and earthly singers were joined in common praise. This ideal appears in the eighth distinction of Caesarius of Heisterbach's *Dialogus Miraculorum*, where he recounts a vision experienced in a monastery in Saxony during the performance of the *Te Deum laudamus*, a non-scriptural hymn sung at the end of matins on Sunday and feast days. A young girl (presumably an oblate or novice) who was allowed to attend matins only on high feast days was compelled by her tutor to leave before the conclusion of the service so as to retire to bed. Remaining near the choir so as to listen, she saw the singers taken up to heaven when the *Te Deum* began. As the performance progressed, at each reference in the text to apostles, prophets, and so on, the girl saw the corresponding group revealed on high; during the concluding phrase of the chant, the choir descended to earth and the heavens closed.[49] This literal illustration of the text reflects the ideal joining of celestial and earthly choirs that was a common theme of medieval liturgical commentary.[50] An earlier *exemplum* in the Cistercian *Collectaneum Exemplorum* recounts that some of those in the choir saw angels circulating among them during the singing of the *Te Deum*, rejoicing in the devotion of the singers. According to this brief text, the vision signifies that

one must take great care to sing with devotion <...> pausing briefly after

---

[48] *Exordium Magnum*, 2.3, ed. Griesser, p. 75.

[49] *Dialogus Miraculorum*, 8.90, ed. Strange, ii, pp. 157–8.

[50] See G. Iversen, *Chanter avec les anges. Poésie dans la messe mediévale. Interprétations et commentaires* (Paris, 2001). For a recent study showing the realization of this idea in musical practice, see L. Kruckenberg, 'Neumatizing the sequence: special performances of sequences in the central middle ages', *Journal of the American Musicological Society*, lix (2006), 243–317.

each phrase and slightly lengthening both the words and the syllables (*Unde magnopere curandum est ut cum deuotione cantetur <...> per clausas breuiter pausando et uoces et sillabas aliquantulum protrahendo*).[51]

It is no coincidence that the language of the conclusion echoes twelfth-century Cistercian legislation on singing as well as the short treatise attributed to Bernard of Clairvaux: in this monastic tradition, a particular style and technique of singing had specific spiritual implications. It may be significant that the closely related narratives in the *Exordium Magnum* and *Dialogus Miraculorum* (both from the early thirteenth century) do not employ the technical language of chant performance, in contrast to the earlier *Collectaneum Exemplorum*, compiled a few decades after the completion of the Cistercian chant reform.[52] All, however, reflect the ideal of angelic participation in the liturgy. The *exempla* concerning the involvement of angels in the *Te Deum* formed part of the same liturgical theology as those on demonic interference in the monastic office. All reinforced the fundamental concept that made the performance of the office such a central focus of Cistercian endeavours: the ancient and powerful belief that by singing together they forged a living link between the monastic community and the divine.

---

[51] *Collectaneum Exemplorum*, 3.15, ed. Legendre, pp. 257–8. The ellipsis reflects the erasure of eight letters in the manuscript.

[52] *Exordium Magnum*, 2.4, ed. Griesser, p. 76.

Inside and outside the medieval laity: some reflections on the history of emotions*

John H. Arnold

The historiography of medieval popular religion has recurrently drawn upon the language of emotions. Authors have talked of 'the religious emotions of traditional Christianity', of 'deeply felt' communitarian impulses, of the elevation of the Host being the 'emotional peak' of the mass, of the 'desperate desire' people had for intercessionary masses and the 'great comfort' they received from Christ's sacrifice.[1] The development of 'affective piety' in the late middle ages brings with it – in the source material itself, and in modern commentaries upon it – a rich vocabulary of love, fear, desire and the pull and sway of transcendent feelings. But historians of religion have not yet considered 'emotion' as an analytical category in its own right. Emotions have, rather, tended to be taken as transparent and transhistorical experiences shared by all human beings; and hence can be used to explain the need for religious beliefs and practices (in regard to the fear of disease and death, for example), or as a useful basis upon which to forge sympathetic connection with religious experiences from past cultures (in the case of ecstatic mystics, for instance).[2] One potential exception

* My thanks to Miri Rubin and the conference participants – not least Christopher and Rosalind Brooke – for their comments on this paper. An earlier draft was aired at the Leeds International Medieval Congress in 2006, and I am similarly grateful for responses from that audience, particularly Frances Andrews and Rob Lutton (who first prompted me to address the topic). Thanks also to Peter Biller, Victoria Howell, Caroline Jewers, Lucy Riall and students on the MA in Historical Research at Birkbeck.

[1] J. Bossy, *Christianity in the West, 1400–1700* (Oxford, 1985), p. 75; E. Duffy, *The Stripping of the Altars* (New Haven, Conn., 1992), p. 92; R. N. Swanson, *Religion and Devotion in Europe, 1215–1515* (Cambridge 1995), p. 141; C. Harper-Bill, *The Pre-Reformation Church in England* (Harlow, 1989), pp. 70, 66.

[2] This is implicit, e.g., in Barbara Newman's methodological statement of intent in her *From Virile Woman to Woman Christ: Studies in Medieval Religion and Literature* (Philadelphia, Pa., 1995), pp. 16–17; it similarly informs various contributions to *History in*

J. H. Arnold, 'Inside and outside the medieval laity: some reflections on the history of emotions', in *European Religious Cultures: Essays offered to Christopher Brooke on the occasion of his eightieth birthday*, ed. M. Rubin (London, 2020), pp. 105–27. License: CC-BY-NC-ND 4.0.

to the rule – Jean Delumeau's magisterial *Sin and Fear* – does place an emotion centre stage, but similarly assumes that the nature and meaning of the emotion itself remain static and unchanged, his analysis tracing instead the ways in which fear was evoked and aroused by developments in western religious culture.[3]

However, recent work in other fields has more closely questioned the nature of emotion, and explored the possibility of providing it with a history.[4] In areas such as early medieval politics, high medieval spirituality, and late medieval law, historians have sought to demonstrate the importance of certain emotions in particular situations, the wider cultural meanings carried by the expression of emotions, and the historically- and culturally-specific 'content' of emotions such as friendship, anger and hatred.[5] For medieval historians, an abiding concern has been to revise or refute the position of our period within the grand narrative of a 'civilizing process' famously propounded by Norbert Elias. Thus Daniel Smail's study of the 'consumption' (as he nicely terms it) of law in Marseille emphasizes that the development of legal processes did not work to repress or discipline emotion, but rather the opposite: hatred (the key emotion here discussed) was a 'social institution' which could be amplified, shaped and elaborated through legal dispute. In a different fashion, Barbara Rosenwein has sought to emphasize, for the governing and literate elite of the early middle ages, a succession of variant 'emotional communities' with particular norms of behaviour and affect. There is, Rosenwein argues, no smooth upward curve from unfettered emotionality to disciplined, rational 'civilization', but rather a succession of different emotional 'styles' particular to successive groups. The contours of these emotional communities can be traced through their lexicons: the available set of 'emotion words', whether sincere

the Comic Mode: Medieval Communities and the Matter of Person, ed. R. Fulton and B. W. Holsinger (New York, 2007).

[3] Jean Delumeau, *Le peche et la peur: la culpabilisation en occident entre XIIIe et XVIIIe siècles* (Paris, 1983); English translation, *Sin and Fear: Western Guilt Culture, 13th to 18th Centuries*, trans. E. Nicholson (New York, 1990).

[4] For a detailed overview, see B. H. Rosenwein, 'Worrying about emotions in history', *American Historical Review*, cvii (2002), 921–45.

[5] E.g., *Anger's Past: the Social Uses of an Emotion in the Middle Ages*, ed. B. H. Rosenwein (Ithaca, N.Y., 1998); D. Boquet, *L'ordre de l'affect au moyen âge: autour de l'anthropologie affective d'Aelred de Rievaulx* (Caen, 2005); *Emotions and Material Culture*, ed. G. Jaritz (Vienna, 2003), particularly the essays by Daniel Smail, Gabor Klaniczay, Michael Goodich and Piroska Nagy; P. Hyams, *Rancor and Reconciliation in Medieval England* (Ithaca, N.Y., 2003). It is worth noting that 'love' has long been analysed from a broadly 'culturalist' perspective (C. S. Lewis, *The Allegory of Love* (Oxford, 1936); D. de Rougemont, *Passion and Society*, trans. M. Belgion (2nd edn., 1956)).

or commonplace in any particular source, indicate the field of potential emotions, and social valuations attached to those emotions.[6]

These key works, and others following their lead, have taken their cues from anthropology, a discipline which for some decades has been arguing about the analysis of emotions and the consequent social, cultural, political, juridical, epistemological and ontological issues.[7] Since the late nineteen-seventies, anthropologists have been exploring some core topics which map rather well onto historical study: whether emotions are innate or socially constructed, involuntary or strategically deployed; whether certain societies or groups (natives/medievals) are intrinsically more 'emotional' than others (westerners/moderns); and the methodological challenges presented by 'reading' emotion and emotional languages from the available data (fieldwork/historical texts). Given their disciplinary position as a social science, it is perhaps unsurprising to find that anthropologists are somewhat ahead of historians in considering how psychological studies might intersect with – and be critiqued by – fieldwork analysis. Some have also begun to consider whether a focus on language and culture can truly escape dealing with issues of embodiment and materiality, envisaging embodiment not as an alternative or rebuttal to language, but its necessary complement, 'the existential ground of culture'.[8]

It is worth noting just how much conceptual and methodological apparatus anthropology already proffers in this field; historians need not reinvent all the theoretical wheels for this particular bandwagon. At the same time, however, historical work has attempted to grapple with an issue which anthropologists are often able to leave to one side: the question of change over time. Do emotions themselves – in the sense of the interior bodily affects experienced by individuals – change over time, or is it only the wider cultural systems, within which emotions are expressed and interpreted, that move diachronically? And do emotions (whether transhistorical or transitory) play a role in historical change? William Reddy, a historian of eighteenth-century France, has answered the latter question with a strong affirmative, arguing that the potential dissonance between individual

---

[6] D. L. Smail, *The Consumption of Justice: Emotions, Publicity and Legal Culture in Marseille, 1264–1423* (Ithaca, N.Y., 2003), particularly pp. 244–5; B. H. Rosenwein, *Emotional Communities in the Early Middle Ages* (Ithaca, N.Y., 2006), particularly pp. 191–203.

[7] A helpful overview of past work is given in the introduction to *Mixed Emotions: Anthropological Studies of Feeling*, ed. K. Milton and M. Svašek (Oxford, 2005), upon which the following remarks are largely dependent.

[8] T. J. Csordas, 'Embodiment as a paradigm for anthropology', *Ethos*, xviii (1990), 5–47, at p. 23; see also T. J. Csordas, 'Somatic modes of attention', *Cultural Anthropology*, viii (1993), 135–56.

emotional need and governing 'emotional regimes' (such as pertained at the royal court of the *ancien régime*) can in themselves provoke change: in this case, the French revolution.[9] For Reddy, the expression of emotion constitutes a particular kind of speech act: 'emotives' (as he terms them) are, like the 'performative utterances' noted by the linguistic philosopher J. L. Austin, words which 'do' the thing they denote; but, going further than Austin's sense of performatives, Reddy's 'emotives' also *change* the thing they perform – 'emotives are themselves instruments for directly changing, building, hiding, intensifying emotions'.[10] For Reddy, this further means that the inner feeling can never fully be 'represented' by the emotive utterance; and that this, therefore, places a limit on the fluidity of cultural construction, because the sense of human interior affect clearly precedes and exceeds the available bounds of language. Without wanting to assert a genetic, programmed, unvarying emotional constitution for all human beings, Reddy nonetheless argues that a set of interior dispositions remain essentially constant across history. What changes are the emotional regimes which shape and encourage – or, more often, discourage – emotional expression.[11]

All of this is exciting and stimulating work. But in bringing some elements of the history of religion in conjunction with the history of emotions, I do not wish to use the latter simply as a template for interpreting the former. My aim is more critical and dialectical, and I want to conclude this introductory section by raising some questions and problems with regard to the current work on emotions, responses to which will be further explored below. Reddy, Rosenwein and Smail, albeit in slightly different fashions, all seek to assert or demonstrate some 'core' of transhistorical emotional stability: that, beyond language, something which nonetheless

[9] W. M. Reddy, *The Navigation of Feeling: a Framework for the History of Emotions* (Cambridge, 2001).

[10] W. M. Reddy, 'Against constructionism: the historical ethnography of emotions', *Current Anthropology*, xxxviii (1997), 327–52, at p. 331. See J. L. Austin, *How to Do Things with Words* (2nd edn., Oxford, 1975).

[11] See further W. M. Reddy, 'Emotional liberty: politics and history in the anthropology of emotions', *Cultural Anthropology*, xiv (1999), 256–88; W. M. Reddy, 'The logic of action: indeterminacy, emotion, and historical narrative', *History and Theory*, xl (2001), 10–33. At the heart of Reddy's critique of constructionist perspectives is a desire for a universal ontological basis for political action: to put it crudely, a desire that one be allowed to intervene in a situation arising within a different cultural context, on the basis of a universally shared need for 'emotional liberty'. I recognize some of the force of this desire, but Reddy's assumption that politics *primarily* consists of those from 'liberal' emotional regimes (i.e., westerners) diagnosing and intervening in the suffering of those from 'repressive' emotional regimes (i.e., everyone else), does strike me as problematic.

coheres to categories such as 'hatred' or 'fear' or 'anger' can be found across time and space.[12] The claim is practically impossible fully to support or refute, but it brings with it a number of other claims – or assumptions – which can be pushed a little. One is that the nature of this inner affect is something which emanates from within the individual human subject. As Rosenwein puts it, 'Let us recall the very definition of emotions: they have to do with appraisals of things *affecting me*' (her emphasis).[13] Emotion here is immanent and individual; as is similarly the case with Smail's legal combatants and Reddy's seekers of emotional liberty. But a key discovery in certain anthropological studies has been the intrasubjective nature of emotions: that not simply the expression but the very experience of certain emotional states can be collective rather than individual.[14] I would like then to ask, what is the nature of emotional subjectivity? That is, in what *kinds of* situations and contexts (within what discourses) do what *kinds of* individuals or groups (subjectivities) experience and express emotion? A particular area of interest here is the relationship between the body and emotion: we may consider whether the body is simply that which 'grounds' emotion (the bit 'beyond language', from whence the essence of feeling arises), or whether there are other ways in which the relationship between body and feeling have been configured in the past. Another issue concerns language, for both anthropological and historiographical enquiries: can any researcher access emotions 'beyond' the cultural expression of the same? And, for that matter, can any person express emotions 'outside' or 'prior to' language and behaviour, or are such expressions, if not bounded by

---

[12] Reddy and Smail turn, at certain points, to psychological and neurophysiological studies in order to undergird this. One cannot reject these out of hand, but it is not clear to me how one avoids a circularity of argument here, if wishing to project the empirical findings of brain- and body-response back into the past. We cannot study the brain of a fourteenth-century litigant to see which parts respond in what ways to what situations; and given that neuropsychological studies suggest that there is considerable 'feedback' between external (cultural) stimuli and interior (biological) affect, this leaves us begging further questions. On the latter point, see A. Damasio, *Descartes' Error: Emotion, Reason and the Human Brain* (New York, 1994), quoted by Smail, p. 244, n. 1; and for an interesting appraisal of the general issues, G. E. R. Lloyd, *Cognitive Variations: Reflections on the Unity and Diversity of the Human Mind* (Oxford, 2007).

[13] Rosenwein, *Emotional Communities*, p. 166.

[14] One might view the experience of 'grief' within early modern Iroquois society in this light, as the emotion is experienced as a wound to the 'household' and tribe, bringing practical and affective reactions from the group rather than just the individual. See D. K. Richter, *The Ordeal of the Longhouse: the Peoples of the Iroquois League in the Era of European Colonization* (Chapel Hill, N.C., 1992), particularly pp. 32–6. In general, see further Milton and Svašek.

such constraints, always at the very least *liable* to (culturally-informed) interpretation by others?

To turn to a more specific methodological aspect of this latter question, how securely does a study of emotional lexicons (including their elisions and silences) in historical sources allow one to map an 'emotional community' or 'regime'? There is a further issue here beyond the matter of genre-specific rhetoric (the stock language of *amicitia* in letters, for example) and 'sincerity'.[15] We may further need to consider at what points, and in what contexts, different discourses and their textual practices deem the expression and recording of emotional language to be necessary and appropriate; the reasons for so doing not necessarily being limited to emotional issues in and of themselves. Here is an example, from a body of sources I know well: inquisition trials. The registers of inquisition depositions from early fourteenth-century France contain intermittent mention of emotions, or emotionally-charged actions, ascribed both to deponents themselves and to others whose past deeds they narrate. But these aspects are almost non-existent in inquisitorial registers from the mid thirteenth century. What changed over that period was not, I would suggest, a shift in emotions themselves, nor 'emotional community' or 'regime', but an alteration in the textual practices of inquisition, with regard to the production and textualization of 'truth', legal verisimilitude, and the nature of the subject producing the confession.[16] Writing down what was 'true' about a subject confessing in the early fourteenth century could, at some points, include writing down what they said about feelings; what changed was how a conception of 'truth' got textualized, not the emotions in and of themselves.

To explore further some of these issues, the remainder of this paper traces a path through some aspects of later medieval religion, concentrating upon two interconnected areas: the language of confession and penance developed in the late twelfth and thirteenth centuries; and vernacular literature slanted towards the late medieval English laity – initially indirectly via the parish priest, but latterly directly to a (relatively elite) literate laity.[17]

[15] Rosenwein, *Emotional Communities*, pp. 26–9, 193–6.

[16] See J. H. Arnold, *Inquisition and Power: Catharism and the Confessing Subject in Medieval Languedoc* (Philalelphia, Pa., 2001), particularly ch. 3. Readers of Mark Gregory Pegg's sparkling monograph *The Corruption of Angels: the Great Inquisition of 1245–6* (Princeton, N.J., 2001) may be led to believe that mid thirteenth-century records were full of emotional expression; a glance at the Latin sources, however, reveals the extent to which this is Pegg's imaginative and engaging reconstruction of what lies 'beyond the text'.

[17] Given my present purposes, I will not rehearse here the wider historical picture of these devotional developments, attempt to describe the full range of confessional literature, or map the precise relations between thirteenth-century Latin texts and fourteenth- and

As an initial foray, this makes no claim to completeness either empirically or conceptually, and some important aspects – such as the roots of penitential discourse prior to the twelfth century – have been left completely aside. Nonetheless, this smattering of sources provides a useful arena for the exploration of some aspects of lay religion and emotion. My aim is to note not only *what* emotions, but the wider discursive context within which such emotions are placed: what kind of subject, in what position, at what time, is supposed to experience them – and to what end? As this suggests, a key argument for this paper is that emotions need to be analysed in terms of the cultural discourses they inhabit, both because (as we shall see) there are good reasons for seeing particular emotional expressions arise, historically, within changing cultural demands; and because, as historians, any claim we make to move 'beyond' such realms is problematic.

* * *

A key aspect to medieval lay piety was its basis in collective action: the rituals of mass, processions, feasts, the marking of parish bounds, the corporate beneficence of guilds and confraternities, the journeys of groups of pilgrims, and so forth. These collective activities have, alongside other aspects, an emotional component: friendship, charity, peace, joy, and so forth. These are thus, within these contexts, sets of emotional ideals and performances which come *only* in collective expression – and, one might argue, are experienced only as part of that collectivity. If one reads the laity's experience of the mass in line with John Bossy's picture of a moment of communal transformation, this central Christian ritual is thus an 'intrasubjective' emotional ritual.[18] And even if, to demur somewhat from Bossy's perspective, one wishes to consider the minority of medieval people who avoided mass or looked critically or doubtfully at its central mystery,[19] it is clear that their sense of 'individual' reaction (and whatever emotions this entailed) was nonetheless framed by their awareness of what they assumed to be the larger, collective experience of Eucharistic piety; this again constituting a different kind of 'intrasubjective' emotion.

---

fifteenth-century English ones. For an introduction to issues of this kind, see L. E. Boyle, 'The fourth Lateran Council and manuals of popular theology', in *The Popular Literature of Medieval England*, ed. T. Heffernan (Knoxville, Tenn. 1985), pp. 30–43.

[18] J. Bossy, 'The mass as a social institution, 1200–1700', *Past & Present*, c (1983), 29–61.

[19] On such reactions, see J. H. Arnold, 'The materiality of unbelief in late medieval England', in *The Unorthodox Imagination in Medieval England*, ed. S. Page (Manchester, forthcoming).

The emotionality of the regular parish mass is perhaps more assumed than demonstrated, but it is clear that other aspects of liturgy addressed a sense of collective engagement, and implicitly sought to activate a collective emotional response. Take, for example, the Rogation days: having fasted for three days, the parish then went on procession and held a feast, in celebration of Christ's Ascension. A sermon that the late fourteenth-century priest John Mirk wrote for the occasion emphasizes how important it was to join in, that failure to contribute was as sinful as absence from the mass. Moreover, he says, there are 'fiends that float in the air' who, when they hear the thunder of the spring storms, cause mischief upon the earth, attacking the fabric of the community in various ways. To ward off these effects, Mirk says, the parish fasts and then goes upon procession:

> For just as when a king goes to battle, trumpets go before and the banner is displayed and comes after, then comes the king and his host following him; just so in Christ's battalion the bells, that are God's trumpets, ring, banners are unfurled and openly borne on high in the air. Then the cross in Christ's likeness comes, as a king of Christian men, and His host, that is Christ's people, follow him.[20]

Although not using any 'emotion words', Mirk's rhetorical appeal is clearly predicated upon the prompting of audience affect, by evoking an excited, purposeful, communal effort against an external threat. Again, I would argue, the emotions which this seeks to activate assume a collective subjectivity and affect; one cannot, alone, feel part of a collective 'host'. The argument could be similarly extended to other rituals, and there is indeed explicit discussion of, and injunction regarding, collective emotion in the case of guild records. The annual Easter feast of the Guild of Holy Cross (Stratford-upon-Avon), for example, was to be held 'in such a manner that fraternal love shall be enriched between [its members] . . . and true amity upheld'.[21] Once again, you cannot have 'fraternal love' without a fraternity; it is, in its very conception, intrasubjective. One might make a similar claim about that central Christian virtue, the very essence of Christian community: *caritas*. We often translate *caritas* as 'charity', which imbues it for modern

---

[20] John Mirk, *Festial: a Collection of Homilies*, ed. T. Urbe (English Early Text Soc., extra ser., xcvi, 1905), p. 150: *For ry3t as a kyng, when he gope to batayle, trompes gon before, þe baner ys desplayde and comyþ aftyr, þen comyþ þe kyng and his ost aftyr sewyng hym; ryght so in Cristys batagyle þe belles, þat ben Godys trompes, ryngen, baners byn unfolden, and openly born on hegh yn þe ayre. Then þe cros yn Cristys lykenes comyth as a kyng of cristen men, and his ost, þat ys Cristys pepull, sewyþe hym.*

[21] *English Gilds*, ed. T. Smith and others (English Early Text Soc., old ser., xl, 1870), pp. 216–17.

readers with a sense of top-down beneficence. But this is the usage of a later age; within a medieval context it could more simply be rendered as 'love', and the most important form of love, one focused on spiritual amity between people. *Caritas* might again be seen as something which can only exist intrasubjectively, as its very essence is a sense of community.

In line with my introductory comments, I make no claim here one way or another regarding the 'real' experience of the emotions of those participating in such rituals. Nor am I arguing that medieval people could only feel emotions as part of corporate bodies. My point is that the particular discourses which attempt to prompt these affective responses are predicated upon a collective, rather than an individual, experience. One is further reminded that a long-held tenet of Christian piety (for all but the most extraordinary) was to 'fit in', to adhere to one's place precisely as part of a collectivity. 'It is pride which makes a man stand out among the common herd', as the twelfth-century writer Alain de Lille put it.[22] As Caroline Walker Bynum pointed out some time ago, medieval identity, and the appropriate spiritual (and hence emotional) states that accompanied it, was largely conceived as one's location within an available set of collective models.[23] The practice of annual confession has sometimes been seen as an exception to this pattern, or as a key element in a shift toward a more 'modern', individual and interiorized subjectivity. The remainder of this paper will focus on confessional discourse, and principally upon the advice given to the individual about to confess (or the confessor about to receive that confession). But it is important to note that this 'individual' was not an immanent historical presence 'set free' by the extension of confessional practices following the Fourth Lateran Council of 1215. It is, rather, that confessional discourse constructs a particular kind of subjectivity, deems necessary a set of interior operations, demands and codifies some key emotional responses, and invites the narration of a certain 'individuality' – albeit always within the framework of the highly collective and universalized categories of sin.

* * *

Let us turn, then, to confession and emotion, and let us begin with an early text that maps appropriate modes of comportment, Robert of Flamborough's *Liber Poenitentialis* (written *c.*1208). In the opening chapters

---

[22] Alain de Lille, *The Art of Preaching*, trans. G. R. Evans (Kalamazoo, Mich., 1981), p. 54.
[23] C. W. Bynum, 'Did the twelfth century discover the individual?', in C. W. Bynum, *Jesus as Mother: Studies in the Spirituality of the High Middle Ages* (Berkeley, Calif., 1982), pp. 82–109.

of his treatise, Robert explains that the necessary starting points for penance are that one is Christian, and that one is penitent. By 'penitent', he explains, one must be feeling sorrow (*dolor*) for what has gone before, caution toward the future, one must make honest and naked confession, and one must be obedient. (Feeling and action are intrinsically conjoined – emotion is not simply about emotion, but also consequent reform.) An imaginary dialogue between confessor and penitent then amplifies the issue:

'Are you frequently sorry for your sins?'

'Sometimes'

'One should indeed always apply oneself (*studeas*) to sorrow; because the essence of penance is sorrow and contrition . . .'[24]

The importance of emotion is similarly found in other texts on confession from the same period. See, from some time prior to 1236, the *De Modo Confitendi* of Cadwgan, bishop of Bangor (here copying from the Paris theologian Robert of Courçon's *Tota Celestis Philosophia*, 1208 × 13):

He is penitent only if he grieves (*dolet*) and is ashamed for sin, and grieves for it, and humbles himself for that same sin, which is moreover of three grades. For all principal sins are of three kinds: pleasure, shamelessness, pride. And against this, because opposites cure opposites, penitence must be love, shame and humility.[25]

Three things can be noted. First, it is clear that this confessional discourse presents a kind of pedagogy – something which one studies, develops, applies oneself to. Hence, we are talking here about an ongoing *process*, a self-making or self-reforming; not the freeing or revelation of a prior individual self that was just awaiting the moment, but the production and continued development of a better and different identity from that held before. Second, this self-making is conducted within a wider system: most obviously the larger system of sin (usually depicted by medieval theologians as the tree of sin, with ever-subdividing branches), but also a system of

---

[24] Robert of Flamborough, *Liber Poenitentialis*, ed. J. J. F. Firth (Toronto, 1971), i. 5–8 (58–61): *Sacerdos: Frequenter doles de peccatis tuis? Poenitens: Aliquando. Sacerdos: Immo semper studeas ad dolendum; quia summa poenitentia est dolor et contritio.*

[25] J. Goering and H. Pryce, 'The *De modo confitendi* of Cadwgan, bishop of Bangor', *Mediaeval Studies*, lxii (2000), 1–27, at p. 16: *Ille siquidem penitens qui dolet pro peccato et uerecundatur, et dolet pro eo, et se humiliat pro eodem peccato, iam est in tribus gradibus. Nam in omni peccato precipue sunt tria: delectatio, inpudentia, superuia. Et contra hec, quia contraria contrariis curantur, debet penitentia esse amara, uerecunda, et humilis.*

complementary and balanced emotions. Thus, in Cadwgan/Courçon we have not only 'sorrow' but love, shame and humility. Third, it is clear that emotion is not merely a by-product of confession but an essential element, and indeed the guarantor of something: that grief, shame and so forth are indications of penitence. But as it asserts this claim, it simultaneously provides the grounds for doubt: is this particular claim of penitence emotionally correct? Does the inner disposition match the request for absolution? Emotion is simultaneously the mark of authenticity, and the measure against which a true comportment can be distinguished from a false, feigned or failed one.

These are discourses developed initially within a monastic setting (well before 1215), and there is some question over how quickly these ideas were disseminated at parish level, in terms of regular, lay, annual confession. But by the later thirteenth century, there are, at the very least, vernacular texts dealing with confession: most famously the much reproduced French texts *Somme Le Roi* and the *Manuel des Peches*, and also, to pick a contemporary English example, the *South English Legendary* (c.1280). Here, from the latter text's discussion of Lent, we find familiar advice further amplified:

That man tells his sin with his mouth, and be sorry thereto

And that he be not in despair (*wanhope*). And that he carry out penance.

[. . .]

For without sorrow of heart, no sin is forgiven.

A man would be better off if he is sorry for his sin, but unconfessed,

Than make confession without sorrow; and better should be forgiven.[26]

Being sorry (*sori*) but in despair (*wanhope*), the text goes on to explain, is also no good – for that was the state into which Judas fell after betraying Christ. The penitent is thus confronted with a particular kind of task, requiring a particular kind of agency – circumscribed within the demands of confession, and with the possibility of failure. This is not, however, simply the failure to feel, but the possibility that one might feel *wrongly*.

---

[26] *South English Legendary*, ed. C. d'Evelyn and A. J. Mill (Early English Text Soc., ccxxxv–ccxxxvi, 1956), i. 131: *Þat man telle is sunne mid is mouþ. & be[o] sori þerto / And þat he in wanhope ne be[o] noȝt. & þat he penance lede [. . .] / For wiþoute sorwe of heorte. no sunne nis forȝive /A mon were betere for is sunne be[o]. sori and vnssriue / Þan issriue wiþoute sorinesse. & bet ssolde be[o] forȝive.*

Later texts provide further refinement of the emotional field demanded of the penitent, and its differentiations. John de Burgo's fifteenth-century *Pupilla Oculi* (an influential adaptation and expansion of William of Pagula's even more influential early fourteenth-century work of pastoral care, *Oculis Sacerdotalis*) explains that absolution cannot happen without the appropriate inner state: 'contrition is moreover sorrow voluntarily taken up (*dolor voluntarie assumptus*) for sins, with the intention of making confession and satisfaction'; again, a little later: 'and contrition is said to be voluntarily taken-up sorrow, to differentiate it from natural sorrow (*dolor naturalis*) which has neither merit nor demerit for sins'.[27] The *Book of Vices and Virtues* (*c.*1375), a Middle English translation of *Somme Le Roi*, maps out a still wider emotional terrain. It emphasizes the necessity of 'hating' sin, another emotional disposition that can be learnt:

> Forget your body once a day, and go into hell whilst you are alive, so that you do not go there when you are dead. And holy wise men often do thus. There you shall see all that the heart hates and flees: lack of all goodness, and a great plenty of all wickedness, burning fire, stinking brimstone, foul storms and tempests, rutting hideous devils, hunger, thirst that may never be staunched, all manner of torments, weepings, sorrows more than any heart may think of or any tongue may devise, and [all this] lasting evermore without end.[28]

These horrors are balanced by the 'joy' of Heaven, discussed in the following pages, full of the precise opposites to Hell's various torments, namely feasts and so forth, 'wiþ songes and ioye wiþ-outen ende'.[29] The meaning, compass and mechanism of 'hate' is interesting here. While the penitent is being

---

[27] John de Burgo, *Pupilla Oculi* (n.p., 1510), fo. 27v(b): *Est autem contritio dolor voluntarie assumptus pro peccatis cum proposito confitendiae satisfaciendi . . . Et dicitur contritio dolor voluntarie assumptus: ad differentiam doloris naturalis qui nec meritoris nec demeritoris pro peccatis.*

[28] *The Book of Vices and Virtues*, ed. W. Nelson Francis (Early English Text Soc., old ser., ccxvii, Oxford, 1942), p. 71: *Forȝet þi body ones a day, and go in-to helle while þou lyvest, þat þou come not þere what þou art ded. And þus doþ ofte the holy wise men. Þere þou schalt see al þat herte hateþ and fleeþ: defaute of al goodnesse, and gret plente of al wikkednesse, brennynge fier, stynkynge brymston, foule stormes & tempestes, routynge ydousedeueles, hunger, þryst þat may neuere be staunched, many manere of turmentrye, wepynges, sorwes more þan any herte may þenke or any tunge may deuyse, and euere-more wiþ-outen ende lastynge.* The Middle English text closely parallels the original French: *Oublie ton cors une fois le iour, va enfer a ton vivant que tu in wises en mourut. Ce sont souvent li saint home e li sage. Illec verras tu quanques cuers het et fuit. Sante de tous o biens plete de tous maus [. . . etc. . .] divers tourmens pleurs et doleurs plus que cuers ne porroit penser de langue deviser et tous iours duiront sans fin* (British Library, MS. Royal 19 C ii fo. 28r(a), *Somme le Roi*).

[29] *Vices and Virtues*, p. 73.

encouraged to foster it as a feeling toward sin, the depiction of Hell makes it clear that 'hate' is also an automatic and involuntary reaction toward certain external elements (fire, storms, hunger, etc.). The relationship between 'body' and 'emotion' is configured here in a notably different fashion from more modern discourses: 'hating' is an innate bodily affect with regard to certain external physical phenomena, but one which can be encouraged, tended and then harnessed in service of spiritual reform. In a similar fashion, in the *Book of Vices and Virtues*' lengthy final section on 'soberness',[30] the regimen for achieving this state of control is notably external, focused upon speech, clothes, eating and drinking – and is not about the kind of interior state of affect or humour that a later notion of 'sobriety' might assume.

These discourses on sin, penitence and confession thus map a complex emotional landscape which must be negotiated in order to achieve absolution. There may be a particular complication for the laity in this regard, owing to the way in which the system of confession and penance was presented. Cadwgan (again copying from Robert of Courçon) tells us that

> true penance can be known by that which Augustine teaches in his book of penance, which establishes that there are fifteen worthy steps of penance ascending to the celestial Jerusalem. A step moreover, according to Augustine, is nothing other than progress; in truth, to ascend is nothing other than the act of making progress.[31]

Penance is, in other words, a skill to be mastered, as part of an ongoing discipline; as Cadwgan/Courçon present it, a reassuring programme of self-development. In contrast, one can compare the later (*c.*1434) instructions on confession, written by a cleric from Beccles for children he was schooling in Latin:

> In every man's heart, dwelling in a wretched vale of tears, it is necessary to make spiritual labour and work (*gostly labour & trauayle*) in relating his conscience at this holy time of Lent, which is deputed and ordained for the reformation of souls. For, following the proverbs of old men, whosoever is not holy in Lent or busy in harvest is not likely to thrive. Every man therefore, beating his breast in

---

[31] Cadwgan, *De Modo Confitendi*, p. 16: *Notandum quod uere penitentes possunt agnosci per hoc quod docet Augustinus in libro de penitentia, quibus elicitur quod xv gradibus dingne* [*sic*] *penitentie ascenditur in Ierusalem celestem. Gradus autem, secundum Augustinum, nichil aliud est quam profectus; ascendere vero nichil nisi proficere.*

compunction, should rise up mightily to spiritual works.[32]

The notion of *labour & trauayle* lies at the heart of other vernacular treatises, and provides the governing central metaphors of the confessional texts *Handlyng Synne* (c.1303) and *Jacob's Well* (c.1440): the former tells one to 'handle' (that is, work with) sin in all that one does, the latter presents the metaphor of a 'foul pit' (the body) which must constantly be excavated in search of spiritual cleanness. The *Book of Vices and Virtues*, following *Somme Le Roi*, presents the possibility of spiritual work to the laity, but repeatedly references the 'wise holy man' who can *really* do it properly; the assumed subject position of the reader is to be in proximate relationship with this figure, not to inhabit the holy man's transcendent status. Thus, while one strand – an originary, monastic strand – of confessional discourse presents it as a skill to be mastered (or, at least, developed with some proficiency), as this becomes vernacularized, the reader or auditor is often presented instead with a continuation of labour, and never-ending labour at that. This would suggest (though it can only be suppositional) that the emotional disposition of the lay penitent toward his or her 'labour' is likely to be of a different order from that of an assured, intellectual, Latinate penitent.

It is clear that all of the aspects discussed above – the act of confession, the emotional dispositions it requires, the relationship between body and affect it works through – are *taught* rather than innate. Confessional discourse is a pedagogy, with all the issues of power relations that pedagogy involves. As noted above, emotion (sorrow, principally) is positioned as the key marker of authenticity. It permits a kind of diagnostic knowledge on the part of the confessor; and the relationship between 'inner' and 'outer' is therefore not a binary choice, but a necessarily dualistic system. John de Burgo explains that contrition can be so great as to completely remit sin, but:

> nevertheless, it is required that confession be made and the enjoined penance be completed, because of the precepts of the church and moreover because of *uncertainty*, because no one can be certain that his contrition was sufficient to lift his guilt [my emphasis].[33]

---

[32] S. B. Meech, 'John Drury and his English writings', *Speculum*, ix (1934), 70–83, at p. 76: *In every manys herte dwellyng in wrecchid vale of teris is nedful to ben foundyn gostly labour & trauayle in telying of his concyens þis holy tyme of Lent, deputid and ordeynyd to reformacion of soule. For after þe prouerbe of olde men, ho so is not holy in Lente or besi in hervest is not lykly to thryve. Every man perfore knowyng his bryst in compunccion rise vp mytyly to gostly werkis.*

[33] John de Burgo, *Pupilla Oculi*, fo. 28r (b): *Nihilominus tamen requiritur confessio et penitentie iniuncte expletio proter preceptus ecclesie et etiam propter incertitudine quia non est quis certitudine quod sua contritio fuerat sufficiens ad totum reatum tollendum.*

Furthermore, as a thirteenth-century text (attributed to Robert Grosseteste) enjoins, the priest should be aware that any circumlocution on the part of a penitent may indicate the presence of a hidden sin. Similarly, an anonymous confessors' manual from the same period warns that if the priest 'see[s] the penitent stumbling and doubtful and going along as if feeling the way', he should encourage him to speak openly, as something important is being hidden.[34] Thus an essential part of the confessor's task is the interpretation of the emotional state and actions of the confessing penitent.

* * *

The genre of confessional discourse flowered in late medieval Europe, extending itself well beyond the fairly concise and practical advice of early thirteenth-century confessors' manuals. One direction this took was the call, directed toward the literate laity, for individual reflection upon their interior selves. Here, for example, is the so-called Goodman of Paris, in a text purportedly written for his young wife *c.*1393:

> The third article [of this book] says that you should love God and keep yourself in His grace. On which, I counsel you that immediately and laying aside all other tasks, you refrain from drinking or eating at night or vespers, even a very little bit, and you remove all earthly and worldly thoughts, and while coming and going you put and hold yourself in a secret place, alone and far from people, and think of nothing but hearing your mass early the next morning, and after that giving account to your confessor of all your sins by a good, full and thoughtful confession.[35]

While there is no specific emotional instruction involved in this passage, the idea of an individual, interior response – this 'secret place, alone and far from people' that one sustains while 'coming and going' – is clearly drawn. The sense of having to make a spiritual 'space' within the demands

---

[34] 'Robert Grosseteste's treatise on confession *Deus est*', ed. S. Wenzel, *Franciscan Studies,* xxx (1970), 218–93, at p. 247; 'The *Summa Penitentie Fratrum Predicatorum*: a thirteenth-century confessional formulary', ed. J. Goering and P. J. Payer, *Mediaeval Studies,* lv (1993), 1–50, at p. 27.

[35] *Le Menagier de Paris*, ed. G. E. Brereton and J. M. Ferrier (Oxford, 1981) (hereafter *Menagier*), p. 12: *Le tier article di que vous devez amer Dieu et vous tenir en sa grace. Surquoy je vous conseille que incontinent et toutes euvres laissies vous vous desistez de boire ou mengier a nuyt ou vespre, se trespetit non, et vous ostez de toutes pensees terriennes et mondainnes, et vous mectez et tenez alant et venant un ung lieu secret, solitaire et loing de gens, et ne pensez a riens fors a demain bien matin oyr vostre messe et aprez ce rendre compte a vostre confesseur de tous voz pechiez par bonne, meure et actrempee confession.*

of domestic duty may strike some chords across time; but such resonances should not make us collapse culture into nature. The Goodman's text is quite clearly *instruction*: he is here explaining how, and in what way, to construct an 'interior', and to what end it should be put.

Medieval interiority is, in other words, not simply the revelation of an innate human condition, long-hidden by 'the dark ages' or awaiting a coming Renaissance. There are, rather, medieval *interiorities*, constructed within different discourses for different functions. One interior, which intersects both the language of confession and certain aspects of emotional response, is the interior from whence 'affective piety' may be seen to spring. This 'interior' is individual, relatively private (though, as in the case of the highly-visible mystic Margery Kempe, prone to dramatic self-publicization), founded upon emotional responses – but also an 'interior' strongly connected to the exterior plenitude of Christ and the Virgin Mary; or, in a different inflection, to the coming Judgement and inescapability of death. It is, in other words, an individual interior notably aware of, and connected to, certain exterior elements. A brief example, extracted from an early sixteenth-century manuscript of poems, can stand in for a much larger field: 'To see þe maydyn wepe her sonnes passion / It entrid my hart full depe with gret compassion'.[36] What is important here, with regard to the argument of this article, is the connection between bodies, interiors and emotions. The Virgin's emotion is apprehended through outward bodily display; it 'enters' the body of the auditor; and through entering, it provokes affect which is always, to some degree, bodily. Take another Marian example, again drawn from John Mirk's sermon collection. Mirk's sermon for the salutation of the Blessed Virgin Mary tells the story of a nun who every day said as many *Ave Maria* prayers as there are psalms in the psalter. The Virgin appears to her one day, thanks her for her worship, but then tells her that she can please Mary better: leave aside half of the number of *Ave*s and say the remaining half 'in trete' – meaning something like 'in full thought' or 'all sincerity'. Mary continues her advice:

and when you come to the words 'God is with thee', then say that with all thy heart and in full thought (*and all in trete*). For there is no tongue that may tell the joy that I have in my heart, when that word is said to me devoutly; for I think that I feel my son Jesus with that word playing in my body, and that is so high a joy that it pleases me beyond all other joys.[37]

[36] *Songs, Carols and other Miscellaneous Poems*, ed. R. Dyboski (Early English Text Soc., extra ser., ci, Oxford, 1908), pp. 41–2 (no. 51); see similarly various other Marian poems in these extracts from Richard Hill's commonplace book.

[37] Mirk, *Festial*, pp. 299–300: *and whan þou comyst to þis worde 'God is syth þe' þan say þat*

Mirk invites a dazzling combination of emotional and bodily empathy here (and one more clearly appropriate for the expected experiences of a lay audience than a nun). It is once again notable that what might be first seen as a text describing or encouraging innate feeling, in fact works through the conjunction of bodily experience and exterior prompt. Indeed, much like the way the hatefulness of Hell was figured in the *Book of Vices and Virtues* as an inevitable response to exterior conditions, for Mirk's Mary the fact of the child playing in her womb *is* joy – not a prompt to joy, but joy itself. But it comes from an exterior source (the prayer); and in Mary's visitation to the nun (and in Mirk's performance of the *exemplum* to a parish audience) it is once again, and necessarily, externalized.

For all its focus upon interior response, the externalization of affective piety – whether joyful or sorrowful – is an intrinsic part of its system. Take, for example, the advice given to an unknown 'devout and literate lay man', in a late fourteenth-century text:

> At the door when you go out say: 'All the men of this city or town from the greater to the lesser are pleasing to God, and only I am worthy of hell. Woe is me. Welawey.' Let this be said from all your heart so that the tears run; you need not always say it with your mouth; it is sufficient to say it with a groan.[38]

Here, as elsewhere, interiorized emotion is undoubtedly present. But it is produced in concert with a spiritual adviser, and making the inner feeling visible or audible is essential, because it undergirds the key role of the confessor. The body and emotion (explicit and implicit) play a key role here too. As an early manual explains, once the penitent has confessed everything that they are able,

> one begins to censure, namely by showing the magnitude and enormity and badness of what they have confessed, and the goodness of God that should lead them to penance. Warn the confessant and say 'Brother, do you regret this crime you have perpetrated . . . ?[39]

wyth alle þine herte and all in trete. For þer is no tong þat may telle þe ioy þat I haue in myn herte, whan þat worde is sayde to me deuoutely; for me thynkeþe þat I fele my son Ihesu wyth þat worde pleying in my body, and so þat is so hegh a ioye þat it gladuth me passing alle othur ioyes.

[38] 'Instructions for a devout and literate layman', ed. and trans. W. A. Pantin in *Medieval Learning and Literature*, ed. J. G. Alexander and M. T. Gibson (Oxford, 1976), pp. 398–422, at pp. 398–9, 420: *Ad hostium <exeundo dicatur>: Omnes homines huius civitatis <vel ville> a maiori ad minorem placent Deo, et ego solus dignus sum inferno. Ve michi. Welawey: dicatur ex toto corde, ita ut lacrime currant; non semper proferatur ore: sufficit quod gemendo.*

[39] 'Summa penitentie', ed. Goering and Payer, p. 39.

Bishop Cadwgan explains that the manner in which one confesses should include confessing 'cheerfully' (*hillaris*); that is,

> not done with sorrow and only fear of punishment, but from a greater love of virtue; ... and scrupulously (*morose*), not in saying everything in a never-ending line – I committed this sin, and this, and this ... – but as one sharply pricked and greatly crushed [by sin], when with great diligence and scrupulousity he vomits [them up].[40]

Thus one's bodily and emotional experiences – and it is again unclear whether there is any meaningful difference between 'bodily' and 'emotional' here – are key elements in bringing forth full confession and contrition. The *Book of Vices and Virtues* further elucidates:

> Repentance requires great sorrow and great regret in [one's] heart of that [deed through which] we have made Our Maker wrathful . . . You must say 'well away' with truly deep heart, so that the heart will melt and bring forth all thy tears with great sorrow, and with great weeping and deep sighing [you] shall cry God's mercy, as His thief, His manslaughterer and murderer, that deserves to be hanged in Hell . . . Such tears drive away the devil, just as scalding hot water makes a hound flee the kitchen.[41]

---

[40] Cadwgan, *De Modo Confitendi*, pp. 16–17: *Hillaris, ne fiat cum tristitia et solum timore pene, set magis uirtutis amore; tristitia enim seculi mortem operatur, ut dicit Augustinus, contritio uero salutem. Morosa, ne in transcursu fiat sic: 'Ego commisi hoc peccatum, et hoc, et hoc,' ad modum combinatorum numero per innumeras numero; ut acutius pungant et cum magis tereant, cum maxima diligentia et morositate euomantur.*

[41] *Vices and Virtues*, p. 172: *Repetaunce askeþ grete sorwe and grete oþenkynge in herte of þat þat we have wrapped our maker ... þei schulle seye 'weil-awey' wiþ riȝt deep herte, so þat þe herte mowe melte and brynge forþ ale þe teeres wiþ grete sorwe, and wiþ grete wepynge and sore syȝhing schal crie God mercy as his þef, as his mansleer and murþerour, þat þat haþ deserued to be honged in helle ... Suche teeres dryuen awey þe deuel, riȝt as þe scolde hot watre makeþ an hound flee þe kychene.* This again follows the source text, including the final domestic metaphor, but with some slight amplification (such as, like the 'Devout and literate layman', sighing 'weil-awey'): *Repentance requiert grant doleur et grans gemissemens de cuer de ce que leu a couroucie son creatour ... Eu qui a dieu couroucie par pechie mortel u doit gemir du parfont du cuer si que li cuers li fonde tous en lermes. Et a grans pleurs et agrans lour pirs doit crier a dieu merci come son larron, son murtrier, son tiruteur, qui a desserui le gibet denfer... Teles lermes chacent le dyable hors du cuer comme lyave chaude chace le chien de la cuisine* (*Somme le Roi*, fo. 68v). The word *gemissemens*, translated by the *Vices and Virtues* author as *oþenkynge* (regret), could be rendered as 'moaning', which further emphasizes the externalizing aspect here (see *Dictionnaire de l'ancien français, jusqu'au milieu du XIVe siècle*, ed. A. J. Greimas (2nd edn., Paris, 1968)).

Once again, we see a complex interplay between exterior and interior: the words which must be said in order to soften the heart, so that sorrow can be felt; that sorrow itself being expressed through the external sign of tears; those tears acting to drive away the exterior threat of the devil. The body is hence not simply the inner seat of emotion, nor emotion an innate affect; learning how to confess and be penitent requires a kind of 'work' involving body, emotion, interior and exterior. All are necessary elements, and none is dominant.

Perhaps most importantly, because of these factors, the body is an important sign for the confessor, a means of reading and identifying emotion, devotion, and hence penitential diligence. Thomas of Chobham, another very influential thirteenth-century writer, explains the matter through a common metaphor:

Just as a doctor of the body examines many signs and indications of a patient's illness to see whether he can be cured or not, so a doctor of the soul should consider many signs around a penitent, of whether he is truly penitent or not, for example if he sighs, if he cries, if he blushes, and does other such things. Or if he laughs or denies that he has sinned or defends his sin or similar things.[42]

The emotional displays of the body are a kind of simple language, which the confessor must decode. Contrition is an inner state – but its only guarantee, within a system of confession and penance imposed from without, is its external, bodily affect. Yet another thirteenth-century manual explains that 'If [the penitent] appears strenuous in penance, by the grace of the bishop a milder penance can be given'.[43] The specific case discussed here is parricide – a serious crime – but the principle of potential leniency extends throughout the penitential system. Indeed, the Goodman of Paris explains the very nature and necessity of contrition to his young wife via the model of a condemned man begging his judge for mercy: 'how he would implore him in good heart with great tearfulness, with moaning and great grindings of heart, without thought to anything else'.[44] So too should one implore God (and His earthly representatives, the clergy), via these external signs, for clemency. How well,

---

[42] Thomas of Chobham, *Summa Confessorum*, ed. F. Broomfield (Analecta Namurcensia, xxv, Louvain, 1968), pp. 240–1: *Et sicut medicus corporalis multa signa et indicia inquirit de morbo patientis utrum possit curari vel non, ita medicus spiritualis per multa signa debet considerare circa penitentem si vere peniteat vel non, veluti si gemat, si ploret, si erubescat, et cetera talia faciat. Vel si rideat vel se peccasse neget vel peccata sua defendat et similia.*

[43] 'The *Summa de Penitentia* of Magister Serlo', ed. J. Goering, *Mediaeval Studies*, xxxviii (1976), 1–53, at p. 17.

[44] *Menagier*, p. 15: *il le prieroit de bon cuer en grans pleurs, en gemissemens et grans contrictions de cuer sans penser autre part.*

or otherwise, these emotions are externalized – or, perhaps we should say, how these emotions, *constituted as externalizations*, are interpreted – will affect both the spiritual fate of the sinner, and, more immediately, his or her treatment by those who wield power.

* * *

I began this paper by invoking the somewhat unexamined importance of emotions to the historiography of lay religion. The material cited above traces a path – not, I think, too idiosyncratic or unrepresentative a path – through a very much wider terrain. It has demonstrated the presence of explicit discussion of emotion, notably in the sacrament of confession and penance, and has suggested the implied presence of emotion, particularly as a desired affect on the part of an audience or readership, in other areas as well. At the same time, I have sought to show that these emotional performances are not simply innate, unchanging, ahistorical experiences. Expectations of lay emotion change over time, and the degree to which emotion is understood to underpin lay spirituality depends upon both the historical moment and the genre of spiritual experience. To take the most prominent example, affective piety was not a 'discovery' of previously unseen or ignored emotionality; it very clearly seeks to prompt, develop and nurture a particular *kind* of emotional response. In other words, emotions are called forth within particular discursive contexts, which provide disciplines and maps for the experience of affect. Take the example of Marian poems and stories, many more of which could be cited than the sparse evidence given above: it is perfectly possible, indeed likely, that some medieval laypeople would have felt an automatic empathy for Mary, focusing perhaps on the shared experiences of motherhood and loss. But the texts to which we, as historians, have access clearly sought to teach and disseminate such an empathetic reaction, and to mould the emotional expression into its correct shape. There is no unmediated access available to us. Similarly, it is perfectly possible that one might innately feel bad about anti-social things that one has done; but the process of feeling the *right* kind of sorrow for what is recognized as *sin* depends upon a particular penitential pedagogy. In each case, the shaping of human experience should not be collapsed back into something innate, 'beyond' culture and politics; for it is precisely in these operations of penitential and spiritual reform that we see 'history turned into nature', as the anthropologist Pierre Bourdieu would put it.[45]

For these reasons and more, it is not clear to me that there is any possibility

---

[45] P. Bourdieu, *Outline of a Theory of Practice*, trans. R. Nice (Cambridge, 1977), p. 78.

of accessing something other than cultural constructions. The issue has a further inflection for historians: our access to any of this comes only through surviving textual sources. On what basis, other than our individual sympathy and whimsy, do we claim to reach 'beyond' those sources to past suffering or joy? I would further argue that there is no clear *point* to such a project, even if one wishes, for political and humanistic reasons, to hold that cultural construction is not 'all there is'. Were we to transcend culture, bypass language and plunge ourselves somehow into the raw emotional maw of a singular historical individual – what would we then do with what we found? It would certainly not explain that individual within her or his historic circumstances, since those circumstances would entail a return to the cultural and linguistic constructions from which we are somehow fantasizing our escape. And at any moment in which we begin to talk or write about our imagined experience of the unmediated individual, we once more rejoin the games of language, culture and mediation.

What we can do instead is look at how different discourses, in different cultural contexts and at different points in time, make use of emotions. In this respect, there are some specific aspects to the ways in which medieval religious culture constructs emotion that have interesting implications for the wider history of emotions. The extent to which emotions, within this field, could be 'individual' is dependent on a historical shift: the amplification and refinement of penitential discourse, with regard to the laity, which first flowered in the late twelfth century, and found its fullest expression only by the late fourteenth. At the same time, this move did not constitute a simple shift from corporatism to individuality, as some later historians and critics still tend to imagine. The collective experience of emotion – which one might see as intrasubjective affect – continued to play an essential part of lay religious life (as it still did, of course, after the Reformation). The conceptual tools used by the current historians of emotion are predicated upon a bedrock of individual, interior affect; what does the possibility of collective subjectivity do to their arguments?

A particular contribution that medievalists can make to the history of emotions is to remind ourselves that much of the vocabulary of western emotion is drawn from the language of sin, confession and penance. As the sketch that I provide above attempts to demonstrate, some important implications follow from this. One is that emotion, within this confessional discourse, even while being carved into some interior place, must be exteriorized, because of issues of legibility and control. A frequently recorded preaching *exemplum* tells of a priest who was granted the ability to discern the state of men's souls by their faces. As his parishioners came up to receive the Host, he could see the nature of their sin: lecherers had blackened faces, those with red faces were full of ire, those in charity shone brightly like the sun.[46] The tale does not simply illustrate a medieval belief in the exteriority of interiors, but more the unfulfilled *desire* that lay at the heart of confessional processes; an inescapable lacuna that is the very engine of that discourse. No priest could see the interior person written so clearly upon the body. Hence the necessity of schooling penitential subjects in how they should externalize their inner feelings, and of schooling their confessors to inspect and interpret those external signs they could discern.

A further implication is thus that the emotions studied in this paper were but one element within a wider system: a regime of spiritual discipline. 'Regime' is used here not in as strong a fashion as that evoked by Michel Foucault for later discourses of sexuality and medicine; nor in William Reddy's sense of a system of governance focused upon the emotions; but a regime – a spiritual *regimen* perhaps – nonetheless, one making relatively strong claims upon the individual subject (within a medieval context), and one that sits at the intersection of several overlapping discourses (confession, medicine, governance, and so forth). What is important here is that these discourses are not primarily about emotion. Emotion is, rather, but one element within a number of wider fields. Confessional discourse maps a variety of potential emotional responses, but it is not interested in discussing *all* emotion, only those particular to its terrain; and it is also concerned to interpret and prescribe other elements of public and private behaviour, and further modes of speech and comportment. The emotions it does discuss are thus linked to other matters, of social and self-discipline, reputation and scandal, salvation and damnation, clerical and lay identity, and so forth. Prioritizing 'emotion' among these issues is to distort the shape of the discursive field.

It seems to me, then, that while we surely cannot 'get at' the past emotional experience of individuals in an unmediated fashion – we can never meaningfully say whether a particular person really, truly *felt* an emotion, even if we have managed to decide what precisely we mean by all those terms – we can instead explore the conditions of possibility for all such experiences, and the variety of experience contained within such regimes. Such cultural constructions are thus never 'mere'; they are the

---

[46] Robert Mannyng of Brunne, *Handlyng Synne*, ed. I. Sullens (Binghampton, Medieval and Renaissance Texts and Studies, 1983), pp. 253–5, ll. 10165–256. The tale probably originates in the *Vitae Fratrum*, and the power was originally ascribed to an abbot or a bishop; Mannyng's translation of the gift down the ecclesiastical scale to the parish may indicate something of the changes in expectation of lay spirituality (see F. C. Tubach, *Index Exemplorum: a Handbook of Medieval Religious Tales* (Helsinki, 1969), nos. 1959, 1960).

very structures of individual experience. We might further recognize that asking what someone 'really truly felt' carries with it very strong echoes of confessional discourse and its desire for legibility. Finally, we might further ask whether a 'new history of the emotions', as a delimited sub-field of historiography, is actually the best way of studying and understanding the conditions within which human affect is experienced and expressed. Do we actually need histories of individual emotions, or emotional regimes? Or would we be better served by seeing emotions as but *one* part of the larger, ongoing, historical flux of language, subjectivity and power – and hence always best studied in the wider contexts of those other factors?

'The whole company of Heaven': the saints of medieval London

Caroline M. Barron

By the end of the twelfth century the city of London was already divided up into over 100 parishes, or even more when the parishes in the extramural suburbs are included in the count. The role played by these parishes in 'shaping the city' – the phrase used by Christopher Brooke to describe the evolving topography of London between 800 and 1216 – was extremely important. In a characteristic passage he configures the different ways in which these parishes may have evolved:

> Let us imagine two circumstances. A man builds a church on his own property, his own soke; it is in the first instance a personal possession, its priest his chaplain; his tenants, the men under the jurisdiction of his soke – whatever that means – will naturally worship in his church, perhaps have an obligation to do so; and he will expect them to contribute to its building fund and to help him keep it in repair. The other case is of a group of pious craftsmen, living in the same neighbourhood, who decide to build themselves a little church for their own use and to support a priest in it. The Church and the priest will serve a community which may from the first be quite clearly defined; but it is of its nature (unlike the first example) a voluntary community, not a conscript congregation.[1]

These churches were dedicated, whether by a lord, or a group of pious craftsmen, to chosen saints. In this way they can be seen to express some of the priorities and preferences of the men – English, Danish and Norman – (and perhaps women also) who lived in London in the tenth to the twelfth centuries. What is unusual about London is that there survive records to tell us about the dedications of these early parish churches which make it possible to map the popularity of the different saints' cults. Why certain

[1] C. Brooke with G. Keir, *London 800–1216: the Shaping of a City* (1975), p. 131.

saints were chosen and others not is an interesting question which is not easy to answer. Christopher Brooke, in his study of medieval cults in Cambridge and Avignon, argued convincingly that in both these very different towns, relics played a very minor role in the choice of cults.[2] The interventions by the saints in the lives of local people, the predilections of the local bishops, and the enthusiasms of returning pilgrims, may all have played a part. But these early commitments are now lost to us.

We can, however, even at this distance, observe some of these early preferences and enthusiasms. For this analysis the saints of London will be divided into four categories: biblical saints, martyrs and early European saints, British and Anglo-Saxon saints, and other dedications. It is clear from the table (see appendix) that the Virgin Mary was already outstandingly popular in twelfth-century London: twenty-one (16 per cent) of all the churches in London were dedicated to her.[3] She had twice as many dedications as her nearest rival, the catch-all dedication to All Saints. The cult of St. Michael was widely popular in Anglo-Saxon England and in Normandy, and so it is not surprising to find that the heavenly standard-bearer was commemorated in eight London churches. In fact there are few surprises among the dedications of the London churches although there are some distinctive features. Six of the eleven churches in medieval England dedicated to St. Olaf were to be found in London; St. Christopher had only six other dedications, St. Mildred only five, St. Alphage four, St. Agnes three, and St. Owen and St. Magnus just two. The parish church in Foster Lane was dedicated to St. Vedast, the bishop of Arras who died in 539 and is otherwise commemorated in England only at Tathwell in Lincolnshire; and the church in Fish Street commemorated St. Wandrille (Wandregisilus), an abbot who, in 657, established a monastery at Fontenelle in Normandy which came to be known as St.-Wandrille. This saint is only otherwise commemorated at Bixley in Norfolk.[4] One London dedication is unique: the little church in Broad Street is dedicated to St. Ethelburga (d. 675), the abbess of Barking and sister of St. Erkenwald the saintly bishop of London whose place of burial in St. Paul's cathedral became a shrine.

It is possible that the church in Coleman Street, which was at first only a chapel, was originally dedicated to St. Colman of Lindisfarne (d. 672 ×

[2] C. Brooke, 'Reflections on late medieval cults and devotions', in *Essays in Honour of Edward B. King*, ed. R. G. Benson and E. W. Naylor (Sewanee, Tenn., 1991), pp. 33–45.

[3] Brooke, *London 800–1216*, p. 141. For the numbers and dedications of parish churches elsewhere in England, see F. A. Foster, *Studies in Church Dedications or England's Patron Saints* (3 vols., 1899), esp. ch. 2.

[4] Foster, iii, appendix 1. Foster notes that there were, of course, more churches dedicated to these saints in the eighteenth and nineteenth centuries.

675) and that it was the dedication of the chapel which gave the name to the street. But by 1214 the chapel had developed into a parish church and the dedication had changed to St. Stephen.[5] Some of the other dedications to British or Anglo-Saxon saints also disappeared: by 1250 the church at Newgate, originally commemorating the king and martyr St. Edmund (d. 869), had been re-dedicated to the Holy Sepulchre; the church in Honey Lane which at first commemorated St. Alphege, the eleventh-century archbishop of Canterbury who was murdered by the Danes, by 1235 was dedicated to All Hallows or All Saints.[6] The church in Friday Street in the eleventh century was dedicated to St. Werburga, an abbess who had died *c*.700, but by the mid fourteenth century she had been joined by St. John the Evangelist, and by the fifteenth century St. Werburga had been lost sight of altogether.[7] The popularity of these pre-Conquest saints is, however, attested by the fact that they secured nearly a quarter of all the twelfth-century London dedications. Moreover only four of these dedications were supplanted in the succeeding centuries which suggests a deep affection and conservatism.

A small church or chapel near St. Clement Danes in the Strand was dedicated to the Holy Innocents.[8] This is interesting because only four other English medieval churches were given this dedication: Adisham near Canterbury, Great Barton in Suffolk, Foulsham in Norfolk and Lamarsh in Essex.[9] Near to the chapel of the Holy Innocents was another small church dedicated to the Virgin, the church of St. Mary le Strand which belonged to the bishop of Worcester.[10] In 1326 the body of the murdered bishop of Exeter, Walter Stapleton, was taken *ad quandam ecclesiam Sanctorum Innocentium quae prope fuit praedictam ecclesiam Sancti Clementis derelictam et omnino destructam.*[11] So, by this date, the church of the Holy Innocents was derelict and its parish – if it had had one – was merged with that of St.

---

[5] E. Ekwall, *Street-Names of the City of London* (Oxford, 1954), pp. 84–5.

[6] *Cartulary of St. Mary Clerkenwell*, ed. W. O. Hassall (Royal Historical Soc., 1949), p. 166.

[7] Henry Harben, *A Dictionary of London* (1918), pp. 523–4, 619–20.

[8] This church belonged to Abingdon abbey (see *The History of the Church of Abingdon*, ed. J. Hudson (2 vols., Oxford, 2002), ii. 18–21, and 266–7, where the church of the Holy Innocents is confused with St. Mary le Strand).

[9] Foster, iii. 367.

[10] See the presentation by the bishop of Worcester to Thomas Becket in the 1150s, in *Materials for the History of Thomas Becket*, ed. J. C. Robertson (7 vols., Rolls ser., lxvii, 1867–85), iii. 17. I am very grateful to Christopher Brooke for help in elucidating the relationship between the churches of the Holy Innocents and St. Mary le Strand.

[11] *Chronicles of the Reigns of Edward I and Edward II*, ed. W. Stubbs (2 vols., Rolls ser., 1882–3), i. 317.

Mary le Strand, and the advowson became a source of dispute in Worcester between the bishop and the Benedictine abbey.[12]

If we consider the pattern of the church dedications in London at the end of the twelfth century we can see that the dominant group (38 per cent) was comprised of the early Christian martyrs together with the saints of the Gallic church such as St. Denis (bishop of Paris, d. c.250), St. Martin (abbot and bishop of Tours, d. 397), St. Vedast (bishop of Arras, d. 539), St. Benedict (abbot, d. c.550), St. Wandrille (abbot, d. 668), St. Ouen (bishop of Rouen, d. 684) and the hermit St. Giles from Provence (d. c.710). These dedications testify to the strong influence in England of the early martyrs and also to the lasting influence of the Gallic church. A further quarter of the church dedications were to the British and Anglo-Saxon saints, most of them heroes of the conversion of the English following the Gregorian mission led by St. Augustine. The Virgin Mary claimed 16 per cent of all the churches and the other saints of the Bible a further 14 per cent, including six of the Apostles (Simon Peter, James, Andrew, Bartholomew, Matthew and Thomas), John the Baptist and Mary Magdalene. At this comparatively early date there were only a small number of 'other dedications': eight churches were dedicated to All Saints, and one each to the Holy Innocents, the Holy Trinity, the Holy Sepulchre and, the chapel on the new stone bridge spanning the Thames, dedicated to the most recent of all the saints, St. Thomas Becket.

When we move forward into the later middle ages, it is possible to construct another league table demonstrating the popularity of different saints by analysing the dedications of the numerous – some 270 – new chapels and altars and parish and craft fraternities which were formed in these years. The figures in the second column of the table (see Appendix) are much less secure than those for the earlier period. Our knowledge of these later dedications is derived from more fragmentary and more diverse evidence. We know of the existence of these new fraternities and chapels from the returns made to the guild enquiry of 1388, from the Chantry Certificate of 1548, from licences to hold land in mortmain, from the surviving churchwardens' accounts and, above all, from references in wills.[13] There are thousands of London wills in these years enrolled in a variety of ecclesiastical courts and there has been no systematic reading or analysis of

---

[12] *English Episcopal Acta*, xxxiii: *Worcester 1062–1185*, ed. M. Cheney, D. Smith, C. Brooke and P. A. Hoskin (British Academy, 2007), pp. xliii and n. 57, 78–80.

[13] See C. Barron, 'The parish fraternities of medieval London', in *The Church in Pre-Reformation Society: Essays in Honour of F. R. H. Du Boulay*, ed. C. Barron and C. Harper-Bill (Woodbridge, 1985), pp. 13–37.

them. When a will that has been read records a fraternity or altar in a London church then the dedication has been included in the analysis. This means that although the *trends* in the popularity of different saints are reasonably clear, the exact rankings can only be tentative. In this analysis, all known dedications of fraternities, guilds, chapels and altars have been included but not dedications simply to lights or images. Also, the dedications of, and in, the religious houses of London have also been excluded. Most of the early religious houses were founded not by Londoners but by members of the royal family or the aristocracy and so the choice of saint may not represent the particular concern of Londoners.[14] Likewise, at the end of the period, when fraternities were founded in religious houses these seem often to have been inspired by the houses themselves, rather than by the Londoners.[15] In any case the number of fraternities founded in the religious houses is very small: almost all the London guilds and fraternities were based in the parish churches. The dedications of these parish guilds and fraternities were often fluid: fraternities might be combined, or additional saints added to the dedication, so the figure of 275 represents the number of times a saint is commemorated in a London fraternity, not the number of such fraternities.

The response to different saints can be seen to have varied a good deal since the twelfth century. The enthusiasm for the Virgin Mary has become even more marked: nearly a quarter of all the new dedications were made in her honour. The popularity of St. John the Baptist is also very evident, as is the enthusiasm for the new cult of St. Anne, whose feast was made obligatory in England in 1383, in part out of respect for Richard II's young queen, Anne of Bohemia.[16] The martyrs and early European saints also retained their share of the market, but with some unusual, or unexpected, additions to their company, such as St. Amand from Poitou, a monk and a missionary who died in *c.*675. He joined St. Vedast in the dedication of the fraternity of that parish church. Among the early martyrs, three newly popular saints stand out – St. Christopher, St. Katherine and St. George – and their popularity was by no means confined to London. St. Christopher protected travellers and those in danger of sudden death, St. George was linked to the Order of the Garter and the chapel at Windsor which, together with his support for the English at Agincourt, led to his feast day being raised to a principal feast in 1415. St. Katherine, the bride of Christ, was the protectress of the dying and her cult was very widely spread

[14] *The Religious Houses of London and Middlesex*, ed. C. M. Barron and M. Davies (2007), pp. 7–8

[15] Barron and Davies, pp. 19–20; Barron, 'Parish Fraternities', pp. 17–18.

[16] R. W. Pfaff, *New Liturgical Feasts in later Medieval England* (Oxford, 1970), p. 2.

throughout Europe, especially in the later middle ages.

By contrast, there is a very marked decline in the popularity of British and Anglo-Saxon saints. Indeed this decline is even more marked than it appears because six of the twelve fraternities were, in fact, dedicated to the patron of the parish church (St. Alban, St. Augustine, St. Bride, St. Dunstan (2) and St. Mildred) and so these represent old loyalties rather than new enthusiasms. The guild dedicated to St. Erkenwald at St. Paul's cathedral seems to have been deliberately, and unsuccessfully, promoted by Robert Braybrook when he was bishop of London. It never attracted any significant support among the Londoners.[17]

What is striking, if not unexpected, is the expansion of the range of dedications to embrace some of the new devotions. There were eight new cults including the widely popular cults of Corpus Christi and the Name of Jesus.[18] But there were also some more unusual enthusiasms, reflecting, perhaps, interest in Christian virtues and attributes, rather than in the personalities of the saints themselves. In 1414 John Stanton, a chaplain at St. Magnus near London Bridge left 4d to each brother of the guild dedicated to St. Charity.[19] In the College of Priests at St. Michael Paternoster Royal, a fraternity of the Holy Wisdom was established in 1490 in honour of Jesus Christ, The Virgin Mary, St. Paul, St. John the Evangelist, St. Jerome, St. Augustine of Hippo and St. Mary Magdalene. The purpose of this fraternity was to provide a solemn public reading, or lecture, freely in the college 'so that divine doctrine and fruitful preaching may be presented to God's people'.[20] Here the Holy Wisdom, one of the gifts of the Holy Spirit, and synonymous with the incarnate Word of God, or the Logos, incorporates in the dedication the virtues and characteristics of a number of saints ranging from the Virgin, to the doctors of the early church and to Mary Magdalene. The most popular new feast, however, was that of the Holy Trinity, a festival that had been particularly promoted by Thomas Becket, who had ordained that the Sunday after Whitsun should be dedicated to 'The Holy, Blessed and Glorious Trinity'; and the Black Prince had a lifelong devotion to the

---

[17] See *St. Paul's: the Cathedral Church of London 604–2004*, ed. D. Keene, A. Burns and A. Saint (New Haven and London, 2004), pp. 40, 114–21.

[18] See M. Rubin, *Corpus Christi: the Eucharist in late Medieval Culture* (Cambridge, 1991); Pfaff, ch. 4; E. A. New, 'The cult of the Holy Name of Jesus in late medieval England, with special reference to the fraternity in St. Paul's Cathedral London c.1450–1558' (unpublished University of London Ph.D. thesis, 1999).

[19] Guildhall Library, Archdeacon of London's Register, MS. 9051/1 fo. 14v. I am grateful to Robert Wood for this reference.

[20] *The Register of John Morton, Archbishop of Canterbury 1486–1500*, ed. C. Harper-Bill (3 vols., Canterbury and York Soc., 1987–2000), i. 18–19.

Holy Trinity and chose to be buried in the Trinity chapel at Canterbury.[21]

There were, as might be expected, regional variations in the popularity of different saints. In London's three 'home counties' of Middlesex, Surrey and Essex the Blessed Virgin, St. Katherine, St. John the Baptist and the Holy Trinity were among the most popular dedications, as they were in London.[22] Further afield there were some shifts of loyalty. In Norfolk and Essex St. Peter is notably more popular than he is in London, and in Cambridgeshire the feast of Corpus Christi was the second most popular dedication after the Virgin Mary.[23] The popularity in London of St. Anne, St. George and St. Christopher appears to have been distinctive compared with other areas of England. The cult of St. Thomas Becket, although reasonably popular in London, was by no means unique to the city. The chapel on London Bridge was dedicated to St. Thomas (possibly to help with money-raising in the initial phases of construction) but the London churches already had their saints by the time of Becket's martyrdom. However, in the rest of England, sixty-nine churches were dedicated to England's newest saint.[24] It might have been expected that the Londoners would have formed fraternities and dedicated altars to St. Thomas Becket, who was born in the city; in fact, only six such dedications are recorded.[25]

What may well have played a part in determining which cults were popular in London was the compendium of saints' lives which came to be known as *The Golden Legend*. The Latin version of the stories of the saints written by Jacobus de Voragine appeared first in 1260, and a French version by Jean Belet was produced early in the next century. In 1380 Jean de Vignay produced his *La Legende Dorée* in which he added a substantial number

---

[21] See *Age of Chivalry: Art in Plantagenet England 1200–1400*, ed. J. Alexander and P. Binski (1987), pp. 478–9; C. Wilson, 'The medieval monuments', in *The History of Canterbury Cathedral*, ed. P. Collinson, N. Ramsay and M. Sparks (Oxford, 1995), pp. 451–510, esp. pp. 494–5.

[22] This statement is dependent upon the unpublished work of other scholars who are working on the fraternities in these counties: Dr. Jessica Freeman in Middlesex; Dr. Matthew Groom in Surrey; and Dr. Janet Cooper in Essex. I am grateful to all three of them for generously sharing their work with me.

[23] See K. Farnhill, *Guilds and the Parish Community in Late Medieval East Anglia, c.1470–1550* (Woodbridge, 2001), p. 38. Farnhill provides a table comparing the popularity of different saints in Norfolk, Suffolk, Yorkshire, Cornwall, London and Cambridgeshire. St. Christopher does not appear on the list, perhaps because he was not particularly popular in Norfolk which provided Farnhill's template, but the numerous surviving wall paintings of St. Christopher in churches suggest that he was, in fact, widely venerated.

[24] Foster, iii. 24.

[25] At St. Dunstan in the East; St. Magnus; St. Margaret, Southwark; St. Martin in the Vintry; St. Mary Aldermary; St. Mary Islington.

of new legends to the original corpus. A group of 'clerks and doctors' translated de Vignay's text into English in 1438 and this compilation was known as the *Gilte Legende*.[26] The different versions varied considerably in their selection of saints' lives. When Caxton came to print his *Golden Legend* in 1484 he used all three versions of the text and added a number of legends of his own, including accounts of the lives of some of the Anglo-Saxon saints such as Alphege, Dunstan, Edmund, Swithin and Erkenwald.[27] Of the seventy-seven saints and festivals commemorated in the churches and fraternities of London, only about a third of them do not appear in any of the known versions of the *Golden Legend*. As will be clear from the table, those saints who did not appear in the *Golden Legend* were almost all British and Anglo-Saxon: in fact only four of these nineteen British and Anglo-Saxon saints appeared in the pre-Caxton versions of the *Golden Legend*, which is not surprising since it was a compilation largely made in Italy and France. However most of the Gallic saints venerated in London appear in the *Golden Legend*, except St. Ouen, the bishop of Rouen who died in 694; St. Faith, the virgin and martyr of the third century; St. Wandrille; St. Eloi, the bishop of Noyon who became the patron saint of metal workers; and St. Erasmus, a third-century bishop from Campagna who came to be considered as a patron of sailors and of children with stomach problems. Caxton, however, did include St. Erasmus in his printed version of the *Golden Legend* and he also included St. Barbara who, very surprisingly, given the numerous surviving images of her, does not appear in either the *Golden Legend* or the *Gilte Legende*.[28] As might have been expected several of the non-saintly dedications did not have accounts in the *Golden Legend*: the Holy Trinity, St. Sepulchre, St. Charity, Corpus Christi, the Five Wounds, the Holy Wisdom and the Name of Jesus. But it remains the case that the extremely popular *Golden Legend* appears to have exerted a considerable influence on the devotional preferences of men and women in London.

But neither the *Golden Legend* nor a strong local connection can explain the popularity in London of an Italian servant girl saint who lived in Lucca, hundreds of miles away from London. St. Zita (or Sithe as she was known in England) was unlike other home-grown English saints. On the whole England did not go in for popular canonization. There were a number of

[26] *Gilte Legende*, ed. R. Harmer (3 vols., Early English Text Soc., 2006–7), i. xi.

[27] See W. Blades, *Biography and Typography of William Caxton* (new edn., 1971), p. 277; N. F. Blake, *England's First Publisher* (1976), p. 117.

[28] See Jacobus de Voragine, *The Golden Legend: Readings on the Saints*, trans. W. Granger Ryan (2 vols., Princeton, N.J., 1993); Harmer, *Gilte Legende*. For a list of the saints added to Caxton's edition of the Golden Legend, see *The Golden Legend or Lives of the Saints as Englished by William Caxton* (7 vols., 1922), vii. 276–80.

unsuccessful attempts to secure canonization for failed political leaders promoted by their supporters: men such as Simon de Montfort, Thomas of Lancaster, Edward II, Richard Scrope, archbishop of York, and Henry VI.[29] The successful canonizations were those of bishops and theologians such as Hugh of Lincoln (d. *c.*1200), Richard of Chichester (d. 1253) and Thomas of Hereford (d. 1282) and their cults were usually fairly local.[30] St. Zita was completely different. She was a poor peasant girl, born at Monsegrati in the countryside north of Lucca, who came to work in the household of the Faitinelli family where she lived an exemplary life. When her devotions, or her charitable activities, might have caused trouble with her employers, Zita was spared their wrath by divine intervention. When she prayed too long in church and forgot to put the bread in the oven, she found it ready baked when she returned home. When she gave away some of her master's supply of beans to feed the poor, the sacks were replenished. When her master lent her his fur cloak to wear in church on a cold night, Zita gave it to a beggar who, miraculously, returned the cloak the next day. Zita practised many forms of mortification including beating her breast with a small stone. When she died in 1278 the Faitinelli family promoted her cult in the local church of San Frediano where Zita's tomb became a shrine.[31] The cult was sufficiently popular to challenge the long-established cult of the Volto Santo in the cathedral in Lucca.

There were already strong links between England and Lucca, and especially strong links between Lucca and Bury St. Edmunds. This may explain the presence of an altar in the abbey dedicated to Zita already by 1299, only twenty-one years after her death.[32] Moreover the earliest surviving copy of a life of Zita is found, not in Lucca, but in a manuscript (Bodley MS. 240) compiled at Bury before 1377.[33] It is not surprising, therefore, that the Bury poet, John Lydgate, wrote a three-verse hymn to St. Zita in the fourteen-twenties in which he drew attention to two of her attributes in particular: the little stone with which she was accustomed to beat her breast and the fact that she helped those who invoked her aid to find objects which they had lost. This latter aspect of her piety is not to be found in the accounts of

[29] S. Walker, 'Political saints in later medieval England', in his *Political Culture in Later Medieval England* (Manchester, 2006), pp. 198–222.

[30] For the development of central ecclesiastical control over the process of canonization, see R. Bartlett, *The Hanged Man* (Princeton, N.J., 2004), esp. ch. 2.

[31] For a translation of the life of St. Zita and a discussion of her cult, see D. Webb, *Saints and Cities in Medieval Italy* (Manchester, 2007), pp. 160–90.

[32] See C. M. Barron, 'The travelling saint: Zita of Lucca and England', in *Freedom of Movement in the Middle Ages*, ed. P. Horden (Donington, 2007), pp. 186–202, esp. p. 199.

[33] Barron, 'The travelling saint', pp. 190–1.

her life, nor is it apparent in the numerous miracles which were attributed to her in Italy.[34] But, in England, this would appear to have been her defining attribute. Images of her (and there are some seventy surviving in books of hours, stained glass, alabasters, carvings, wall paintings and vestments) show her in a variety of guises. Sometimes she is depicted clasping the small triangular stone with which she beat her breast; or with a bunch of keys or a purse hanging from her girdle. Whereas St. Petronilla usually has a single key, or pair of keys held upright, St. Zita's keys hang in a bunch at her waist or dangle from her wrist. Often she holds a rosary or a book and, occasionally, three loaves of bread. She may be dressed as a servant with an apron or more grandly: often she is shown wearing the expensive cloak which she borrowed from her master. Her hair may be covered with a wimple-like headdress or flowing freely in locks falling over her shoulders. Occasionally she appears to be holding flowers in her apron, or they may be the replenished beans. The many ways in which Zita is presented suggest that she spoke to many needs and aspirations.

Although Zita's cult may have reached England with some monks of Bury returning home from Lucca, the enthusiasm for the new cult must have received some encouragement from the Lucchese silk merchants who did business with the London mercers. Many of these mercers lived in Cheapside and as early the thirteen-forties there was a chapel dedicated to St. Zita in the church of St. Benet (Benedict) Sherehog, a small parish at the eastern end of Cheapside. By 1356 the rector of the church was known as the 'rector of St. Sithe's' and this title was again used in 1358 and 1373. John Fresshe, a London mercer who died in 1397, asked to be buried in the church of St. Sithe in the parish of St. Benet Sherehog, and the lane leading to the church was known as 'Sise lane' as early as 1357.[35] So, for a time at least, the cult of St. Zita ousted the original dedication to St. Benedict. In the parish church of St. Andrew Holborn there was a fraternity dedicated to St. Sithe by 1394 and several references in the wills of parishioners show that this fraternity was the main one in that church, was well-endowed with lands and maintained a priest who celebrated daily at St. Sithe's altar. The fraternity continued to attract support from parishioners right up to the fifteen-forties.[36] There was another fraternity dedicated to St. Sithe in the church of All Hallows on London Wall. This was a small parish and there are no surviving wills which refer to the fraternity, but the churchwardens'

---

[34] Barron, 'The travelling saint', pp. 201–2.

[35] See Barron, 'The travelling saint', pp. 192 and 197 and references there cited.

[36] C. M. Barron and J. Roscoe, 'The medieval parish church of St. Andrew Holborn', *London Topgraphical Record*, xxiv, (1980), 31–60, esp. pp. 37–8.

accounts reveal that by 1469 there was an image of 'sent sithe' in the church and it seems likely that the 'Brotherhood of St. Sithe' which rented the hall of the Carpenters' Company on some twenty occasions between 1468 and 1500 was the fraternity in the nearby church of All Hallows. In 1509 'Sente Sythis clothe' (that is, hearse cloth) was rented out for 1*d* 'for the berying of moder Adams hosbonde', and as late as 1538 the churchwardens acknowledged receipt of 31*s* 10*d* from the wardens of 'sante Sythys brethehed'. It is clear from these accounts that this brotherhood dedicated to Saint Sythe was the main fraternity in the church of All Hallows.[37]

In addition to these two fraternities there were also altars dedicated to the Italian servant saint. In 1490 Margaret Croke, the wealthy widow of the London alderman and skinner John Croke, chose to be buried before the image of St. Sythe in the London Dominican house at Blackfriars, and in 1518 the pope granted an indulgence for the altar in Blackfriars which was, rather improbably, jointly dedicated to St. Thomas Aquinas and Beata Scita the Virgin.[38] In 1527 Margaret Sale, the widow of a London baker, bequeathed her funeral torches to burn in her parish church of St. Margaret Pattens before the images of Our Lady, St. Katherine, St. Anne and St. Sithe.[39] So, we know of two fraternities, two altars and an image dedicated to St. Sithe in medieval London.

Elsewhere in England we have further evidence of the popularity of the cult of St. Zita. She was commemorated in over 100 churches from Devon to Norfolk and from Sussex to Cumberland, as well as in Scotland and in Ireland. It seems clear that Zita could be fashioned, or imagined, as her worshippers desired. She could be depicted as a servant, as a woman of religion or as an attractive, even elegant, young girl. Indeed there are some indications that the cult of St. Zita was beginning by the end of the fifteenth century to attract more aristocratic patrons. This may be a reflection of the presence of merchants from Lucca in England in the later part of the fifteenth century. Two cousins, Giovanni Gigli (d. 1498) and Silvestro Gigli, from the Lucchese merchant community succeeded each other as bishops of Worcester from 1497 until Silvestro's death in 1521. They were men who exercised considerable influence in England, and at the

---

[37] *The Churchwardens' Accounts of the Parish of Allhallows, London Wall ... 1455–1536*, ed. C. Welch (privately printed, 1912), pp. 12, 36, 40, 48, 59, 61; B. Marsh, *Records of the Worshipful Company of Carpenters*, 7 vols. (Oxford, 1913–68), ii, pp. 41, 43, 45, 50, 51, 56, 63, 69, 74, 103, 111, 130. I am grateful to Doreen Leach for this reference.

[38] K. Lacey, 'Margaret Croke, d. 1491', in *Medieval London Widows*, ed. C. Barron and A. Sutton (1994), pp. 143–64, esp. p. 161; *Calendar of Papal Registers*, xx, ed. A. P. Fuller (2005), no. 1295 and n. 109 (at p. 578).

[39] S. Brigden, *London and the Reformation* (Oxford, 1989), p. 9.

royal court.[40] The Lucchese family of Buonvisi were also active in England and commissioned several expensive copes and chasubles from English workers for chapels in Lucca, on which St. Zita was depicted alongside the Volto Santo.[41] As a result, perhaps, of this renewed Lucchese influence in high places, the popular veneration of St. Zita was reinforced by a new enthusiasm for her to be found among the English aristocracy. William Lord Hastings commissioned a beautiful book of hours in Flanders in about 1480 in which Zita is depicted as a charming young girl stepping delicately through a flowered landscape while she reads a book with her keys dangling from her belt.[42] Richard III included a prayer to St. Sitha in his own book of hours and he also specified that she was to be represented among the saints at his projected college at Middleham in Yorkshire.[43] At Croft castle in Herefordshire, on the fine alabaster tomb of Sir Richard Croft, who had been a faithful servant of the Yorkist and Tudor dynasties for fifty years, St. Zita is again to be found alongside St. Margaret.[44] And she is also included among the army of saints raised in protective solidarity around the tomb of Henry VII in the Lady Chapel of Westminster abbey.[45]

It is difficult to assess what it was about St. Zita that made her so attractive to people of all social and economic conditions. It was certainly not only women and servants who remembered Zita in their prayers and devotions. Her ability to find lost objects must have made her popular, but that cannot have been all. It was perhaps her very ordinariness that appealed to people. Unlike the heroic martyrs of the early church, she lived a normal life and did not need to mutilate herself in order to be able to live

[40] See J. B Trapp, 'Gigli, Giovanni (1434–98)', *Oxford Dictionary of National Biography* (Oxford, 2004) <http://www.oxforddnb.com/view/article/10670> [accessed 30 Sept. 2008]; and C. H. Clough, 'Gigli, Silvestro (1463–1521)', *O.D.N.B.* <http://www.oxforddnb.com/view/article/10671> [accessed 30 Sept. 2008].

[41] See the chasuble now at Stonyhurst College which has the arms of the Buonvisi family and also depicts St. Zita and the Volto Santo. See F. Pritchard, 'A pair of late fifteenth-century orphreys embroidered in a London workshop for a Lucchese merchant family'. I am very grateful to Dr. Pritchard for allowing me to see a typescript of her unpublished paper.

[42] British Library, Additional MS. 54782 fos. 66v.–7.

[43] Lambeth Palace Library, MS. 474; and see A. F. Sutton and L. Visser-Fuchs, *The Hours of Richard III* (Stroud, 1996), esp. p. 47. For the statutes for Middleham College see J. Raine, 'The statutes ordained by Richard, duke of Gloucester, for the College of Middleham, dated 4 July 18 Ed. IV (1478)', *Archaeological Journal*, xiv (1857), 160–70, esp. p. 169.

[44] See C. S. L. Davies, 'Croft, Sir Richard (1429/30–1509)', *O.D.N.B.* <http://www.oxforddnb.com/view/article/47535> [accessed 30 Sept. 2008].

[45] Royal Commission on Historic Monuments, *Westminster Abbey* (1924), p. 65; J. T. Micklethwaite, 'Notes on the imagery of Henry the Seventh's chapel, Westminster', *Archaeologia*, xlvii (1883), 361–80.

in a pious, God-fearing and useful manner, alleviating the needs of her poor neighbours and providing succour for all who came to her for help. If we look at the representation of St. Zita in the Hastings Hours we can observe a simple vignette of Christian charity: a young woman (not so much a servant) holding her book to symbolize her regular attendance at church, and with her keys and her purse hanging from her belt to demonstrate her housewifely duties, who moves serenely through the temptations of the vacuous and pleasure-seeking activities of the courtiers on the opposite page. Whether to the poor and needy, or to wealthy aristocrats, the life of Zita was a reminder that it was possible, however disadvantaged by poverty or wealth, to live a good Christian life amid the temptations of earthly experience.

St. Zita's presence among the fifty or so saints who were commemorated by fraternities or altars in London in the later medieval period is distinctive and unusual. St. Zita was not a biblical saint, nor a Gallic bishop, nor a martyr of the early church, nor a hero of the evangelization of the English. She was not even English and, until 1748, she was not officially a saint, and yet her unofficial and popular cult flourished not only in London but throughout England. There is no evidence that Zita's cult took root outside Italy, and indeed there is very little evidence of veneration for her outside Lucca.[46]

The shifting patterns of popular devotion in London at the end of the middle ages show that there was still a place for saints whose lives were exciting and fantastical, such as St. Christopher, St. George and St. Katherine. But the popularity of the devotions to the Holy Trinity, to Corpus Christi and to the Name of Jesus show that there was also support for the more abstract, more symbolic, aspects of the Christian faith. And in the popularity of the cults of St. Anne and St. Zita we can detect an appreciation of patterns of accessible piety and of saints in whose footsteps ordinary Christians might walk and so find a pathway to Heaven.

Appendix

The dedications of London parish churches in the eleventh and twelfth centuries compared with dedications of fraternities and altars in London in the fourteenth and fifteenth centuries

The names in italics are those saints who were included in *The Golden Legend/Gilte Legende*. Those indicated with a C were added by Caxton to the *Golden Legend* in the fourteen-eighties. M indicates a martyr.

Saints	11th c. and 12th c. church dedications		14th c.–16th c. altars and fraternities	
BIBLICAL SAINTS				
St. Andrew	4			
St. Bartholomew	1			
St. James	1		3	
St. John the Baptist	2		18	
St. Mary Magdalene	2		3	
St. Matthew	1			
St. Paul	1			
St. Peter	5		1	
St. Thomas	1		1	
St. Anne			16	
St. John the Evangelist			3	
	18	14%	45	16%
Virgin Mary	21	16%	59	22%
MARTYRS AND EARLY EUROPEAN SAINTS				
ᵃ*St. Agnes* M	1			
St. Anthony/Antholin	1		2	
ᵇ*St. Benedict/Benet*	4			
St. Christopher M	1		11	
St. Clement M	2		4	
St. Denis/Dionis	1			

Saints	11th c. and 12th c. church dedications	14th c.–16th c. altars and fraternities
St. Ewan/Ouen	1	
St. Faith M	1	
St. George M	2	14
St. Giles	1	1
St. Helen	1	
St. Katherine M	1	23
St. Lawrence	2	5
St. Leonard	3	2
St. Margaret M	6	4
St. Martin	6	
St. Michael	8	3
St. Nicholas	3	7
St. Pancras M	1	
St. Stephen M	1	4
St. Vedast	1	
ᶜSt. Wandrille	1	
St. Amand		1
St. Augustine of Hippo		1
St. Barbara M C		1
St. Cornelius M		1
St. Eloi/Eligius/Loy		2
St. Erasmus M C		2
S Fabian and Sebastian M		1
St. Gabriel		1
St. Jerome		1
St. Sebastian		1
St. Ursula M		3
	49 38%	95 35%

Saints	11th c. and 12th c. church dedications		14th c.–16th c. altars and fraternities	
BRITISH AND ANGLO-SAXON SAINTS				
St. Alban C	1		1	
St. Augustine	3		1	
dSt. Alphage/Aelfheah C	2		1	
St. Bridget/Bride	1		1	
St. Botolph	4			
eSt. Coleman	1			
St. Dunstan C	3		2	
fSt. Edmund C	2			
St. Ethelburga	1			
St. Gregory (Pope)	1			
St. Magnus	1			
St. Mildred	2		2	
St. Olaf/Olave	6			
St. Swithin C	1			
gSt. Werburga	1			
St. Erkenwald C			1	
St. Hilda			1	
St. Etheldreda			1	
St. Patrick			1	
	30	22%	12	4%
OTHER DEDICATIONS				
All Hallows/Saints	8		5	
Holy Innocents	1			
Holy Trinity	1		18	
St. Sepulchre	1			
St. Thomas Becket	1		6	
All Souls			1	
St. Charity			2	

Saints	11th c. and 12th c. church dedications		14th c.–16th c. altars and fraternities
Corpus Christi			12
Five Wounds			1
Holy Cross/Rood			5
Holy Wisdom			1
Name of Jesus			9
Resurrection of Christ			1
St. Sithe/Citha/Zita			4
	12	10%	65	23%
TOTAL	130		276

[a] By 1467 the church was dedicated to St. Anne.

[b] St. Benet Sherehog was known as St. Sithe in the later fourteenth century, see p. 139, above.

[c] By 1181 the church was dedicated to the Blessed Virgin.

[d] By 1235 the church was dedicated to All Saints.

[e] By 1214 the church was dedicated to St. Stephen, see p.132, above.

[f] By c.1250 St. Edmund outside Newgate was dedicated to St. Sepulchre.

[g] By 1349 the church was dedicated to St. John the Evangelist.

Epilogue

Christopher Brooke

The papers gathered in this volume are striking evidence that the religious culture of medieval Europe is a central field of current historical research. That a group of professional historians can be gathered to illustrate this in so satisfying a manner reflects the efficacy of Miri Rubin's magic wand – but is also a sign of the times. It is not so much that the interests represented in these papers are wholly new, but it is novel that they represent in their diversity a unified field of enquiry.

What part does an octogenarian scholar play in this adventure? I had supposed that he was, and ought to be, a mere spectator, enjoying a feast celebrating the end of a long career. I vividly recall Sir Frank Adcock, retired Professor of Ancient History at Cambridge, commenting on his successor's inaugural lecture: he had been over the same evidence some years before and come to a different conclusion, and 'I have reached the age when one does not have to change one's mind'. As a young man, I was deeply shocked and still am – though I can make more allowance now for the self-irony. But there is much to be said for the view that over seventy, still more over eighty, scholars should be restrained from interfering, or anyway keep quiet. Shakespeare's Jaques reckoned seven ages to the life of man; Alexander Pope, more succinctly, reduced them to two. The millions who, like bees, gather in throngs in *The Temple of Fame* (ll. 290–1) comprise a variety of types of men, 'and boasting youth and narrative old age'. The natural tendency of old age is to be resisted.

Yet perhaps we have a role, though a very delicate one. Fashions change; scholarly standards remain, and of these the elderly can be guardians. But the first duty of an elderly don is to listen to his younger colleagues, to help them to realize their own vocations – not to do his bidding. From this I exempt Giles Constable, who is only by a small margin younger than me, but as the doyen of American medievalists – and with contacts in many European academies – he represents a width of scholarly experience with which I could not compete.

C. Brooke, 'Epilogue', in *European Religious Cultures: Essays offered to Christopher Brooke on the occasion of his eightieth birthday*, ed. M. Rubin (London, 2020), pp. 147–51. License: CC-BY-NC-ND 4.0.

Paul Binski's work has a breadth of a different kind. It is not, in the fashionable cliché, interdisciplinary: he simply tramples on the supposed boundary between history and art history – and with a delightful, and very moving, flattery lays the blame on me. What I find particularly attractive about this piece is the way great scholarship from the past – Robert Willis, Edmund Bishop – is reconciled with modern fashions prudently and sceptically interpreted. He cites the importance of the clerical elite surrounding the archbishops of Canterbury at the turn of the twelfth and thirteenth centuries who encouraged their masters in the attempt to form a secular rival to their monastic cathedral. He might have added that the clerks of the bishop of Ely, faced with a similar lack of status and income in Ely itself – and left without occupation by the Interdict their bishop had pronounced on behalf of Pope Innocent III – took to founding a new university in Cambridge in 1209 or so to fulfil their aspirations and occupy their time.[1]

I still boldly call Dame Janet Nelson a younger colleague, for all that she has been president of the Royal Historical Society and vice-president of the British Academy. With great subtlety and delicacy she sketches the role of some leading figures of the Carolingian age who changed their manner of life when they were, in Bertie Wooster's phrase, 'well stricken in years, fifty if a day', and shows how many aspects of politics and society were touched by the pious retreat into Benedictine care homes. Of special interest to me is St. William, ex-count of Toulouse, who settled in later life amid what Orderic Vitalis called 'the countless rocky crags of the valley of Gellone', in a place now adorned with the beautiful Romanesque church of St.-Guilhem-le-Desert.[2] As with his master Charlemagne, he flourished after his death in a different setting, in the *chansons de geste* – and it was his final, ironical destiny to be the hero of one of the greatest of medieval epics, the *Willehalm* of Wolfram von Eschenbach. There is perhaps in this chapter a message of hope for the elderly: when a man can no longer 'mount a horse in manly fashion, wield his weapons vigorously …' he may live in comparative comfort in a monastery he has built for his old age, and earn a reputation for sanctity – or in our own world, an elderly scholar may sit back and rejoice in the prowess of his colleagues.

---

[1] See C. N. L. Brooke, 'What happened in 1209?', in *The University of Cambridge: an 800th Anniversary Portrait*, ed. P. Pagnamenta (2008), pp. 33–5.

[2] Orderic Vitalis, *Ecclesiastical History*, ed. and trans. M. Chibnall (6 vols., Oxford, 1969–80), iii. 218–19. The church is portrayed in a photo by the late Wim Swaan (plate 1 of C. N. L. Brooke, *Rise and Fall of the Medieval Monastery* (Folio Soc., 2006; 3rd edn. of *The Monastic World* of 1974), p. xviii).

Virginia Davis, head of the department of history at Queen Mary, University of London in which the colloquium was held, gave us a foretaste of her biography of William of Wykeham – as I was brought up to call him when I enjoyed his hospitality. The episode of his late vocation to orders is a notable instance of lessons to be drawn from ordination lists in episcopal registers – and it is fascinating to see the supreme arranger of the fourteenth century arranging his own life.

The sources for the early crusades have been familiar territory since my first serious encounter with them as general editor of Nelson's Medieval Texts, steering Rosalind Hill's *Gesta Francorum* through the press; and I supposed that I had little more to learn about them. I was quite mistaken: William Purkis has shown beyond cavil how much is still to be learnt from the exceptionally rich mine of early crusading literature – and he ties his findings, most convincingly, to contemporary literature on pilgrims and pilgrimage.

That great classic Edmund Bishop's *Liturgica Historica* (1918) is among my treasured possessions, often re-read; but my knowledge of medieval liturgy is skin-deep, of music more superficial still – which has been a serious failing. In both Susan Boynton is expert, and she gives us a fascinating insight into their potential, guided by devils and angels, and drawing in Radulfus Glaber, Hildegard and Peter the Venerable – and including, on the day of the colloquium, a recording of the voice of the Devil.

The boundaries of history and literature have long been one of my hunting grounds; but where I am an amateur, John Arnold is a professional, and he opens many windows into the world of lay spirituality. It is interesting to compare his account of the village mass as a triumphal community act with the popular religious movements of an earlier age, which had between about 950 and 1200 filled the English countryside with tiny, intimate churches – and the towns with even more, London to the tune of well over 100 (ninety-nine within the walls), Winchester with over fifty, and so forth, in which small communities could meet their parson and share his Eucharist. I am also intrigued to compare his early thirteenth-century penitentials with the classic literary presentation of confession from the same era – albeit to a lay hermit – when Parzival confesses to his uncle Trevrizent in Book 9 of Wolfram's *Parzival*.

Many years ago Gillian Keir and I published a book on the history of London in the mid middle ages, and I collaborated with Caroline Barron in work for the London volume of the *British Atlas of Historic Towns*. I have often written and lectured on urban church dedications and it is a pleasure to be reminded of those of London. By drawing in guild chapels and the like she has greatly enlarged our knowledge of late medieval dedications;

and with St. Zita (of whom I had never heard) Caroline Barron has done more, in adding delightfully a dimension to our understanding of how obscure cults developed and prospered in the late middle ages.

Giles Constable, in his masterly overview of the whole field of medieval church history – which it was a privilege to hear and is a delight to re-read – rightly observed how unfashionable it was among many professional historians in our early days. I say many, because my own personal experience was rather different. I embarked on historical research in my teens in apprenticeship to my father, Zachary Brooke, whose own career had begun in the world of Pope Gregory VII, and in later years was engaged with Dom Adrian Morey in editing the letters of Gilbert Foliot and in laying the foundations for the prosopography of the twelfth-century English church. Under my father's inspiration I gave up collecting engine numbers and took to collecting medieval archdeacons and abbots. The archdeacons, to my great delight, were taken up by Diana Greenway, Joyce Horn and others in the new Le Neve of the Institute of Historical Research. The abbots led to my first meeting with David Knowles – later to be one of the most powerful influences on my studies – which issued many years later in our first volume, with Vera London, of *Heads of Religious Houses,* a series now completed in two more volumes, partly based on Vera's work, by David Smith. The interests represented by these projects have stayed with me all my life, and it has been a particular satisfaction to see the standards and aims of the best scholarship of the early and mid twentieth century continued and advanced. The guidance of David Knowles led me, as a student, to study St. Francis and so to meet my wife, Rosalind, and to labour, not just for seven years, like Jacob, but for sixty, as her assistant. Giles Constable started his career, as I did, editing a twelfth-century letter collection: he gave us too modest a reminder of his work, which is fundamental for the understanding of the monastic world and the friendship networks on which so much has been built since then. All the studies in this book illustrate the basic importance of the proper use and understanding of historical sources – texts, craftsmanship, architecture, music, drama and sermons – and the ways in which they can be woven together. They also illustrate the value of collaborative research, which has been particularly evident to me in my recent work in support of the editors of *English Episcopal Acta of the Twelfth and Thirteenth Centuries,* in which under the direction of David Smith and Philippa Hoskin we have been guided in palaeography by Theresa Webber, in sigillography by Sandy Heslop, in detecting forgery – a common occupation of the period – by Martin Brett and Julia Barrow, and so forth. The elderly can help to ensure that the best standards and insights of former times are preserved; younger scholars can find new expertise, new interests and fashions and insights to build on them.

To build on them: textual study, to which most of my life has been dedicated, as editor, general editor or assistant, is the crucial foundation for the interpretation and understanding of numerous aspects of medieval culture; and even so mundane an activity as precise chronology has unexpected lessons to teach us. Giles Constable referred to the re-editing and re-assessment of the early Cistercian constitutions. Some recent work in this field has ignored the vital observation, made long ago by Christopher Holdsworth, that the early constitutional documents are not necessarily a reliable guide to the practice of the early Cistercians.[3] My own work on *Heads* revealed to me that the Cistercians were the only medieval religious order whose members could tell us the exact day on which each house was founded. Doubtless in practice a foundation took months and years to complete; but some crucial event, commonly (one supposes) the entry of the monks to the monastic choir, was carefully remembered, and recorded in the lists of the abbeys of the order which survive from the late twelfth century and later. Evidently they were intended as a guide to seniority in an order whose members met annually in general chapter – were a guide to order of seating, a vital matter in the eyes of twelfth-century religious. But it is manifest that the memory of these exact dates went back to a very early period in the history of the order – a clear indication, I would think, that the general chapter (in some form) was a primitive feature of it.[4] If so, it is an interesting case in which a careful study of chronology throws a gleam of light on the practices of medieval religious not revealed by their constitutional documents. Medieval culture is a palace with many entries: the more we use the fuller will be our understanding of the treasures within.

Thus far an old man's reflection on the riches which Miri Rubin and her accomplices have gathered for me – and for a wider audience: I am exceedingly grateful. The colloquium from which this book emerged began in the Institute of Historical Research under the baton of David Bates, and finished in Queen Mary, University of London under the guidance of Miri Rubin and Virginia Davis – to them I owe special and heartfelt thanks.

---

[3] On the interpretation of the early Cistercian statutes, Holdsworth's chapter in *Cistercian Art and Architecture in the British Isles*, ed. C. Norton and D. Park (Cambridge, 1986), pp. 40–55 is still fundamental. For the texts see note in Brooke, *Rise and Fall*, p. 281, n. 12, and for their interpretation, cf. Brooke, *Rise and Fall*, p. 254.

[4] This is contrary to the indications of the earliest copies of the constitutional documents of the order. See the discussion in Brooke, *Rise and Fall*, pp. 254–5 and 282, nn. 19–21.

INSTITUTE OF HISTORICAL RESEARCH | SCHOOL OF ADVANCED STUDY UNIVERSITY OF LONDON

The Institute of Historical Research (IHR) is the UK's national centre for history. Founded in 1921, the Institute facilitates and promotes innovative research via its primary collections library, and its programme of training, publishing, conferences, seminars and fellowships. The IHR is one of the nine humanities research institutes of the School of Advanced Study at the University of London.

'IHR Shorts' is a new Open Access publishing series from the Institute of Historical Research at the University of London. Insightful and concise, IHR Shorts offer incisive commentaries on contemporary historical debates. Titles typically range from 15,000 to 50,000 words with a focus on interdisciplinary approaches to the past.

1. Dethroning historical reputations: universities, museums and the commemoration of benefactors
   edited by Jill Pellew and Lawrence Goldman (2018)

2. Magna Carta: history, context and influence
   edited by Lawrence Goldman (2018)

3. Suffrage and citizenship in Ireland, 1912–18 (The Kehoe Lecture in Irish History 2018)
   Senia Pašeta (2019)

4. European Religious Cultures: Essays presented to Christopher Brooke on the occasion of his eightieth birthday
   edited by Miri Rubin (2020 [2008])

Lightning Source UK Ltd.
Milton Keynes UK
UKHW021828040820
367696UK00004B/157